Aboriginal Policy Research

Moving Forward, Making a Difference

Volume V

Aboriginal Policy Research

Moving Forward, Making a Difference
Volume V

Edited by

Jerry P. White, Erik Anderson, Wendy Cornet, and Dan Beavon

THOMPSON EDUCATIONAL PUBLISHING, INC.
Toronto, Ontario

Information on how to obtain copies of this book is available at:
Website: http://www.thompsonbooks.com
E-mail: publisher@thompsonbooks.com
Telephone: (416) 766–2763
Fax: (416) 766–0398

Library and Archives Canada Cataloguing in Publication

Aboriginal Policy Research Conference (2nd : 2006 : Ottawa, Ont.)
     Aboriginal policy research : moving forward, making a difference / edited by Jerry P. White ... [et al.].

Papers presented at the 2nd Aboriginal Policy Research Conference, held in Ottawa, Mar. 20-23, 2006.
"Volume III", "volume IV", "Volume V".
ISBN 978-1-55077-162-6 (v. III).--ISBN 978-1-55077-164-0 (v. IV)
ISBN 978-1-55077-165-7 (v. V)

     1. Native peoples--Canada--Social conditions--Congresses.
2. Native peoples--Canada--Government relations--Congresses.
3. Native peoples--Canada--Congresses. I. White, Jerry Patrick, 1951- II. Title.

E78.C2A1495 2006   305.897'071   C2006-
906523-3

Managing Editor: Jennie Worden
Production Editor: Katy Harrison
Cover/Interior Design: Tibor Choleva
Copy Editor: Rachel Stuckey
Proofreader: Crystal J. Hall
Cover Illustration: Daphne Odjig, *A Time Revisited*, 1999
                          acrylic on canvas 24" × 20"
                          Reproduced by permission of Daphne Odjig.
                          Courtesy of Gallery Gevik, Inc. (Toronto).

Every reasonable effort has been made to acquire permission for copyrighted materials used in this book and to acknowledge such permissions accurately. Any errors or omissions called to the publisher's attention will be corrected in future printings.

We acknowledge the support of the Government of Canada through the Book Publishing Industry Development Program for our publishing activities.

Printed in Canada. 1 2 3 4 5 6 09 08 07 06

Table of Contents

Acknowledgements

The Bill C-31 and First Nations Membership pre-conference workshop was a truly collaborative effort of many dedicated and talented individuals. Primarily, the workshop was a partnership between Indian and Northern Affairs Canada (INAC) and Status of Women Canada (SWC). These departments were both central actors in the policy discussion and debate that led to the development of Bill C-31 in 1985, and it was most fitting that they join forces to examine the history, impacts, and future policy development of Indian status and First Nation membership from sometimes complementary and sometimes different perspectives. Erik Anderson managed the process, and Jennifer Becherelle, Ritu Sood, Joanne Chambers of INAC, and Maureen Williams and Zeynep Karman of SWC helped develop the workshop over a period of many months. Brenna Grafton, a student of Bill C-31 and Aboriginal governance from Winnipeg, acted as note taker and sounding board during the conference workshop. Special thanks is reserved for all of the presenters whose varied perspectives and experience made for an extremely informative and thought-provoking session, and for Wendy Cornet who stepped up to fill the role of facilitator at the last minute, keeping the proceedings on track and the discussion focussed. Finally, we must thank the many participants themselves who contributed to the success of the workshop by sharing their many insightful comments and personal experiences.

The editors also wish to thank all of the contributors to this volume of Bill C-31 pre-conference proceedings for turning their presentations and reports into well-crafted papers under tight timelines. Specifically, a huge thanks is reserved for the women involved in the Nova Scotia Native Women's Society Bill C-31 research project, for their courage and openness in sharing their personal stories with us.

We would like to thank some of the many people who poured so much energy into this conference and helped make it a great success. First, we want to acknowledge the tireless efforts put forward by the coordinator, Sylvain Ouelette; it could not have been done without his amazing energy and commitment. At the National Association of Friendship Centres, Executive Director Peter Dinsdale, co-chair of the conference, was a central leader as was Alfred Gay and President Vera Pawis Tabobondung. Many others contributed, but we wanted to specially note the work of Sandra Commanda.

At Indian and Northern Affairs Canada Strategic Research and Analysis Directorate, we would like to thank Éric Guimond, Erik Anderson, Patricia Millar, Bob Kingsbury, Norma Lewis, and Norma Chamberlain. At the University of Western Ontario (UWO) we want to thank President Paul Davenport, Vice President (Research and International Relations) Ted Hewitt, and all the people in accounting and purchasing who played a role. From the Aboriginal Policy Research Consortium at Western, we want to acknowledge Susan Wingert and Nicholas Spence.

For those we have not named directly, we know how much you too have given. And to our families: thanks for giving us the chance to do this project, we know you have picked up the extra. Thank you.

The covers of all five volumes in the Aboriginal Policy Research series have featured artwork by Daphne Odjig, a celebrated Aboriginal artist who was one of eight recipients of the Governor General's Awards for Visual and Media Arts in March of 2007.

Introduction

Jerry White, Dan Beavon, and Susan Wingert

The legal terrain changes quickly and dramatically. Shortly before this book went to press a major legal decision was delivered that will have an impact on many First Nations peoples. The B.C. Supreme Court rejected part of the existing legal definition of who can claim status under the Indian Act. They decided that those who trace their aboriginal ancestry through their female relatives have been discriminated against in current legislation. The current rules force people to look at only father or grandfather to determine Indian status.

Potentially, many hundreds of thousands of people may now qualify to be added to the Indian registry. Ms. Sharon McIvor, and her son Jacob Grismer, made the case that they were excluded and rejected from their community. In the ruling the court said: "I have concluded that the registration provisions embodied in [Section 6] of the 1985 Indian Act continue the very discrimination that the amendments were intended to eliminate," The ruling goes on to say that the current provisions favour males and their descendants while discriminating against the descendants of female First Nations.

This decision simply reinforces the arguments that you find in this very timely book

Introduction

In March 2006, the second triennial Aboriginal Policy Research Conference (APRC) was held in Ottawa, Canada. This conference brought together over 1,200 researchers and policy-makers from across Canada and around the world. Aboriginal and non-Aboriginal delegates (representing government, Aboriginal organizations, universities, non-governmental organizations, and think tanks) came together to disseminate, assess, learn, and push forward evidence-based research in order to advance policy and program development. The conference was a continuation of the work begun at the first APRC held in November of 2002. The 2002 conference was co-hosted by Indian and Northern Affairs Canada (INAC) and the University of Western Ontario (UWO),[1] with the participation of nearly 20 federal departments and agencies, and four national, non-political Aboriginal organizations. By promoting interaction between researchers, policy-makers, and Aboriginal people, the conference was intended to expand our knowledge of the social, economic, and demographic determinants of Aboriginal well-being; identify and facilitate the means by which this knowledge may be translated into effective policies; and allow outstanding policy needs to shape the research agenda within government, academia, and Aboriginal communities.

The 2002 Aboriginal Policy Research Conference was the largest of its kind ever held in Canada, with about 700 policy-makers, researchers, scientists, academics, and Aboriginal community leaders coming together to examine and discuss cutting-edge research on Aboriginal issues. The main portion of the conference spanned several days and included over fifty workshops. In addition to and separate from the conference itself, several federal departments and agencies independently organized pre- and post-conference meetings and events related to Aboriginal research in order to capitalize on the confluence of participants. Most notably, the Social Sciences and Humanities Research Council (SSHRC) held its first major consultation on Aboriginal research the day after the conference ended. These consultations led to the creation of SSHRC's Aboriginal Research Grant Program which supports university-based researchers and Aboriginal community organizations in conducting research on issues of concern to Aboriginal people.[2]

The Impetus for the First Aboriginal Policy Research Conference

The idea for holding a national conference dedicated to Aboriginal issues grew from simple frustration. While there are many large conferences held in Canada every year, Aboriginal issues are often only an afterthought or sub-theme at best. More frequently, Aboriginal issues are as marginalized as the people themselves and are either omitted from the planning agenda or are begrudgingly given the odd token workshop at other national meetings. While Aboriginal peoples account for only about 3% of the Canadian population, issues pertaining to them occupy a disproportionate amount of public discourse. In fact, in any given year, the Aboriginal policy agenda accounts for anywhere from 10–30% of Parliament's time, and litigation cases pertaining to Aboriginal issues have no rival in terms of the hundreds of billions of dollars in contingent liability that are at risk to the Crown. Given these and other policy needs, such as those posed by the dire socio-economic conditions in which many Aboriginal people live, it seems almost bizarre that there are so few opportunities to promote evidence-based decision making and timely, high-quality research on Aboriginal issues. Hence, the 2002 Aboriginal Policy Research Conference was born.

In order to address the shortcomings of other conferences, the APRC was designed and dedicated first to crosscutting Aboriginal policy research covering issues of interest to all Aboriginal people regardless of status, membership, or place of residence. Second, the conference was designed to be national in scope, bringing together stakeholders from across Canada, in order to provide a forum for discussing a variety of issues related to Aboriginal policy research. Finally, in designing the conference, we specifically sought to promote structured dialogue among researchers, policy-makers, and Aboriginal community representatives.

The first conference was seen worldwide as an important and successful event.[3] The feedback that we received from participants indicated that the conference provided excellent value and should be held at regular intervals. It was decided, given the wide scope and effort needed to organize a conference of this magnitude, that it should be held every three years. In March, 2006, the second APRC was held.

Aboriginal Policy Research Conference 2006

The 2006 APRC was jointly organized by Indian and Northern Affairs Canada, the University of Western Ontario, and the National Association of Friendship Centres (NAFC).[4] The 2006 APRC was intended to 1) expand our knowledge of Aboriginal issues; 2) provide an important forum where these ideas and beliefs could be openly discussed and debated; 3) integrate research from diverse themes; 4) highlight research on Aboriginal women's issues; 5) highlight research on urban Aboriginal issues; and 6) allow outstanding policy needs to shape the future research agenda.

Although the 2002 APRC was quite successful, we wanted to raise the bar for the 2006 event. During and after the 2002 conference, we elicited feedback, both formally and informally, from delegates, researchers, sponsors, and participating organizations. We acted on three suggestions from these groups for improving the 2006 conference.

First, we made a concerted effort to ensure that Aboriginal youth participated in the 2006 conference, because today's youth will be tomorrow's leaders. The NAFC organized a special selection process that allowed us to sponsor and bring to the conference over 30 Aboriginal youth delegates from across Canada. The NAFC solicited the participation of Aboriginal youth with a focus on university students or recent university graduates. A call letter was sent to more than 100 of the NAFC centres across Canada. Potential youth delegates were required to fill out an application form and write a letter outlining why they should be selected. The NAFC set up an adjudication body that ensured the best candidates were selected and that these youth represented all the regions of Canada. The travel and accommodation expenses of these Aboriginal youth delegates were covered by the conference.

A parallel track was also put in place in order to encourage young researchers to participate at the conference. A graduate-student research competition was organized and advertised across Canada. Aboriginal and non-Aboriginal graduate students were invited to submit an abstract of their research. Nearly 40 submissions were received, and a blue-ribbon panel selected 12 graduate students to present their research at the conference. The travel and accommodation costs of these graduate students were also covered by the conference. The research papers of the 12 graduate students were judged by a blue-ribbon panel and the top five students were awarded financial scholarships of $1,000 to help with their studies.

Second, at the 2002 conference, research sessions and workshops were organized by the sponsors. The sponsors (government departments and Aboriginal organizations) showcased their own research, or research that they found interesting or important. At the 2002 conference, there was no venue for accepting research that was not sponsored. For the 2006 conference, we wanted to attract a broader range of research, so a call for papers was organized and advertised across Canada. Over 70 submissions were received from academics and community-based researchers. About half of these submissions were selected for inclusion in the conference program.

Third, the 2002 conference focused solely on Canadian research on Aboriginal issues. For the 2006 conference, we accepted research on international Indigenous issues, and many foreign scholars participated. In fact, the UN Permanent Forum on Indigenous Issues held one of its five world consultations at the conference. This consultation brought experts on well-being from around the globe and greatly enhanced the depth of international involvement at the 2006 APRC.

The APRC is a vehicle for knowledge dissemination. Its primary goal is to showcase the wide body of high-quality research that has recently been conducted on Aboriginal issues in order to promote evidence-based policy-making. This conference is dedicated solely to Aboriginal policy research in order to promote interaction between researchers, policy-makers, and Aboriginal peoples. It is hoped that this interaction will continue to facilitate the means by which research or knowledge can be translated into effective policies.

Of course, many different groups have vested interests in conducting research and in the production of knowledge and its dissemination. Some battle lines have already been drawn over a wide variety of controversial issues pertaining to Aboriginal research. For example, can the research enterprise coexist with the principles of "ownership, control, access, and possession" (OCAP)? Are different ethical standards required for doing research on Aboriginal issues? Does Indigenous traditional knowledge (ITK) compete with or complement Western-based scientific approaches? Does one size fit all, or do we need separate research, policies, and programs, for First Nations, Métis, and Inuit? Many of these issues are both emotionally and politically charged. These issues, and the passion that they evoke, render Aboriginal research a fascinating and exciting field of endeavour. The APRC provides an important forum in which these ideas and beliefs can be openly discussed and debated, while respecting the diversity of opinions which exists.

The APRC was designed to examine themes horizontally. Rather than looking at research themes (e.g., justice, social welfare, economics, health, governance, demographics) in isolation from one another, an attempt was made to integrate these themes in the more holistic fashion that figures so prominently in Aboriginal cultures. By bringing together diverse research themes, we hoped that more informed policies would be developed that better represent the realities faced by Aboriginal people.

This conference was also designed to ensure that gender-based issues were prominent. In addition to integrating gender-based issues with the many topics of the conference, specific sessions were designated to address issues of particular importance to policies affecting Aboriginal women. This included, for instance, a one-day pre-conference workshop on gender issues related to defining identity and Indian status (often referred to as Bill C-31). This book contains papers from this pre-conference workshop, it is the third volume of the 2006 proceedings and the fifth volume in the *Aboriginal Policy Research* series.

The conference also gave considerable attention to the geographic divide that exists between rural and urban environments. Nearly half of the Aboriginal population lives in urban environments, yet little research or policy attention is devoted to this fact. Specific sessions were designated to address research that has been undertaken with respect to Aboriginal urban issues.

The conference engaged policy-makers and Aboriginal people as active participants, rather than as passive spectators. By engaging these two groups, research gaps can be more easily identified, and researchers can be more easily apprised of how to make their work more relevant to policy-makers. In addition, the conference promoted the establishment of networks among the various stakeholders in Aboriginal research. These relationships will provide continuous feedback, ensuring that policy needs continue to direct research agendas long after the conference has ended.

In the end, 1,200 delegates participated at the conference from Canada and numerous countries in Europe, Asia, Latin America, North America, and the South Pacific. The conference planning included 20 federal government departments and organizations,[5] seven Aboriginal organizations,[6] four private corporations,[7] and the UWO. Feedback from participants and sponsors indicates that the 2006 conference was even more successful than the previous one. This was not too surprising, given that in addition to the plenary sessions there were over 90 research workshops in which delegates met to hear presentations and discuss research and policy issues.[8]

Breaking New Ground

While the APRC brought people from many nationalities and ethnicities together, it also provided a forum for showcasing Inuit, Métis, and First Nations performing arts. The conference delegates were exposed to a wide variety of cultural presentations and entertainment: Métis fiddling sensation Sierra Nobel energized delegates with her youthful passion and the virtuosity of her music; different First Nations drum groups invigorated the audience; Juno and Academy Award winner Buffy Sainte-Marie entertained and mesmerized everyone. We saw demonstrations of Métis fancy dancing, and the skill and artistic splendour of two-time world champion hoop dancer, Lisa Odjig; we heard the rhythmic and haunting sounds of Inuit throat singers, and Karin and Kathy Kettler (sisters and members of the Nukariik First Nation); and we laughed uproariously at the humour of Drew Haydon Taylor (the ongoing adventures of the blue-eyed Ojibway). The conference was indeed a place where diverse Aboriginal cultures met, and the artistic talents of the aforementioned performers were shared with delegates from across Canada and around the world.

Research, Policy, and Evidence-based Decisions

It was Lewis Carroll who said, "If you don't know where you are going, any road will get you there."[9] Knowing where you are going requires a plan, and that can only be based on understanding the current and past conditions. The first APRC, and the 2006 conference, was centred on promoting evidence-based policy-making. We stated previously that, in part, our conference was designed to deal with the communication challenges that face social scientists—both inside and outside of government—policy-makers, and the Aboriginal community. Could we bring these different communities of interest together to develop a better understanding of the problems and processes that create the poor socio-economic conditions facing Aboriginal people in Canada? And equally, could we find the basis that has created the many successes in the Aboriginal community? Could we develop the co-operative relations that would foster evidence-based policy-making and thereby make improvements in those conditions? And equally, could we develop those relations in order to promote the "best practices" in terms of the successes? We are acutely aware that policy-makers and researchers, both those in and out of government, too often live and work in isolation from each other. This means that the prerequisite linkages between research and policy are not always present. This linkage is something we referred to in earlier volumes as the research-policy nexus.[10]

Our aim has been to strengthen that research-policy nexus. The APRC is first and foremost a vehicle for knowledge dissemination and, with a captive audience of many senior federal policy-makers,[11] the conference was able to enhance dialogue between researchers and decision makers and, ultimately, promote evidence-based decision making. More broadly, both the 2002 and 2006 conferences succeeded in helping to raise the profile of Aboriginal policy research issues, including identifying research gaps, promoting horizontality, and enhancing dialogue with Aboriginal peoples.

Moreover, in order to produce superior quality research, there is much to be gained when researchers, both in and out of government, work in co-operation on problems and issues together. Beyond just disseminating the results of research, the APRC was also about the discussion and sharing of research agendas, facilitating data access, and assisting in analysis through mutual critique and review.

We feel strongly that the highest quality research must be produced, and that that research must be communicated to policy-makers for consideration in formulating agendas for the future. If you wish to make policy on more than ideological and subjective grounds, then you need to help produce and use high calibre research understandings. It is simply not enough to delve superficially into issues or be driven by political agendas that have little grounding in the current situation. The APRC is designed to challenge ideologically driven thinking and push people past prejudice, superficiality, and subjectivity.

Policy that affects Aboriginal people is made by Aboriginal organizations, Aboriginal governments, and Aboriginal communities. It is also made by national and provincial governments and the civil service and civil society that attaches to those systems. We encourage all these peoples and bodies to embrace the realities they face with the best understandings of the world that evidence can give them.

Volume Five—The Contents of the Proceedings

by Jerry White, Erik Anderson, Wendy Cornet, and Dan Beavon

Bill C-31, an *Act to Amend the Indian Act*, was made into law 22 years ago in 1985. Bill C-31 was intended to bring the *Indian Act* into conformity with gender equality rights provided under section 15 of the Canadian Charter of Rights and Freedoms and section 35(4) of the *Constitution Act*, 1982. It changed the rules for Indian registration under the *Indian Act* and substantially increased the numbers of individuals eligible for registration. It also allowed First Nations to have limited control over their memberships, but only after certain individuals who had lost Indian status under the *Indian Act* prior to 1985 were granted reinstatement upon application to both Indian status and First Nation membership.

The *Indian Act* has had a profound historical impact on shaping Aboriginal identities, and the 1985 amendments have resulted in both continuing and new challenges. The challenges that Bill C-31 has posed for Aboriginal women, First Nation communities, and different levels of Aboriginal and non-Aboriginal governments are many and diverse. They include the continuing effects of gender discrimination from previous versions of the *Indian Act*, competing notions of "Indianness" in the face of shifting demographics, and a renewed debate over First Nation control of membership and Registered Indian status in the context of self-determination and sovereignty. Control is increasingly at the forefront of any discussion of First Nation membership, and is often couched in terms of citizenship and nationhood.

In the end, Bill C-31 attempted to strike a balance between ending all gender discrimination under the *Indian Act* while respecting First Nations' control of membership. Much has been written about the impacts of Bill C-31 from a number of competing viewpoints since 1985, but commentators by and large agree that it has failed on both of these counts. While Bill C-31 has been much maligned and criticized over the years, it has perhaps been less easy for commentators to develop workable solutions to the complex confluence of Aboriginal control in the face of attempts to correct for an historical gender discrimination not of their making.

And yet this is exactly where we find ourselves 22 years after the creation of Bill C-31—in need of a different solution and a different approach to these issues.

Both Indian and Northern Affairs Canada (INAC) and Status of Women Canada (SWC) have supported research programs on Bill C-31 issues. In September 2003, the Research Directorate of SWC through the Policy Research Fund held a targeted call for proposals on "Bill C-31—Membership and Status." The Research and Analysis Directorate at INAC has undertaken Bill C-31 research since the mid-1990s. The second Aboriginal Policy Research Conference (APRC) presented an ideal opportunity to showcase recent research funded through these programs, as well as other current research initiatives. INAC and SWC joined forces to lead development on a full-day pre-conference workshop on March 19, 2006, that brought together historical, demographic, and legal scholars, as well as First Nation community representatives. A lot of care was taken with numerous partners in the development of an interactive workshop with a well-balanced mix of presentations.

The decision to develop a book of proceedings from this workshop as part of the *Aboriginal Policy Research* series was an easy one to make. All of us involved agreed that a thorough and up-to-date review of historical, legal, and policy issues was very much needed. In addition, as pressure to amend the *Indian Act* on other topics continues, unresolved policy questions concerning the 1985 amendments will continue to percolate, as they touch on almost every aspect of the *Indian Act*. This body of work examining the range and complexity of Bill C-31 issues under a single volume will be extremely useful to anyone concerned with the future of the *Indian Act*, and the ongoing dialogue on self-government rights, human rights, and collective rights.

Additionally, this book tells the stories of women impacted by Bill C-31, interspersed between the sections. These stories are based on research conducted by The Nova Scotia Native Women's Association (NSNWA) in 2005 and complied in a project entitled *Bill C-31 Women's Profiles: A Personal Impact*. This project was funded by Status of Women Canada.[12]

Clara Gloade, the president of the NSNWA, presented the results of this project at the pre-conference workshop, noting that the interviews represent a form of oral history providing insight into how the 1985 amendments affected Native women then and now. She noted that in conducting the interviews, the NSNWA found many of the women to be very bitter about their experiences and wanted their stories told. Reinstated women said they are still being treated in a discriminatory way—now because of their status as persons reinstated under Bill C-31.

Clara Gloade asked those listening to her speak to imagine ourselves in the place of these First Nations women. Imagine being told that if you fell in love and married a non-First Nation man, she said, the Government of Canada can take away your birthright, your identity, and what few rights you have as a First Nations person.

So that the reader may imagine his or herself in the place of these First Nations women, we present these thoughtful and personal accounts that speak eloquently to the impacts on the women and their communities.

The opening two chapters provide some historical foundations for the reader. The first chapter, "The Search for Consensus: Legislative History of Bill C-31, 1969–1985" (Chapter 1) by Gerard Hartley, examines the legislative history of Bill C-31 and describes the social and political context in which federal *Indian Act* policy developed during the period from 1969–1985. His paper on the legislative history of Bill C-31 traces the struggle for gender equality by women who married non-Indian men from the Lavell and Bedard cases in the 1970s, through the Lovelace case and inclusion of gender equality under the Charter in the early 1980s, to the development of Bill C-31 in 1985. This story is one of a series of obstacles to a debate over gender equality both within the federal government and within the Aboriginal community. Importantly, this struggle is set against the backdrop of the failed 1969 assimilationist White Paper policy, which significantly increased fears and mistrust within the Aboriginal community toward any government-led initiative to amend the *Indian Act*. This historical analysis is critical to an understanding of the challenges facing any further policy development in this area, especially in the context of continued developments in Aboriginal autonomy and self-governance. Hartley covers, not only the origins of the debate over Aboriginal women's rights in Canada, but also the emergence of competing viewpoints within the Aboriginal community: Who should or could be members? The paper follows these debates and traces the evolution of government thinking on *Indian Act* policy, by explaining the influence of various Aboriginal viewpoints on the policy considerations. The chapter lays out the rationale for Bill C-31, the different Aboriginal views of the bill, and makes the case that despite years of consulting with Aboriginal leaders on how to amend the *Indian Act*, the federal government passed Bill C-31 in 1985 without the consent of these leaders. He traces the possible reasons why there was a failure to achieve a consensus among Aboriginal peoples and leaders and why the bill was eventually opposed by many in the communities. Hartley argues that it was political considerations, such as the creation of an equality provision in the Canadian Charter of Rights and Freedoms and a United Nations ruling on the loss of status by Sandra Lovelace, that led to the passage of the Bill.

Chapter 2 by Martin Cannon, is framed as a "history of injustice surrounding the 1985 *Indian Act* amendments." Given the legislation is predicted by most to have impacts on many very central issues, such as land rights, citizenship, and Aboriginal identity, the author sets out to develop discussions on each of these three. Cannon discusses his current qualitative research to explore the "involuntary enfranchisement" of Status Indians in Canadian policy. He argues that legal assimilation is less threatening to individuals who understand Aboriginal identity and Aboriginal community in its multiple facets but even individuals who are knowledgeable are unable to prevent the legal assimilation of Status Indians and their reserve lands in Canada today. He concludes that Bill C-31 is not about women, nor was the process really about women's identity. It has become clear to Cannon that it is about Aboriginal identity, because the legislation has an impact on both men and women and affects the whole Aboriginal community.

Considerable time has passed since the enactment of Bill C-31, but arguably the issues of paramountcy or "sequencing" between collective and individual rights remain: the debate over whether the issue of residual gender discrimination should take priority over the issue of First Nations governance or whether First Nations control should take priority, leaving individual rights to be decided on a First Nation by First Nation basis.

Also critical to any policy development today is an understanding of the impacts Bill C-31 has had at the community level. If there is one piece that has been missing from the debate, it is this dynamic. Bill C-31 had specified that INAC would report back to parliament in two years time on the impacts that it has had. This period was ultimately stretched to five years time, based on the finding that the full impacts of the bill had not yet been felt. In 1992, 47 communities were examined for impacts from the bill, but the final report concluded that still insufficient time had passed for a full accounting of impacts. This analysis, however, represents the last attempt by government to monitor the community-level impacts of its bill. For this reason, a large portion of the Bill C-31 pre-conference workshop was devoted to discussion of community-level impacts. There are a number of papers within this volume that examine the individual and community-level impacts from different perspectives.

The next paper is chiefly concerned with community impacts. In "Bill C-31: A Study of Cultural Trauma," (Chapter 3) Jo-Anne Fiske and Evelyn George they set out to examine the Bill C-31 impacts in new ways. They saw the previous investigations as centering on gender conflicts arising from the reinstatement of women who lost status through out-marriage, issues of conflict between individual and collective rights, and questions of identity arising from distinctions made between Status and Non-Status Indians. In their paper, they shift the focus of investigation and present Bill C-31 and the attendant policy as cultural trauma. Jo-Anne Fiske and Evelyn George, and our interspersed accounts taken from the Nova Scotia Native Women's Society research headed-up by Clara Gloade, detail the personal and often devastating impacts felt by individuals from Bill C-31. Their look at cultural trauma from Bill C-31 includes an examination of collective stigmatization or rejection that can be felt from one's own culture. Their emphasis is on the imposition of patrilineal identity on matrilineal cultures, and the resulting fragmentation of First Nations identity. They highlight the policy shift in 1985, which required the naming of fathers on birth and Indian registration documents for the purposes of determining Registered Indian status, and made children's status based on both parents. This had a particularly devastating impact on families and communities. Fiske and George conclude that the trauma generated by C-31 arises from the ongoing and persistent destruction of individual well-being and collective continuity. They conclude that "where law and force of the state delegitimizes established forms of family, kin, and identity, law remakes identity." This leads to generations that cannot relate to family in the way they want and on their own terms.

This theme is further developed by Michelle Mann in a later chapter, which further discusses impact analysis and proposed policy options related to this issue.

In the first of his two chapters (Chapter 4) Stewart Clatworthy takes a quantitative approach to the community-level impacts of Bill C-31 on the Brokenhead Ojibway Nation in Manitoba. His paper uses methodology that he developed and refined for over a decade to examine the population increases, real and projected, to both the Registered Indian population and population of band members (see White et al 2003). This type of analysis is critical for helping First Nations and the federal government understand the long-term impacts of their respective policies, and for informing policies that can have profound impacts on future populations. Clatworthy's paper also adapted methodology from earlier government analysis of community-level impacts, by surveying both on- and off-reserve Brokenhead members on a series of issues related to community, family, and individual impacts. This portion of the analysis was treated as a test-case and points to the further need for understanding and monitoring these impacts. He explores a broad range of the potential impacts associated with Bill C-31 including population and demography, First Nations membership, the demand for (and use and costs of) key programs and services, and social and political changes within the community. He concludes that the 1985 *Indian Act* amendments have had significant impacts on the size of Brokenhead's Registered Indian population. Clatworthy found no real impact on services but does conclude that high rates of inter-marriage may result in growing numbers of children who will not have entitlement to Indian registration and consequently will not be members of the community under Brokenhead's current membership rule. The paper argues that the impacts of Bill C-31 will force Brokenhead to address issues related to membership, preserving political and social equality, ensuring access to programs and services, and "differential rights and entitlements of different classes of citizens."

Stewart Clatworthy's second chapter, "Indian Registration, Membership, and Population Change in First Nations Communities" (Chapter 5) demonstrates the population increases and projections of both the Registered Indian and membership populations, at the national level. Clatworthy highlights the important distinction between Indian registration and First Nations membership for many First Nations who have chosen to develop their own membership codes under the 1985 amendments to the *Indian Act*. He begins with a brief examination of different broad categories of membership rules, and undertakes population projections based on these rule types, among other factors, in comparison with Registered Indian population projections. He finds that for some First Nations, the future populations of Registered Indians and First Nation members will begin to diverge sharply in the not-to-distant future, and other First Nations may experience growing classes of reserve residents with membership, but lacking Indian status, or with Indian status but lacking membership. This, he notes, could have significant impacts on future service provision for a number of First Nations. His research findings are particularly relevant for future First Nation policy development in the area of membership or citizenship.

The volume concludes with two chapters that deal with very salient issues. In "Indian Registration: Unrecognized and Unstated Paternity" (Chapter 6), Michelle Mann examines the enormous problem that 19% of all children born to subsection 6(1) registered women have no paternity stated. The INAC registrar demands that there be evidentiary proof of paternity. This, argues Mann, creates the problem that tens of thousands of children have unstated paternity. She examines the various approaches that are open to INAC and concludes that major changes are likely needed. She advocates that INAC consult with Native women's groups, and other stakeholder groups, as well as culturally trained and knowledgeable counsellors. She does advocate changes such as allowing women to swear affidavits on the paternity, which is much simpler than the current requirements.

Wendy Cornet concludes the book with a study of the role of federal law in the chapter "First Nation Citizenship, Kinship, Gender, and Race" (Chapter 7). She points out that Aboriginal people cope with layers of legal identities that are confusing, sometimes contradictory, and always beyond their control. The consequences are dire for those who can not interpret the myriad of laws and regulations. For example, the difference between "being able to reside on-reserve or not, being able to buy a house on-reserve or not, having access to post-secondary education, employment training, and other programs." The level of complexity and arbitrariness governing Indian status and band membership can create difficult barriers and levels of burden that are impossible or impractical for many to deal with. This leads to confusion and conflict for both leaders and individuals.

Wendy Cornet argues that the goal of ensuring the equality and cultural rights of First Nation peoples is not well served by the continued statutory use of the racial term "Indian," and may be better served by First Nation concepts and use of criteria such as culture and family relationships. She points to the increasing arbitrariness of the historical definition of "Indian," culminating in the either/or type classification system based on descent under the current *Indian Act*. The greater the degree of arbitrariness, she argues, the greater the potential for harm to individual identities and rights. She outlines a number of useful social and legal concepts of race, culture, and citizenship as a backdrop to a discussion of the complex mixture of legal definitions of "Status Indian," "band member," or even "treaty beneficiary," with their uniquely associated rights and benefits. Cornet points out several policy alternatives that could revise the Indian status and band membership provisions under the *Indian Act,* including moving towards clearer recognition of First Nations citizenship. These proposals are aimed at eliminating residual sex discrimination, recognizing Indian status entitlement, addressing issues of unstated paternity and discriminatory treatment of children, and eliminating the concept of Indian status.

Endnotes

1 More specifically, the conference was organized by the Strategic Research and Analysis Directorate, INAC and the First Nations Cohesion Project, the Department of Sociology at the UWO.
   Dan Beavon and Jerry White acted as conference co-chairs from their respective organizations.

2 One of the other funding bodies for academic research, the Canadian Institute of Health Research,
   also has a program (the Institute of Aboriginal Peoples' Health) that supports research to address
   the special health needs of Canada's Aboriginal peoples.

3 The Canadian government commented on the importance of the APRC in a speech to the United
   Nations in Geneva on July 22, 2003. More specifically, see the statement by the observer dele-
   gation of Canada to the United Nations Working Group on Indigenous Populations, Twenty-First
   Session, July 21–25, 2003.

4 Consequently, there were three conference co-chairs: Dan Beavon, Director of the Strategic
   Research and Analysis Directorate, INAC; Jerry White, Professor of Sociology and Senior
   Advisor to the Vice President at the University of Western Ontario; and Peter Dinsdale, Executive
   Director of the National Association of Friendship Centres.

5 The federal departments and organizations provided funding support at three different levels.
   Gold: Indian and Northern Affairs Canada, Human Resources and Skills Development Canada,
   Department of Justice Canada, Status of Women Canada, Health Canada, Veterans Affairs
   Canada, Fisheries and Oceans Canada, Canada Housing and Mortgage Corporation, Correc-
   tional Service Canada, Atlantic Canada Opportunities Agency, Canadian Council on Learning,
   Canadian International Development Agency, Public Safety and Emergency Preparedness,
   Social Sciences and Humanities Research Council of Canada, and Canadian Institutes of Health
   Research. Silver: Canada Economic Development for Quebec Regions, the Policy Research
   Initiative, and Canadian Heritage. Bronze: Natural Resources Canada and Statistics Canada.

6 National Association of Friendship Centres, Aboriginal Healing Foundation, First Nations
   Statistical Institute, National Aboriginal Housing Association, Indian Taxation Advisory Board,
   National Aboriginal Forestry Association, and National Aboriginal Health Organization.

7 Public History, Canadian North, VIA Rail Canada, and Canada Post.

8 There were also four all-day pre-conference workshops that attracted nearly 300 delegates. These
   four pre-conference workshops included Harvard University's Research Model on Aboriginal
   governance; Aboriginal demographics and well-being; Bill C-31 and First Nation membership;
   and records management for First Nations.

9 This famous quote is actually a paraphrase of what the Cheshire cat said to Alice in Carroll's
   book, *Alice's Adventures in Wonderland.* Chapter 6, "Pig and Pepper." 1865.

10 The research–policy nexus is built on the foundation of dialogue and discourse between those
   making policy and those discovering and interpreting the evidence that should underscore it.
   When superior quality research is produced and used in making policy, this completes the
   structure.

11 While there are many Canadian cities with larger Aboriginal populations, in terms of both proportions and absolute numbers, Ottawa was selected as the most logical conference site because it
   would have otherwise been difficult to engage the participation of such a large number of senior
   federal policy-makers. In many ways, the conference was about educating and exposing this
   group to the vast array of research that has been done on Aboriginal issues.

12 *Nova Scotia Native Women's Association Bill C-31 Native Women's Profiles* was funded by Status
   of Women Canada's Women Program. The resulting document expresses the views of the authors
   and does not necessarily represent the official policy of Status of Women Canada or the Government of Canada.

Edna May Francis

Edna was born on May 1, 1951, to Mr. and Mrs. Edward Kabatay. She was raised on the Membertou First Nation located near Sydney, Nova Scotia. Edna spoke her native tongue, Mi'Kmaq and her family was steeped in the Mi'Kmaq and Ojibway cultures. Her father Edward and the family were the first Mi'Kmaq dancers and drummers in the area at that time. In 1967 Edna lost her Indian status through 12(1)(b) of the Indian Act. She was no longer considered an Indian or a band member.

After her marriage she received a letter from the Membertou Band Council that stated she was no longer a band member and she was asked to move from the reserve. Edna stated that this was the most devastating news she ever received in her life, and she was very hurt because she felt she was still an Indian and a member of the community, and a stroke of a pen did not change that. Edna refused to move from her community despite of her eviction notice. Edna gives much credit to her grandfather who she lived with, because he told her she was not moving and he informed the Band Council, and clearly made his intentions known that Edna was staying. Edna's marriage ended and she had her son to care for. Edna stated she had tremendous financial and emotional struggles just trying to make ends meet. She didn't receive any financial assistance from the Band.

Edna stated that during this time she had to pay for her own dental, medical, utilities, and education. Over the years she made several moves for employment reasons but always returned to her community. She also completed upgrading and training courses over the years. Edna stated that she is quite bitter against Indian Affairs and the discrimination policy that was imposed on her. She was especially bitter during her dilemma when the same policy was not imposed on the native men who married non-native women. White women gained Indian status and band membership in her community and these very women felt she was not an Indian; they in turn enjoyed all the benefits that she was denied.

In 1985, Edna regained her Indian status and band membership through Bill C-31. She states that she was fortunate to have stayed in the community and held on to her culture and language; she attributes this to her parents, who were very strong and committed to their culture. Edna lost her Indian status and band membership for eighteen years. Edna is employed by the Membertou Band as the assistant manager for the Membertou Gaming Commission. Edna feels that Indian Affairs owes her compensation for her lost rights for eighteen years because of discrimination in the Indian Act.

Part One:
The Historical Dimension

1

The Search for Consensus:
A Legislative History of Bill C-31,
1969–1985[1]

Gerard Hartley

Introduction

Canada's 1985 *Indian Act* amendment, known as Bill C-31, was intended to eliminate discrimination against Indian women by creating a non-discriminatory legal criteria for defining "Indian" under the Act. Before 1985, Indian status under the *Indian Act* was based on a patrilineal system in which a woman's status was dependent on her father or husband's status. Therefore Indian women who married Indian men retained their legal status, whereas Indian women who married non-Indian men lost their legal status and their ability to transmit status to their children. Indian men who married non-Indian women, however, not only retained their status, but also transmitted it to their wives and children. The pre-1985 *Indian Act* provision that removed status from Indian women who "married out" is known as section 12(1)(b).

Many Aboriginal women viewed section 12(1)(b) as a blatant form of discrimination. However, when Aboriginal women's groups began their long campaign in the early 1970s to pressure the government to amend the *Indian Act*, Canadians were generally unaware of and uninterested in their plight. But by the early 1980s, the problem of discrimination against Indian women was widely condemned in Canada and no longer considered acceptable in a society that valued equal rights and equal treatment for everyone.

This paper examines the legislative history of Bill C-31 and describes the social and political context in which federal *Indian Act* policy developed during the period from 1969 to 1985. It begins by examining the origins of the debate over Aboriginal women's rights in Canada in the early 1970s. It then traces the emergence of competing viewpoints within the Aboriginal community on "membership issues",[2] the evolution of government thinking on *Indian Act* policy, and the influence of Aboriginal viewpoints on federal policy considerations. It also examines the rationale for Bill C-31 and Aboriginal people's views of the bill.

The primary impetus for Bill C-31 was the creation of an equality provision in the Canadian Charter of Rights and Freedoms and a United Nation ruling in 1981 in favour of Sandra Lovelace, an Aboriginal woman who had lost her status under section 12(1)(b). However, after years of consulting with Aboriginal leaders on how to amend the *Indian Act*, the federal government failed to achieve a consensus in the Aboriginal community and passed Bill C-31 in 1985 without the consent of these leaders. This paper will examine why Aboriginal groups opposed Bill C-31.

Lavell-Bedard Case: the Origins of the 12(1)(b) Debate, 1969-1973

In 1971, an Ojibway woman from Manitoulin Island named Jeannette Corbière Lavell launched a legal challenge against section 12(1)(b) of the *Indian Act*. When it first began, Indian leaders paid very little attention to the case. But once it reached the Supreme Court of Canada in 1973, Lavell's case had become a *cause célèbre* within the Indian community, leading to bitter divisions between Aboriginal women's groups and many of Canada's largely male-dominated Aboriginal associations. The case also set the stage for the long and contentious 12(1)(b) debate that culminated in Canada's 1985 *Indian Act* amendment, known as Bill C-31.

Lavell's case began in a York County court in June 1971 after her name was struck from the Indian register as a result of her marriage to a "white photographer." She argued that section 12(1)(b) of the *Indian Act* contravened the equality clause of the 1960 Canadian Bill of Rights because it discriminated on the basis of gender. Indian men who married non-Indians retained their legal status; moreover, these men transmitted status to their non-Indian wives and children through section 11 of the *Indian Act*. Section 12(1)(b), however, fully disinherited Indian women of their Indian rights and benefits, including their rights to band membership, to inherit on-reserve property, and even to live on-reserve.[3]

The lower court judge dismissed Lavell's arguments, stating that the matter should be dealt with by Parliament, not by the courts. Undaunted, Lavell appealed her case to the Federal Court of Appeal in October 1971, and won. The Federal Court of Appeal ruled that the *Indian Act* contravened the Bill of Rights because it denied Indian women equality before the law and ordered that 12(1)(b) be repealed.[4]

Following Lavell's victory, a second legal challenge was launched against the *Indian Act* by Yvonne Bedard, a Six Nations woman who had also lost her status under section 12(1)(b). Bedard sought the repeal of the entire *Indian Act*, claiming that it discriminated on the basis of gender and race. The Supreme Court of Ontario ruled in Bedard's favour by declaring section 12(1)(b) inoperative, but declined to rule on the question of whether the entire *Indian Act* should be repealed.[5]

While many Aboriginal women celebrated the Lavell and Bedard rulings, Indian leaders grew fearful that Indian reserves would be opened up to hundreds of native women and their families. As well, some Status Indians felt that "Non-Status" women should have to live with their decision to "marry-out," and therefore resented Lavell and Bedard's efforts to bring about changes to the *Act*. One Indian woman told Bedard: "You have made your bed—now lie in it."[6]

Generally, however, Indian attitudes were rooted in much broader legal concerns over the special status of Indian people in Canadian society and the preservation of Indian culture and land. Indian groups feared that the Lavell and Bedard cases could lead to the abolition of the entire *Indian Act*, which would in turn lead to the disappearance of the Indian reserve system and the destruction of the Indian way of life. In many ways, this reaction stemmed from the psychological impact of a 1969 federal policy proposal that had sought to end the federal government's special relationship with the Indian people.[7]

In June 1969, the Trudeau government shocked Indians by releasing a White Paper on Indian Policy that recommended terminating all special rights for Indians, ending legal status and the Indian reserve system, and repealing the *Indian Act*. The proposed policy was a reflection of Prime Minister Trudeau's promise of a Just Society, with its emphasis on equality and the protection of individual rights, and his general mistrust of collective rights. Indian leaders, however, flatly rejected the White Paper, denouncing it as an attempt by the government to abrogate its legal and moral responsibility to the Indian people. The government's proposed policy created wide-spread fear among Indians, who perceived it as a fundamental threat to the survival of the Indian people.[8]

This fear galvanized the Indian movement in Canada and led to a resurgence of Indian organizations. Indian leaders across Canada joined together to create a powerful new lobby association called the National Indian Brotherhood (NIB) to "negotiate from strength with the federal government." The unity achieved among Indian leaders in the aftermath of the White Paper was unprecedented in the history of Indian-White relations in Canada.[9]

Through the NIB, the Indian people vehemently opposed the White Paper. But the most effective response to the government came from the Indian Association of Alberta (IAA) whose 24-year-old president, Harold Cardinal, published a widely-read condemnation of the White Paper entitled *The Unjust Society*—a mocking reference to Trudeau's Just Society promise. Cardinal warned that the White Paper was just another federal policy amounting to "total assimilation of the Indian people, plans that spell cultural genocide."[10]

In June 1970, the Alberta Chiefs presented the Trudeau government with their own policy proposal, called the "Red Paper," which rejected outright the White Paper, asserting that: "Retaining the legal status of Indians is necessary if Indians are to be treated justly. Justice requires that the special history, rights and circumstances of Indian people be recognized." As a result of these pressures, the Trudeau government jettisoned its proposed policy and publicly promised not to make changes to the *Indian Act* without the consent of the Indian people.[11]

The 1972 Lavell-Bedard rulings brought back many fears for Indian leaders. While the White Paper had failed to end special status for Indians or repeal the *Indian Act*, many in the Indian community believed that the Lavell-Bedard cases might succeed where the White Paper had not. With the objective of preventing abolition of the entire *Indian Act*, the Alberta Chiefs convinced the NIB to intervene against Lavell and Bedard. The federal government appealed the Lavell-Bedard cases to the Supreme Court of Canada, hoping to avoid being forced to revise the *Indian Act*.[12]

Lavell and Bedard, then, were up against both the Government of Canada and a multitude of powerful, well-funded, and politically-organized Indian associations. The two women did receive strong support from a women's group known as Indian Rights for Indian Women (IRIW); however, this organization was less efficient and less influential than the NIB, the IAA, or any of the other Indian associations. The group did not formally incorporate until 1974, and was therefore unable to intervene on behalf of Lavell and Bedard. Instead, Lavell and Bedard were defended before the Supreme Court by the Native Council of Canada (NCC), a national organization for Métis and Non-Status Indians, on behalf of IRIW.[13]

The Lavell-Bedard cases were heard jointly before the Supreme Court of Canada in February of 1973. Lawyers for Lavell and Bedard argued that the *Indian Act* discriminated against Indian women and that the discriminatory provisions should be struck down by the Bill of Rights. The federal government argued that the Bill of Rights could not overrule an Act of Parliament and that the *Indian Act* protected the special status of Indian people. Lawyers for Indian groups argued that the legal banishing of Indian women who married non-Indians was simply following Indian custom in that women traditionally go to live with the men they marry. The *Act*'s inequalities, they maintained, were necessary to protect Indian land and culture. Indian leaders acknowledged the need for *Indian Act* revisions, but asserted that such changes should be made by Parliament, not by the judiciary.[14]

In the end, the court ruled five to four against Lavell and Bedard, dismissing the argument that the Bill of Rights could be used to override the *Indian Act*. In sum, "the *Bill of Rights* is not effective to render inoperative legislation, such as 12(1)(b) of the *Indian Act*, passed by the Parliament of Canada in discharge of its constitutional function under s. 91(24) of the *B.N.A. Act*, to specify how and by whom Crown lands reserved for Indians are to be used."[15]

The ruling against Lavell and Bedard dismayed Aboriginal women. The challenges facing them following their defeat in the Supreme Court were daunting, and yet, there was also a silver-lining: For the first time, Canadians learned about the problem of discrimination against Indian women. The case was highly publicized in the national media, focusing attention on the treatment of Indian women in Canada. Realizing that the 12(1)(b) problem was now a publicly articulated issue, Aboriginal women's organizations refocused their efforts to bring about changes to the *Act* through political pressure.[16]

Initial Attempts to Find an *"Indian Act* Consensus," 1974–77

Although Indian leaders opposed Lavell and Bedards's efforts to bring about an end to section 12(1)(b), they nevertheless believed that work on modernizing the *Indian Act* should be started. While the leaders did not agree on how to change the *Act*, they made it clear to federal officials that any proposals to do so should emanate from the Indian people. In October 1974, the federal government agreed to a unique policy-making experiment called the Joint NIB–Cabinet Committee. The joint committee created two working groups to deal separately with the areas of Aboriginal and treaty rights and *Indian Act* revisions. But Aboriginal women were left out of the entire process. The NIB steadfastly opposed participation on the Committee by Aboriginal women's groups, claiming that the issue of discrimination against Indian women was local and should be dealt with by individual band councils.[17]

By 1977, the Joint Committee had made little progress on any of the issues, including *Indian Act* revisions. Meanwhile, the government was coming under increasingly strong public and political pressure to solve the problem of discrimination against Indian women. Pressure to deal with the status of Indian women was not new—section 12(1)(b) had captured national media attention during the Lavell-Bedard case—but several other events occurred in 1977 that caused the federal government a great deal of embarrassment.[18]

After the government exempted the *Indian Act* from the effects of a human rights bill tabled in the spring of 1977, IRIW denounced the government's actions before the parliamentary committee that reviewed the bill and won the sympathies of many federal politicians. One MP exclaimed that the *Indian Act* is "extremely discriminatory legislation" embodying "blatant cruelty to women." The government, however, retained the provision exempting the *Indian Act* when it passed the *Human Rights Act* in 1977, thereby standing by its 1970 commitment to Indian leaders that changes to the Act would only be made with their consent.[19]

Aboriginal women's groups perceived the removal of the *Indian Act* from the reach of the new human rights legislation as a deliberate attempt to deny Indian women the basic human rights enjoyed by other Canadians, just as the government had failed to protect their rights under the Canadian Bill of Rights three years earlier. With seemingly no where else to turn, a Non-Status Indian woman named Sandra Lovelace from the Tobique Reserve in New Brunswick brought her case to the United Nations Human Rights Committee in December 1977. While it took the government a couple of years to send the UN a response to Lovelace's complaint, officials were still very concerned that discrimination against Indian women in the *Indian Act* was undermining Canada's international reputation for human rights. Indeed, the Lovelace case soon brought international attention to the problem.[20]

IRIW, meanwhile, was gaining prominence as a national organization for Aboriginal women. IRIW's opposition to the exclusion of the *Indian Act* from the effects of the Human Rights Act and its involvement in making represen-tations to the parliamentary committee reviewing the *Indian Act,* increased its awareness of lobbying techniques and the political process. Since its formation during the Lavell case, IRIW had struggled to gain political clout; unlike many Indian associations, Non-Status Indian women's groups were not funded by the federal government. However, after the sympathetic attention brought to IRIW over the exclusion of the *Indian Act* from the Human Rights Act, the voices of Aboriginal women began to be heard by federal officials.[21]

The Aboriginal women's movement gained further momentum when Canada's Human Rights Commissioner, Gordon Fairweather, began publicly supporting their cause. Fairweather warned officials that if the *Indian Act* was not amended to eliminate discrimination against Indian women, his commission would demand that the government make the changes.[22]

Realizing that the problem of discrimination against Indian women could no longer be ignored, Cabinet announced in the fall of 1977 its commitment "to end discrimination on the basis of sex in the *Indian Act*, with particular reference to section 12(1)(b)." Subsequently, federal officials warned Indian leaders that revising the *Indian Act* to remove "discriminations as regards Indian women" was now the government's "top priority issue." However, in April 1978, frustrated with the lack of progress on the agenda items, the NIB withdrew from the process and the Joint Committee collapsed.[23]

Meanwhile, IRIW held a conference in Edmonton in early April 1978 to "discuss the issue of changing the membership sections of the *Indian Act*." Attended by Indian women from status and non-status organizations across Canada, IRIW's conference developed a detailed policy paper that proposed defining Indian status through a "1/4 blood rule" and restoring "full rights" of both status and membership to Aboriginal women who lost it through past discrimination, and to their descendants "who meet the criteria of 1/4 blood." The quarter-blood definition of "Indianness" would be non-discriminatory because it would allow the Indian "bloodline" to be established through "either the mother or father or both," which meant that the grandchildren of mixed unions would retain their Indian status. IRIW sent its proposals to federal officials and Indian leaders across the country.[24]

Department of Indian and Northern Development (DIAND) officials had serious reservations towards the broad scope of IRIW's proposals. During a meeting with IRIW in early June 1978, Indian Affairs Minister James Hugh Faulkner cautioned that IRIW's status criteria and retroactivity proposals were "broader questions" with far-reaching consequences. Initially, explained Faulkner, "the thing we wanted to deal with was 12(1)(b). And so the quarter blood is a concept that was not one that I expected to come out of this resolution." Faulkner also raised concerns over IRIW's retroactivity proposals: "If we adopted the quarter-blood rule and applied it retroactively, I think you would have a fairly major influx of Indians, and I think that raises serious questions about the ability of existing bands to respond to that ... It raises some very fundamental questions about who's an Indian."[25]

Later that month DIAND released an *Indian Act* revision proposal that bluntly rejected the concept of retroactivity.

DIAND Brings Forward its own *Indian Act* Proposal, 1978

In late June 1978, Faulkner presented Aboriginal leaders with a package of *Indian Act* amendments which, he asserted, were derived from "over a hundred meetings" with Indian representatives since 1975. Faulkner viewed tribal government as the centrepiece of his amendment package. The system he proposed would allow a band council to "opt-in" to its own charter and negotiate a "constitution for the purposes of local self-government"; however, its authority—consisting mainly of powers to pass by-laws in areas such as education, housing, and social services—remained subject to federal legislation. Faulkner also emphasized that "whatever else happens in relation to the *Indian Act* revision, the provisions discriminating against Indian women, and in particular section 12(1)(b), must be revised."[26]

Establishing a definition of Indian status that did not discriminate against Indian men, women, or children would be the underlying principle of the government's new membership policy. Options included either taking away status from all Indians (men and women) who marry non-Indians or allowing all Indians who marry non-Indians to keep their status; giving or denying status to non-Indian spouses; giving or denying status to all children of mixed marriages (Indian and non-Indian); allowing the children themselves or the band to decide status; and establishing a status cut-off rule whereby "all children of mixed marriages have registered status as long as they are considered to be ¼ Indian."[27]

Faulkner also considered the possibility of making the membership revisions retroactive, because officials realized that retroactivity would continue to be a priority for Aboriginal women. DIAND officials, however, argued that there were "practical and other difficulties" with the concept, such as "increased demands on Indian lands and cost increases which would result from a larger Indian population." Moreover, "It would be a difficult, if not impossible, task to right all the wrongs of past discrimination."[28]

IRIW denounced Faulkner's proposals, asserting that, "We cannot accept the Government's suggestion that the 'practical difficulties' with 'retroactivity' are too great to overcome."[29]

Indian leaders also bristled at Faulkner's proposal, in particular the concept of local Indian government through band charters. The NIB charged that the proposal "is a far cry from what Indian people are saying in terms of Indian Government." As DIAND focussed its policy efforts on increasing band authority through a legislative framework, the Indian people began to embrace the notion of entrenching Aboriginal rights in a renewed Canadian constitution. Prime Minister Trudeau's conferences on constitutional patriation, which began in 1978, had captured the attention of Indian leaders; soon after, constitutional entrenchment of Aboriginal rights became their top priority.[30]

Ultimately, Faulkner's *Indian Act* proposals were never brought before Parliament. The Liberal government fell in the spring of 1979 before he could even present them to Cabinet, and Canada's first policy initiative to end discrimination against Indian women fell by the wayside.[31]

The 12(1)(b) Problem Becomes a National Debate, 1979–1980

In July 1979, the Women of Tobique Reserve in New Brunswick rekindled national and international awareness of their cause by organizing a "Native Women's March" from Oka, near Montreal, to Parliament Hill "to protest housing conditions on reserves and the treatment of native women in Canada." With enthusiastic support coming from IRIW, the United Church, and Non-Status women's groups across Canada, the Women's March garnered a great deal of favourable media attention, especially after receiving a warm reception from the new Conservative Prime Minister Joe Clark who strongly supported their cause. He promised that the government would act quickly to remove the discriminatory clauses from the *Indian Act* and warned Indian groups that "if there is no action on the part of the NIB in the next four or five months to bring amendments [forward], we will have to do it ourselves."[32]

Prime Minister Clark, however, was prevented from acting on his promise of quick action on the *Indian Act* when the Conservative government fell in December 1979.[33]

Canadian officials then faced international embarrassment in August 1979 when the United Nations Committee on Human Rights found admissible Sandra Lovelace's 1977 complaint that section 12(1)(b) of the *Indian Act* was in violation of certain family, minority, and sexual equality rights protected under the International Covenant on Civil and Political Rights. Subsequently, the UN Committee asked the Canadian government to respond to Lovelace's complaint. The eyes of the international community were now cast upon Canada's treatment of Indian women.[34]

In September 1979, Canada responded that while there were "difficulties" with section 12(1)(b), removing it would change the definition of legal Indian status in Canada, which was essential for the protection of Indian culture, language, and lands. Therefore, it argued, the government's policy was to consult with the "various segments" of the Aboriginal community before making any decisions on how to amend the *Act*.[35]

This stance provoked harsh criticisms from federal parliamentarians. In July 1980, Flora MacDonald, a Conservative opposition member and outspoken critic of section 12(1)(b), rose in the House of Commons to demand that Prime Minister Trudeau take immediate steps to remove section 12(1)(b), pointing out that the Lovelace case "is the first time that Canada's record of human rights has ever been questioned in the United Nations." Trudeau responded that he would not impose a solution on the Indian people; instead, the government would continue its efforts to amend the *Indian Act* with the consent of Indian leaders. He also reminded MPs of his government's White Paper experience, explaining that "it was not wise even to go in a progressive direction over the heads of the Indian leaders themselves."[36]

The prime minister had harkened back to the government's 1970 promise in the wake of the White Paper fiasco that only through the consent of Indian leaders would the *Indian Act* be changed. A consensus within the Indian community on amending the *Indian Act*, however, could not be found and by 1980, the government was still unwilling to make *Indian Act* amendments "over the heads" of Indian leaders. Federal *Indian Act* policy was in a deadlock. However, ending discrimination against Indian women soon became an urgent priority for federal policy makers because of two key events: first, the 1981 United Nation's ruling in favour of Sandra Lovelace; and second, the creation of an equality provision in the 1982 Charter of Rights and Freedoms.

Solving the 12(1)(b) Problem Becomes DIAND's Top Priority, 1981–1983

After returning to power in 1980 and defeating Quebec seccessionists in a referendum on sovereignty, Prime Minister Trudeau immediately began to negotiate with the provinces for patriation and amendment of the Canadian constitution. While federal and provincial politicians clashed over how to amend the constitution, Aboriginal leaders fought furiously for the entrenchment of Aboriginal rights. And in the end, they succeeded. When the Canadian Constitution Act came into force in April 1982, recognition of treaty and Aboriginal rights was secured in section 35. Section 35 was perceived as a great victory by Aboriginal men and women. But more significant for Non-Status Indian women was the enshrinement of a new Charter of Rights and Freedoms. Section 15 of the Charter guaranteed that

> every individual is equal before and under the law and has the right to the equal protection and equal benefit of the law without discrimination and, in particular, without discrimination based on race, national or ethnic origin, colour, religion, sex, age, or mental or physical disability.

Because it would not come into effect until April 17, 1985, section 15 provided the federal government with a three-year period in which to remove all discriminatory legislation. Thus, the Charter served notice that the *Indian Act*'s discriminatory membership provision must be changed.[37]

A ruling against Canada in the Lovelace case only heightened the government's sense of urgency to rid the *Indian Act* of its discriminatory provisions. The United Nations Committee on Human Rights' ruling on the Lovelace complaint, released in July 1981, found that Canada was in violation of Article 27 of the Covenant on Civil and Political Rights—a provision that protects minority rights. The ruling stated that Lovelace was being denied the enjoyment of her cultural community because, as a result of her loss of status under section 12(1)(b), she was prohibited from having band membership. Because Lovelace had lost her status before Canada's ratification of the Convention in 1976, the Committee did not rule on whether section 12(1)(b) violated Lovelace's equality rights.[38]

The Lovelace ruling's greatest significance was its impact on government policy thinking on the retroactivity issue. Canadian officials now believed that the policy to eliminate discrimination against Indian women would have to include, at a minimum, reinstatement of women affected by section 12(1)(b).[39]

The government formalized its consultation process by referring the matter of how to amend the *Indian Act* to a parliamentary committee. On August 4, 1982, the Standing Committee on Indian Affairs and Northern Development (SCIAND) was mandated to study and recommend how the *Indian Act* might be amended to remove its discriminatory provisions. SCIAND was also asked to review the legal and institutional factors related to the issue of self-government.[40]

Shortly after the August 4 all-party agreement, Indian Affairs Minister John Munro released a discussion paper presenting some of the membership policy options being considered by the government. The primary objective of the new *Indian Act* policy would be to create a new system of defining status that did not discriminate "on the basis of sex or marital status." The new policy would also consider the rights of the children born of marriages between Indians and non-Indians and the reinstatement of individuals affected by past discrimination.[41]

Munro's paper provided options for dealing with questions concerning whether the government or individual bands should determine status and/ or membership, rights of the children of mixed unions, rights of non-Indian spouses, and reinstatement; but it made no recommendations.[42]

SCIAND began its deliberations on September 1, 1982. As a reflection of DIAND's priorities, the terms of reference instructed the Standing Committee to deal with discrimination against Indian women before dealing band government issues and report its findings to Parliament before October 27, 1982. Consequently, SCIAND created the Subcommittee on Indian Women and the *Indian Act* to review the discrimination issue separately from self-government. The Assembly of First Nations (AFN)—the newly established Indian association formed out of the NIB—the Native Women's Association of Canada (NWAC), and NCC were all appointed as ex officio members. The AFN convinced the Subcommittee to deal with its first report by September 20 so that it could begin to examine the "broader implication" of Indian self-government.[43]

When Munro appeared before the Subcommittee on September 8, he warned that "time is running out ... we now have to take into account the requirements of the Charter of Rights and Freedoms." He admonished the Subcommittee for cutting short its review of the discrimination issue: "It is surprising, to say the least, that the committee has decided, without significant consultation, to throw this burning issue in with all others related to band government." The government did not oppose the principle of band control of membership, but its immediate priority was to end discrimination against Indian women, he argued.[44]

In his testimony, AFN's National Chief David Ahenakew argued that the *Indian Act* should not be amended before the constitutional entrenchment of the right to self-government: "First, we have to secure our right place in Canada, the rights of our First Nations. Then we would deal with the discrimination against women, by having each First Nation assume its just responsibility by determining its own citizenship."[45]

The next day, NWAC's president Jane Gottsriedson argued that Aboriginal women's rights must not be kept in abeyance while Indian leaders and federal and provincial governments sort out the meaning of Aboriginal constitutional rights. "We are willing to consider band control of membership, but whatever you decide in this area we want reinstatement first." The NWAC supported Aboriginal self-government, Gottfriedson asserted, but explained: "If band control of membership means Indian women must suffer under federal discriminatory legislation for another five or twenty years while you hash out the meaning of Indian government, we will not accept this."[46]

Like the NWAC, the NCC demanded immediate reinstatement of all individuals who lost status through discrimination; the issue of band membership and Aboriginal self-determination, the group argued, should be dealt with later. IRIW recommended full reinstatement of all Indian women affected by the *Indian Act*'s discriminatory provisions and their descendants "up to one-fourth Indian blood"; after this, "local band government should determine membership."[47]

On September 22, 1982, the Subcommittee on Indian Women and the *Indian Act* tabled its report which recommended repeal of section 12(1)(b), reinstatement of women who lost status and their children's right to status and membership, and allowing bands to decide on the residency and political rights of non-Indian spouses. The NWAC and the AFN both publicly supported the Subcommittee's report. The AFN felt that the Subcommittee had supported the right of the Indian people to determine their membership while the NWAC praised it for adopting the group's "bottom line position" on reinstatement.[48]

With the first Subcommittee's hearings complete, the Special Committee on Indian Self-Government began its hearings in December 1982, and until fall of 1983 travelled to every region of the country, hearing from 567 witnesses during 215 presentations. On the membership question, witnesses unanimously supported First Nations control of band membership, but disagreed on whether this should occur before or after Aboriginal women and their children were reinstated. The NWAC, for example, stated: "[Our basic position is that] ... Indian governments determine their own membership, but only after all of those so entitled have been listed or relisted on their band lists." Meanwhile, Indian bands rejected the notion of automatic reinstatement to band membership. The AFN maintained that: "It is up to the Indian governments across the country to resolve that and to put into place some just means of making sure that there is reinstatement or whatever it is they want to do." Several Aboriginal groups recommended a "two-tier" membership system that would allow reinstatement to a general band list, while still allowing bands to decide whether to admit these individuals as band members. Status would remain under the control of the federal government.[49]

The Special Committee's final report (named after the Committee's chairperson Keith Penner) was tabled on November 3, 1983. As its overarching themes, the Penner Report endorsed the establishment of a "new relationship" with Indian First Nations and the entrenchment of Aboriginal self-government in the Constitution. On the question of membership, the Penner Report recommended the use of a General List "as a means of providing special status to people who are Indian for purposes of Indian programs, but who are not included in the membership of an Indian First Nation." The report did not provide recommendations on how to resolve the conflicting views on whether reinstatement to membership should be automatic or controlled by the band. The Penner Report's 58 recommendations were endorsed by all three parties in the House of Commons and were fully supported by the AFN.[50]

While the Special Committee consulted Aboriginal groups between December 1982 and November 1983, the federal government waited for its final recommendations before bringing forward new proposals to amend the *Indian Act*. After the Penner Report was tabled, however, officials had little hope that a consensus could be found within the Indian community on how to end discrimination against Indian women. Moreover, the report's recommendations suggested that federal *Indian Act* amendments should not interfere with Indian government. Officials fully expected opposition to amendments from Indian groups, especially from the AFN, but with the Charter deadline looming, the Canadian government was ready to act.[51]

Bill C-47: Canada's First Attempt to Implement a Non-discriminatory Membership Policy, 1984

In March 1984, federal officials unveiled plans to bring forward two legislative packages—one to deal with ending discrimination against Indian women, the other with Indian band government.

First, on March 5, Munro tabled the government's official response to the Penner Report in the House of Commons. Cabinet rejected the notion of enshrining self-government in the Constitution. Instead, the government would introduce framework legislation to establish Indian government. Indian band government legislation, Munro argued, would be a first step in changing the government's relationship with Aboriginal peoples.[52]

Second, on March 8, Prime Minister Trudeau announced that *Indian Act* amendments to end discrimination against Indian women would, in the near future, be brought forward because the current membership provisions conflicted with the Charter and UN covenants The main components of the proposed amendments included: providing status and membership rights to future children and grandchildren of mixed unions; and allowing "those who lost status and membership as a result of the discriminatory provisions of the Act" and their first-generation children "to be reinstated." In other words, the second-generation descendants (grandchildren) of mixed marriages born *after* the amendments would be eligible for legal status and band membership, whereas those born *before* the amendments, namely the grandchildren of women affected by 12(1)(b), would not be eligible.[53]

Indian leaders were greatly alarmed by the reinstatement proposal, angrily rejecting it in any form. "They're intruding on First Nations government's jurisdiction again. We've made the position very clear. Correct your injustices and stay the hell away from our affairs," exclaimed David Ahenakew of the AFN. NWAC asserted that DIAND's reinstatement proposal didn't go far enough to include all the victims of past *Indian Act* discrimination.[54]

In response to the reaction of Indian leaders, Trudeau withdrew the government's proposed amendments "indefinitely" in May, saying that he wanted to "avoid any suspicion of paternalism" and "grant Indians more time to heal an internal split over the protection of women's rights." While legislators waited and hoped that Aboriginal groups would sort out their differences over how to address the discrimination problem, the AFN and the NWAC met in Edmonton from May 16 to 18 to listen to each other's concerns and attempt to formulate a common position, especially on the dicey issue of reinstatement. Both groups realized that to meet its Charter requirements the federal government would, sooner rather than later, act on its own to amend the *Indian Act* if Aboriginal leaders could not come to an agreement. The NWAC and the AFN succeeded in establishing a consensus, but it was one that cost the AFN much of its support from western Indian leaders.[55]

The main components of what became known as the Edmonton Consensus were a demand that the government reinstate Indian women who lost status and all their descendants (e.g. grandchildren) and that the "newcomers" would be reinstated to a "general" band list from where they could apply for "active" membership in bands. Borrowed from the Penner Report, the general band list would allow bands to determine the criteria for active membership. As explained by AFN representative Gary Potts: "A general list is the list that is primarily kept by Ottawa of people of Indian status," but who may not be "allowed active participation within the community structure."[56]

The IAA, however, was furious that the AFN had accepted any form of reinstatement and left the conference in protest. Most of the chiefs from Manitoba and Saskatchewan also opposed the deal, which they demonstrated by abstaining from voting on the AFN resolution endorsing the Consensus.[57]

Although the AFN would have preferred to "settle the whole business" in the context of self-government, Potts admitted "pressure is being created by the fact that the federal government is bringing in legislation to remove the 12(1)(b) discrimination clauses." The NWAC's Marilyn Kane also acknowledged that government pressure to find some consensus was an important factor in reaching a compromise. She referred to the Consensus as an "interim measure" and was pleased that the AFN "at least agreed to reinstate women to a general list," emphasizing that the NWAC had always supported the right of First Nations to determine their membership. IRIW, who were not invited to the meeting, totally rejected the concept of the general list.[58]

On June 18, 1984, a little more than a week before Parliament adjourned for summer recess, the Liberals introduced Bill C-47, *An Act to Amend the Indian Act*. The main components of the bill were:

- Status and membership would not be determined on the basis of gender;
- Indian status would not be lost or acquired through marriage;
- In the *future*, status and membership would be provided to individuals with at least "one-quarter" descent (e.g. grandchildren) from individuals registered as Indians;
- Indian women who, in the *past*, lost status through the Act's discriminatory membership provisions, and their first-generation children, would be automatically eligible for regaining both status and membership.

DIAND estimated that approximately 30,000 "Non-Status" women and 40,000 children would be eligible for status and membership under Bill C-47. However, the quarter-blood descendants of "12(1)(b) women," would be eligible for neither status nor membership. Also, bands would not be able to control membership; both reinstated women and their children would be automatically transferred to band lists after a two-year waiting period.[59]

When asked why bands were not provided with control over membership, Munro explained: "it was decided that if we're going to conform with the United Nations stipulations that we agreed to, as well as our own charter, we would have to ensure not only that those re-instated women got on the general list, we would have to ensure they got on the band list as well."[60]

On June 26, 1984, three days before summer recess, SCIAND began its review of Bill C-47. During his brief appearance, Munro asserted that, in view of the Lovelace ruling, denying reinstatement to band membership would make a "mere mockery" of the government's objective of "finally doing away with this discrimination" against Indian women. He defended the government's position on restricting reinstatement to first-generation children by arguing that the second-generation individuals were too "remote from the culture of the Indian community." As well, if "you do include grandchildren, and do it on the same basis that we are recommending to the people who lost their status plus their children ... then you are running into a horrendous cost." Furthermore, stated one of Munro's officials:

> The question of reinstatement, the question of dealing with unfairness that may have existed in the past, has been seen not as a matter that the government must deal with because of the Charter but as a matter for policy which the government should deal with as a matter of fairness.[61]

As a reflection of their Edmonton Consensus, AFN and NWAC made a joint presentation that demanded the reinstatement of "all generations who lost status as a result of discrimination" and denounced the bill's encroachment "on the fundamental Aboriginal right of each First Nation to define its own citizenship." Both groups recommended that people of Indian ancestry affected by past discrimination must be entered unto "general band lists" to be administered by DIAND and that bands must control the "active band lists."[62]

When asked by a SCIAND committee member to explain the difference between "general band lists" and "active band lists," AFN National Chief David Abenakew summarized it as follows:

> [The Penner Report] recommended First Nations control over reinstatement to a general list. The AFN proposes to go further than that—and the Native Women agreed with us, on May 17, 1984. They propose the removal of all discrimination, including Section 12(1)(b), the reinstatement in the general list of all generations who lost status or were never registered, the recognition of First Nations' control of and jurisdiction over citizenship. Bands will then determine who gets on active band lists. Bands only will determine the residency of non-Indians and non-members.[63]

On June 27, 1984, Munro tabled Bill C-52, the government's Indian self-government legislation. Yet, Bill C-52 never made it past the first reading in the House of Commons.[64]

After some minor amendments, Bill C-47 received third reading in the House of Commons on June 29, 1984, the last sitting day of the thirty-second Parliament. MPs expressed reservations towards Bill C-47, due in part to the short three-day period allotted to SCIAND to review the bill. They were also loath to block it, however, feeling that to do so would amount to denying Indian women an "historic occasion" to achieve equality.[65]

After its third reading, the bill required unanimous consent for it to be passed in the Senate. However, two senators denied unanimous consent and Parliament adjourned for the summer and Bill C-47 died on the Senate Order Paper when an election was held that September.[66]

After the years of controversy over Aboriginal women's rights and with the imminent deadline of the Charter's equality provision, it may seem surprising that the government waited until the last few days of the parliamentary session to introduce Bill C-47. But it appears that the government was still reluctant to amend the *Indian Act* "over the heads" of Indian leaders. Although Canadian officials no longer expected to achieve a consensus within the Aboriginal community, the angry reaction towards the Liberal amendment proposals was sufficient to make Trudeau temporarily retract them in May 1984.

The Edmonton Consensus of May 1984 was an historic occasion in that it was the first time Aboriginal women and Indian leaders had formally agreed on the highly contentious issue of reinstating women affected by past discrimination. The government, however, rejected the two main tenants of the Consensus: reinstatement of all generations affected by past discrimination; and adding these individuals to a general band list. Government officials believed that the primary objective of Indian policy was to fulfill Canada's obligations under the Charter and the UN covenants. They viewed reinstatement beyond the first-generation children unnecessary to fulfill these obligations; moreover, Munro argued that it was too costly. The general band list was rejected because officials believed that denying reinstated women full membership rights would conflict with UN covenants.

Full reinstatement to status and membership rights of 12(1)(b) women and their first-generation descendants was an unyielding cornerstone of the 1984 policy that led to Bill C-47. Nevertheless, the Liberals failed to pass Bill C-47 into law. The bill satisfied neither Aboriginal women's groups nor Indian associations. As the clock ticked towards the April 1985 deadline for bringing its legislation into line with the Charter's equality provision, officials took note of Aboriginal criticisms of Bill C-47 and began re-evaluating their policy options. The federal election in the fall of 1984 brought to office a new government that was willing to make one more effort to achieve a consensus within the Aboriginal community.

Bill C-31: Canada Adopts a New *Indian Act* Policy, 1985

During the 1984 election campaign, Conservative Leader Brian Mulroney promised that the Tories would deal with the problem of discrimination against Indian women on "an emergency basis." When the Conservatives took office in September 1984, they had only six months to act on this issue. Once the Charter's equality provisions came into effect in April 1985, officials believed that the *Indian Act*'s membership provisions would likely be struck down by the courts. Finding a consensus among Aboriginal groups, especially towards the reinstatement issue, was still the greatest obstacle to amending the *Indian Act*. Nevertheless, David Crombie, the new Minister of Indian Affairs, soon gained popularity within the

Indian community and was optimistic that by consulting widely with Aboriginal groups, a workable solution could be found.[67]

Crombie rejected Bill C-47 as a solution to the "12(1)(b) issue." Bill C-47, he argued, flew in the face of the Penner Report and the principles of self-government, which Crombie fully endorsed, because it did not respect the "integrity of Indian communities to determine their own membership." Crombie set out to develop an amendment package that struck a balance between the rights of Aboriginal women to equality and of Indian bands to self-government, a dichotomy often characterized as individual versus collective rights. In a CBC interview broadcast in October 1984, Crombie outlined the three principles that would form the basis of his government's new amendment proposals:

> One, clearly, that the discrimination must be gotten rid of immediately. Secondly, that the concept and the idea of reinstatement is something that we must consider and accept. Thirdly, that in doing so we must recognize and affirm the integrity of Indian communities to be able to determine their own membership.[68]

Over the next few months, Crombie later contended, he consulted with over 300 "chiefs and councils, [and] many other groups—Indian, Status Indian, Non-Status Indian communities" across the country for suggestions on how to amend the *Indian Act* to end discrimination against Aboriginal women.[69]

On February 28, 1985, Crombie tabled Bill C-31, DIAND's new legislation to amend the *Indian Act*. The main points of Bill C-31 were:

- Removing all discriminatory provisions.
- Preventing anyone from gaining or losing status through marriage.
- Restoring status and membership rights to people who had lost them through past discrimination.
- Restoring status, but not membership, to the first-generation children of those who had lost them through past discrimination.
- Providing band control over membership for the future.
- Respecting rights acquired under the current *Indian Act*. In other words, neither non-Indian women who acquired legal status through marriage nor their children would lose any of their rights.[70]

Bill C-31 defined two main categories of Status Indians:

- Section 6(1) assigned status to all those who were currently Registered Indians and those who had lost status under the discriminatory sections of the *Indian Act* (e.g. 12(1)(b)). Individuals registered under section 6(1) could transmit status to their children regardless of whether they had married an Indian or non-Indian.
- Section 6(2) assigned status to all those with only one Indian parent registered under section 6(1) (e.g. children of 12(1)(b) women). Individuals registered under section 6(2) could only transmit status to their children if they married an Indian registered under either section 6(1)

Table 1.1: Registration Scheme Under Bill C-31

Parent 1		Parent 2		Child
6 (1)	+	6(1) or 6(2)	=	6(1)
6 (1)	+	non-Indian	=	6(2)
6 (2)	+	6(1) or 6(2)	=	6(1)
6 (2)	+	non-Indian	=	non-Indian

or 6(2). In other words, children with one parent registered under section 6(2) and one non-Indian parent would *not* be entitled to legal status.

Section 6(2), then, established a "second-generation cut-off" rule for acquiring Indian status. Therefore, the grandchildren of 12(1)(b) women would not be entitled to Indian status.[71] **Table 1.1** further illustrates the transmission of Indian status under Bill C-31.

Bill C-31 formally separated legal status and band membership for the first time. The federal government would continue to control legal status; however, bands would have the right to determine their own membership for the future, in accordance to their own rules, if they chose to do so. Band control of membership was subject to two principles: 1) band rules must be approved by a majority of band electors, and 2) band rules must protect acquired rights of existing band members and those eligible to have their membership restored—namely Indian women who lost status under section 12(1)(b). Unlike Bill C-47, Bill C-31 did *not* provide automatic band-membership rights to the first-generation children of reinstated women. However, these individuals would be automatically provided with band membership if, following a two-year transitional period which began once Bill C-31 came into force, a band opted not to assume control of its membership.[72]

DIAND officials estimated that the amendments would apply to approximately 22,000 individuals affected by past discrimination and approximately 46,000 first-generation descendants of these people. They also estimated that the Bill C-31 amendments would cost between $295 million and $420 million over a five-year period.[73]

During a press conference on the day Bill C-31 was tabled, Crombie maintained that the basic principles of his bill were the elimination of discrimination, restoration, and band control of membership. Overall, Crombie was satisfied with the new bill. "I think it draws a balance, an acceptable balance between individual and collective rights and I think it passes the test of fairness."[74]

After Bill C-31 was read for a second time in the House of Commons, it was referred to SCIAND for detailed review. Unlike with Bill C-47, Crombie ensured that the Standing Committee was given ample time to hear from all women's groups and Indian associations and bands who wanted to present their views on Bill C-31. When Crombie appeared before the Committee, he cautioned that legislation rarely redresses "past wrongs" and that attempting to remove all of these could create "new injustices and new problems." Crombie also expected that some parliamentarians and Aboriginal groups would raise concerns that the children of reinstated women were not being given automatic membership rights, but he argued that to do so would make a "mockery out of band control of membership."[75]

Over the next several months, Bill C-31 received close scrutiny in both SCIAND and the Standing Senate Committee on Legal and Constitutional Affairs (SSLCA), where Aboriginal bands and organizations from across Canada presented their views on the bill. It soon became apparent that Bill C-31 was in for a rough ride—very few of these groups supported Crombie's amendments.

Generally, Aboriginal women's groups were disappointed with Bill C-31 because it did not, in their view, put them on an equal footing with Indian men. IRIW, for example, feared that band control of membership will "shift the discrimination down to the reserve level" and demanded that children of 12(1)(b) women be registered under section 6(1) and that the children and grandchildren of these women be given automatic membership rights. The Women of Tobique Reserve contended that Crombie's proposed amendments, at best, "merely transpose the effects of discrimination to another generation" because they do not allow the children of reinstated women born before the bill was passed to enjoy the same rights as the children of Indian men and non-Indian women born during the same period.[76]

Marilyn Kane of the NWAC rejected Bill C-31's legal distinction between status and membership arguing that it created more divisions within the Indian community. Committee members were reminded that the NWAC, "in concert" with AFN, had proposed the previous year that all people of Aboriginal ancestry be added to a general band list "with a connection to the appropriate band." When asked by Keith Penner to explain the meaning of the general band list, Kane replied that a person on a general band list "would also have the right to reside in the community, would have the right to own property, to request loans to build a house, to die there."[77]

Kane was also asked about her views on self-government. Ultimately, she stated, recognition of First Nations government in the Constitution is "what Aboriginal groups are after." But because of the problems created by the *Indian Act*, the federal government's first responsibility was to restore status and membership rights to those affected by past discrimination under the Act. "Once that happens, we will be able to re-establish ourselves as our government. We are not talking about the perpetuation of the *Indian Act* system." Other Aboriginal women's groups were even more apprehensive towards self-government. While they supported it in the long term, they believed that the government's primary goal should be full restoration of status and membership rights to victims of past discrimination, and their descendants.[78]

Indian associations were also critical of Bill C-31; in fact, some of these groups completely rejected it. The most common criticism was that the Bill did not provide bands with total control over membership. Nevertheless, the AFN took a moderate view of the Bill. Regional Vice Chief Wally McKay, for example, stated that Crombie's "legislation is acceptable to the First Nations as a transitional step, but not as any substitute for constitutional recognition of an inherent right of the First Nations." Like the NWAC, the AFN felt that the Bill did not conform to the principles of the Edmonton Consensus because it neither fully reinstated "all citizens" of all generations affected by past discrimination nor provided them with "a connection with the appropriate band." But "at the same time, bands must have absolute control over the exercise of active membership lists."[79]

However, many Indian associations were harsh in their criticisms of Bill C-31, not only objecting to the principle of providing reinstated women with an automatic right to membership, but also fearful of the impact that new band members could have on reserve land and resources.[80]

Some of the most negative reaction—and the most concern over the potential for large numbers of returning members—came from Alberta bands. A representative of the Sarcee Nation of Alberta, dismissing the government's premise of employing a legislative solution to the discrimination problem, angrily asserted: "I do not think we are prepared to talk about any changes in Bill C-31. We totally reject it ... So we are not prepared to compromise on any section." The Treaty Six Chief Alliance from northern Alberta warned that if the government imposed the reinstatement policy on to its communities, "we expect that violence will occur." The Indian Women of Treaties 6, 7, and 8 also warned: "it is going to be hell bursting open at the seams ... Band membership is a matter for the band to decide, and one in which only the band should rule."[81]

The priority for these groups was the constitutional recognition of First Nations government, not amending the *Indian Act*. Instead of Bill C-31, recommended the Four Nations of Hobbema, the government should introduce a constitutional amendment to recognize Indian government.[82]

SCIAND's review of Bill C-31, then, demonstrated that Crombie's bill satisfied neither Aboriginal women's groups nor Indian associations. Yet, there was very little common ground among these organizations, especially in relation to their perspectives on reinstatement and self-government. Indian women demanded full restoration of their status as well as membership rights for themselves and their descendants, whereas most Indian associations rejected the entire reinstatement principle, denouncing it as a violation of their right to self-determination. Nonetheless, the AFN and the NWAC attempted to present a common position by arguing that those affected by past discrimination should be reinstated to a general band list with a "connection to the appropriate band." While NWAC believed that reinstated individuals should have automatic rights to live, own a house, and die on-reserve, the AFN asserted that "bands must have absolute control over the exercise of active membership list." The NWAC and the AFN's viewpoints on the membership issue, therefore, appeared to differ on whether or not those affected by past discrimination should have automatic band membership rights.

Crombie had failed to achieve a consensus on amending the *Indian Act*. Bill C-31 was widely denounced by Aboriginal groups, but the reasons for their criticisms were varied and conflicting. However, the time for consultations on how to amend the *Indian Act* was over. On April 17, 1985, section 15 of the Charter came into effect and the government pushed ahead with its legislative proposals, for the most part without the consent of Aboriginal leaders.

When Bill C-31 was read for a third time in the House of Commons on June 12, 1985, its fundamental principles remained intact; the government had accepted some minor amendments recommended by SCIAND, but no major changes were made to the bill's registration and membership provisions. Crombie again expressed his unwavering conviction that Bill C-31 was an appropriate solution to the 12(1)(b) problem. He believed that it was: "a careful balance between two just causes, that of women's rights and that of Indian self-government. ... No one gets 100 percent of what they sought, but each group gets something that is vitally important to them. There was no other fair path to take."[83]

He acknowledged, however, that Bill C-31 did not address the long-standing desire by the Indian people for self-determination. But that would be for another day. Bill C-31 passed in both the House of Commons and the Senate and was enacted into law on June 28, 1985.[84]

Conclusion

The passage of Bill C-31 in 1985 ended a policy deadlock that had existed since 1970 when Prime Minister Trudeau had promised not to change the *Indian Act* without the consent of Indian leaders. Yet when Canada passed Bill C-31, Aboriginal groups were still divided over the question of membership rights. Aboriginal women's groups felt that the government's priority should be restoring full Indian rights to 12(1)(b) women and their descendants, while Status Indian associations strongly opposed any government interference in deciding band membership. The main priority of most Indian groups was the constitutional enshrinement of Aboriginal self-government. Although Aboriginal women's groups also supported the principles of Aboriginal self-government, most Indian women believed that the process for achieving self-government should occur only after the full restoration of their status and membership rights.

After years of consultations with Aboriginal leaders, a consensus on how to amend the *Indian Act* to end discrimination against Indian women eluded federal officials. Instead of an *Indian Act* amendment achieved through consensus among Aboriginal leaders, the main catalysts to Bill C-31 were the creation of an equality provision in the Charter of Rights and Freedoms and the 1981 United Nations ruling in favour of Sandra Lovelace. The Charter and the Lovelace case had an enormous impact on the rationale underlying Canada's *Indian Act* policy. The main pillars of that policy were that the discriminatory provisions of the *Indian Act* must be removed, and that women affected by past discrimination must be reinstated to both Indian status and band membership. These principles can be found in both Bill C-47 and Bill C-31.

Bill C-31 passed with the support of very few Aboriginal groups. Federal officials felt that they had to proceed with amending the *Indian Act* for fear that the discriminatory registration provisions would be struck down by a challenge under the Charter of Rights and Freedoms. Thus, the federal government abandoned its policy of not amending the *Indian Act* without a consensus in the Aboriginal community and provided its own solution to the problem of ending discrimination against Indian women by enacting Bill C-31 "over the heads" of Aboriginal leaders. In the end, Canada's 1985 *Indian Act* amendment pleased neither Aboriginal women's groups nor Indian associations and continued much of the controversy and divisiveness that began with the Lavell-Bedard case in the early 1970s.

Endnotes

1   This article is based on a longer paper prepared for Erik Anderson of the Research and Analysis Directorate of the Department of Indian Affairs and Northern Development. The author wishes to thank Erik Anderson for his insightful comments on early drafts of the paper and for the opportunity to develop it into an article. Special thanks are also due to Aileen Baird, my diligent colleague at Public History, for her invaluable editorial suggestions on both the paper and the article.

2   Prior to the 1985 *Indian Act* amendment, the term "membership provisions" meant registration under the Indian Act as well as membership in an Indian band. Most Registered Indians were also members of an Indian band prior to Bill C-31, therefore, "membership provisions" was a generic term that referred to all the pre-1985 *Indian Act* provisions that deal with Indian status and band membership.

3   Leone Kirkwood, "20 lawyers heard as Lavell case opens before overflow crowd: Reasonable that Indian family's status should be decided by male spouse, Supreme Court told," in *Globe and Mail*, February 23, 1973, p. 13; Sally Weaver, "First Nations Women and Government Policy, 1970–92: Discrimination and Conflict" in Sandra Burt, Lorraine Code, and Lindsay Dorney, eds., *Changing Patterns* (Toronto: McClelland & Stewart Inc., 1993) pp. 97–98; Katherine Dunkley, "Indian Women and the *Indian Act*: a background for parliamentarian," (Ottawa: Library of Parliament, March 1981) pp. 2–5; Kathleen Jamieson, *Indian Women and the Law in Canada: Citizens Minus* (Ottawa: Ministry of Supplies and Services, 1978) p. 1.

4   Weaver, "Indian Women, Marriage and Legal Status," p. 14; Jamieson, *Indian Women and the Law in Canada*, p. 80; Kirkwood, "20 lawyers heard as Lavell case opens before overflow crowd: Reasonable that Indian family's status should be decided by male spouse, Supreme Court told," in *Globe and Mail*, February 23, 1973, p. 13; "Indian rights for Indian women: Debates moves into court," in *Ottawa Citizen*, February 23, 1973, p. 35; Rudy Platiel, "In one corner, the Bill of Rights, in the other, the *Indian Act*," in *Globe and Mail*, February 22, 1973, p. W6; Lilianne Ernestrine Kroswenbrink-Gelissen, *Sexual Equality as an Aboriginal Right: The Native Women's Association of Canada and the Constitutional Process on Aboriginal Matters, 1982–1987* (Germany: Verlag Breitenbach Publishers, 1991), p. 80.

5   Bédard v. Isaac et al. [1972] 2 O.R. 391–397 (OSC); "Two women lose appeal: *Indian Act* biased but valid, court says," in *Globe and Mail*, August 20, 1973, p. 11; Weaver, "First Nations Women and Government Policy, 1970–92, pp. 97–98; Weaver, "Indian Women, Marriage and Legal Status," final revised paper for Professor K. Ishwaran, ed., *Marriage and Divorce in Canada* (Toronto: McGraw-Hill Ryerson, 1978) p. 16; Weaver, "Proposed Changes in the Legal Status of Canadian Indian Women: The Collision of Two Social Movements" (Department of Anthropology, University of Waterloo, 1973) pp. 13–14; Jamieson, *Indian Women and the Law in Canada*, p. 82.

6   Weaver, "Indian Women, Marriage and Legal Status," p. 19; "'Our reserves belong to us', Cardinal says: Indian leader predicts violence if women push too far," in *Globe and Mail*, February 22, 1973, p. W7; Guy Demarine, "'Male chauvinism': Treaty Indians don't want whites on reserves," in *Ottawa Citizen*, February 22, 1973, p. 41; Kroswenbrink-Gelissen, *Sexual Equality as an Aboriginal Right*, pp. 80–82.

7   Harold Cardinal, *Rebirth of Canada's Indians* (Edmonton: Hurtig, 1977) pp. 109–110.

8   "Ottawa plans to abolish treaties, move out of Indian affairs in 5 years," in *Globe and Mail*, June 26, 1969, pp. 1–2; "Indian leaders surprised by move," in *Globe and Mail*, June 26, 1969, p. 3; Canadian Press, "Indian press Ottawa for policy change," in *Globe and Mail*, June 27, 1969, p. 45; J.R. Miller, *Skyscrapers Hide in the Heavens: a History of Indian-White Relations in Canada* (Toronto: University of Ontario Press, 1991) p. 224; Weaver, "Proposed Changes in the Legal Status of Canadian Indian Women," p. 9; Cardinal, *Unjust Society* (Vancouver: Douglas & McIntyre, 1999) pp. 90–99, 111–119; Weaver, "Indian Women, Marriage and Legal Status," p. 11.

9   Miller, *Skyscrapers Hide in the Heavens*, p. 224; Weaver, "Proposed Changes in the Legal Status of Canadian Indian Women," p. 9; Cardinal, *Unjust Society*, pp. 90–99, 111–119; Weaver, "Indian Women, Marriage and Legal Status," p. 11; Presentation by the NWAC on Bill C-31, Canada, House of Commons, Minutes of the Standing Committee on Indian Affairs and Northern Development, March 28, 1985, no. 28, pp. 69–70.

10 Cardinal, *Unjust Society*, pp. 107–119.

11 Rudy Platiel, "'Won't force solution,' Trudeau tells Indians," in *Globe and Mail*, June 5, 1970, p. 1; Cardinal, *Rebirth of Canada's Indian*, p. 108; Miller, *Skyscrapers Hide in the Heavens*, pp. 230–232; Roger Gibbons, "Historical Overview and Background," in J. Rick Ponting, ed., *Arduous Journey: Canadian Indians and Decolonization* (Toronto: McClelland and Stewart, 1986) pp. 32–34; Jamieson, *Indian Women and the Law in Canada*, p. 81.

12 Cardinal, *Rebirth of Canada's Indians*, pp. 108–113; Jamieson, *Indian Women and the Law in Canada*, p. 84; Weaver, "Proposed Changes in the Legal Status of Canadian Indian Women," p. 14; Cardinal, *Unjust Society*, pp. 90–99; Kroswenbrink-Gelissen, *Sexual Equality as an Aboriginal Right*, pp. 82–83; "'Our reserves belong to us', Cardinal says: Indian leader predicts violence if women push too far," in *Globe and Mail*, February 22, 1973, p. W7; Guy Demarine, "'Male chauvinism': Treaty Indians don't want whites on reserves," in *Ottawa Citizen*, February 22, 1973, p. 41.

13 Kroswenbrink-Gelissen, *Sexual Equality as an Aboriginal Right*, pp. 85–88; Weaver, "Indian Women, Marriage and Legal Status," p. 19; Weaver, "First Nations Women and Government Policy, 1970–92," p. 97–100.

14 Cardinal, *Rebirth of Canada's Indians*, pp. 108–113; Kirkwood, "20 lawyers heard as Lavell case opens before overflow crowd: Reasonable that Indian family's status should be decided by male spouse, Supreme Court told," in *Globe and Mail*, February 23, 1973, p. 13; Jamieson, *Indian Women and the Law in Canada*, pp. 79–88; "Indian rights for Indian women: Debates moves into court," *Ottawa Citizen*, February 23, 1973, p. 35; Weaver, "Proposed Changes in the Legal Status of Canadian Indian Women," pp. 13–14.

15 Dunkley, "Indian Women and the *Indian Act*" pp. 2–5; "Two women lose appeal: Indian Act biased but valid, court says," in *Globe and Mail*, August 20, 1973, p. 11; Jamieson, Indian Women and the Law in Canada, p. 85.

16 Kathleen Rex, "Women plan day of mourning for Canada's Bill of Rights," in *Globe and Mail*, September 10, 1973, p. 10; Joe Rosenthal, "Indian Rights," Globe and Mail, September 12, 1973, p. 7; "A Sterile view of rights," editorial in *Globe and Mail*, September 6, 1973, p. 6; Weaver, "First Nations Women and Government Policy, 1970–92," p. 100.

17 DIAND, Main Records Office, File 1/1-8-3, vol. 31, DIAND brief dated 1975 entitled "*Indian Act* Revisions"; Cardinal, *Rebirth of Canada's Indians*, pp. 114–115; Weaver, "First Nations Women and Government Policy, 1970–92," p. 101; Kroswenbrink-Gelissen, *Sexual Equality as an Aboriginal Right*, p. 91; Jamieson, *Indian Women and the Law in Canada*, pp. 2–3, 89–92; Kathleen Jamieson, "Sex Discrimination in the Indian Act," in J. Rick Ponting, ed., *Arduous Journey: Canadian Indians and Decolonization* (Toronto: McClelland and Stewart Limited, 1986) p. 127.

18 LAC, RG 10, Acc. 1995-96/309, Box 12, File E1165-C6, vol. 1, DIAND brief prepared ca. 1977 entitled "Status of Indian Women"; LAC, RG 22, Acc. 1998-01695-1, Box 6, File D1021-J1-1-2, vol. 2, DIAND briefing paper prepared in November 1977; DIAND, Main Records Office, File E4200-8, vol. 1, encl., report prepared ca. November 1979 by NIBentitled "Indian Government, the Land, the People, and the Resources, Report of the Indian Government Program"; Jamieson, "Sex Discrimination in the *Indian Act*," p. 127; *Jamieson, Indian Women and the Law in Canada*, pp. 89–92.

19 LAC, RG 22, Acc. 1998-01695-1, Box 6, File D1021-J1-1-2, vol. 2, DIAND briefing paper prepared in November 1977; Canada, House of Commons, Minutes of the Sub-Committee on Indian Women and the *Indian Act*, September 9, 1982, no. 2, pp. 5–6; Canada, Debates of the House of Commons, June 2, 1977, pp. 6200–6201, 6221; Jamieson, "Sex Discrimination in the *Indian Act*," p. 127; Jamieson, *Indian Women and the Law in Canada*, pp. 89–92; Cardinal, *Rebirth of Canada's Indians*, pp. 114–115; Weaver, "First Nations Women and Government Policy, 1970–92," pp. 101–103. When the Human Rights Act was enacted into law in 1977, the provision exempting the *Indian Act* from the effects of the Act was clause 63(2), which later became section 67. See Canadian Human Rights Commission, *A Matter of Rights: A Special Report of the Canadian Human Rights Commission on the Repeal of Section 67 of the Canadian Human Rights Act* (Ottawa: Minister of Public Works and Government Services, 2005) pp. 5–7.

20 DIAND, Main Records Office, File D1021-J1-1-2MBSHP, vol. 12, NWAC paper

dated September 6, 1980 entitled "Native Women and the Constitution"; LAC, RG 22, Acc. 1998-01695-1, Box 6, File D1021-J1-1-2, vol. 4, government paper entitled "The Federal Government and the Revision of the *Indian Act* as it Relates to Human Rights" prepared ca. 1978; LAC, RG 10, Acc. 1995-96/309, Box 12, File E1165-C6, vol. 1, DIAND brief prepared ca. 1977 entitled "Status of Indian Women"; Weaver, "First Nations Women and Government Policy, 1970–92," pp. 103–104; Jamieson, *Indian Women and the Law in Canada*, pp. 89–92; Canadian Human Rights Commission, *A Matter of Rights*, pp. 5–7.

21 LAC, RG 22, Acc. 1998-01695-1, Box 6, File D1021-J1-1-2, vol. 1, research proposal by National Committee on Indian Rights for Indian Women dated May 1977; LAC, RG 22, Acc. 1998-01695-1, Box 6, File D1021-J1-1-2, vol. 3, policy paper by IRIW dated April 6, 1978 entitled "Some Proposed Changes to the *Indian Act*"; LAC, RG 22, Acc. 1998-01695-1, Box 6, File D1021-J1-1-2, vol. 2, DIAND briefing paper prepared in November 1977.

22 Jeffrey Simpson, "Fairweather finds political touch is hand in Human Rights posting," in *Globe and Mail*, December 29, 1977, p. 9; Canadian Press, "Fairweather brings respect for convictions to new post as human rights commissioner," in *Globe and Mail*, September 12, 1977, p. 2; LAC, RG 22, Acc. 1998-01695-1, Box 6, File D1021-J1-1-2, vol. 2, DIAND briefing paper prepared in November 1977.

23 LAC, RG 10, Acc. 1997-98/374, Box 3, File E1021-J1-1, vol. 3, DIAND speaking notes prepared in ca. 1978; LAC, RG 22, Acc. 1998-01695-1, Box 6, File D1021-J1-1-2, vol. 2, Draft discussion paper dated February 20, 1978; LAC, RG 22, Acc. 1998-01695-1, Box 10, File D1021-J1-1-2-Membership, vol. 4, DIAND memorandum dated September 22, 1978 from Susan Annis, Policy Branch, Policy, Research and Evaluation Group, to Caroll Hurd; DIAND, Main Records Office, File D1021-J1-1-2, vol. 2, draft DIAND discussion paper prepared in ca. April 1978; DIAND, Main Records Office, File D1021-J1-1-2, vol. 8, DIAND brief dated October 3, 1979; LAC, RG 10, Acc. 1995-96/309, Box 12, File E1165-C6, vol. 1, DIAND brief prepared ca. 1977 entitled "Status of Indian Women"; DIAND, "NIB/Committee Separates" in *Indian News*, ca. April 1978; Jamieson, *Indian Women and the Law in Canada*, pp. 89–92; Weaver, "First Nations Women and Government Policy, 1970–92," pp. 101–103.

24 LAC, RG 22, Acc. 1998-01695-1, Box 6, File D1021-J1-1-2, vol. 3, policy paper by IRIW dated April 6, 1978 entitled "Some Proposed Changes to the *Indian Act*."

25 LAC, RG 22, Acc. 1998-01695-1, Box 10, File D1021-J1-1-2-Membership, vol. 2, transcript of June 1978 entitled "Minister's [Indian Affairs] Press Conference—Indian Rights for Indian Women"; LAC, RG 22, Acc. 1998-01695-1, Box 10, File D1021, DIAND letter dated June 29, 1978 from Theresa Nahanee, Chief, Communications, Public Communications and Parliamentary Relations, Indian and Inuit Affairs, to Phil Gibson, Huguette Labelle [Director General, Policy, Research and Evaluation].

26 LAC, RG 22, Acc. 1995-96/308, Box 15, File D1165-C1-12, vol. 2, DIAND paper dated June 13, 1978 entitled "Draft Discussion Paper on the Revision of the *Indian Act*"; DIAND, "Discussion paper for the *Indian Act* Revision" in *Indian News*, November 1978, p. 1; LAC, RG 22, Acc. 1995-96/308, Box 15, File D1165-C1-12, vol. 2, DIAND paper dated June 13, 1978 entitled "Draft Discussion Paper on the Revision of the *Indian Act*"; LAC, RG 10, Acc. 1997-98/374, Box 3, File E1021-J1-1, vol. 3, DIAND speaking notes prepared in ca. 1978; Weaver, "Self-Government for Indians," pp. 4–5.

27 LAC, RG 22, Acc. 1995-96/308, Box 15, File D1165-C1-12, vol. 2, DIAND paper dated June 13, 1978 entitled "Draft Discussion Paper on the Revision of the *Indian Act*"; DIAND, Main Records Office, File D1021-J1-1, vol. 1, DIAND background Paper on discrimination in the *Indian Act* prepared in August 1978; LAC, RG 22, Acc. 1998-01695-1, Box 6, File D1021-J1-1-2, vol. 2, draft DIAND discussion paper dated February 20, 1978.

28 LAC, RG 22, Acc. 1995-96/308, Box 15, File D1165-C1-12, vol. 2, DIAND paper dated June 13, 1978 entitled "Draft Discussion Paper on the Revision of the *Indian Act*"; DIAND, "Discussion paper for the *Indian Act* Revision," in *Indian News*, November 1978, pp. 7–9.

29 LAC, RG 22, Acc. 1998-01695-1, Box 6, File D1021-J1-1-2, vol. 5, paper by IRIW dated January 18, 1979 entitled "*Indian Act* Revision, In Response to the Minister's Discussion Paper: Membership".

30 DIAND, Main Records Office, File E4200-8, vol. 1, encl., NIB report prepared ca. November 1979 entitled "Indian Government, the Land, the People, and the Resources, Report of the Indian Government Program"; DIAND, Main Records Office, File A1025-5/F2, vol. 1, presentation

dated April 28, 1980 by Noel Starblanket, President, NIB, to the First Nations Constitutional Conference; DIAND, Main Records Office, File D4117-2-C3, vol. 4, NIB report prepared in ca. 1980 entitled "Position of the National Indian Brotherhood concerning the Revision of the Canadian Constitution"; Weaver, "Self-Government for Indians, 1980–1990," pp. 5–8.

31 DIAND, Main Records Office, File E4200-8, vol. 1, encl., NIB report prepared ca. November 1979 entitled "Indian Government, the Land, the People, and the Resources, Report of the Indian Government Program."

32 Newspaper article entitled "Indians given deadline for act-change proposals," in *Victoria Times*, July 20, 1979; newspaper article dated July 20, 1979 entitled "Clark will hear protest, Epp tells Indian women," in *Globe and Mail*; newspaper article entitled "Treaty Women's status reviewed," in *Indian Record*, Fall 1980, p. 20; newspaper article entitled "*Indian Act* 'sexism' cut promised" in *Victoria Times*, July 18, 1979, p. 32; newspaper article entitled "Indians meet PM about 'sexist' law; Government 'sympathetic' to their cause," in *The Province*, July 20, 1979; Weaver, "First Nations Women and Government Policy, 1970–92," p. 103.

33 DIAND, Main Records Office, File E4200-8, vol. 1, encl., NIB report prepared ca. November 1979 entitled "Indian Government, the Land, the People, and the Resources, Report of the Indian Government Program."

34 Newspaper article entitled "Indian women's status after marrying whites becomes issue at UN," in *Globe and Mail*, June 14, 1980, p. 13; Weaver, "First Nations Women and Government Policy," pp. 103–104.

35 LAC, RG 22, Acc. 1998-01695-1, Box 10, File D1021-J1-1-2-Lovelace, vol. 2, submission prepared by Canada in ca. April 1980 entitled "Response of the Government of Canada to the Decision of the Human Rights Committee Contained in Document CCPR/C/DR(VII)R.6/24 Dated 19 September 1979 in the Matter Concerning Sandra Lovelace"; and M.J.B. Jones, "Sexual Equality, the Constitution and Indian Status: a final comment on S. 12(1)(b) of the *Indian Act*," [S. l. : s. n., 1983?] pp. 56–57.

36 DIAND, Main Records Office, File E6000-1, vol. 1, excerpt from the Debates of the House of Commons dated July 7, 1980.

37 Miller, *Skyscrapers Hide in the Heavens*, pp. 239–242; Weaver, "First Nations Women and Government Policy," p. 107; Report of the Royal Commission on Aboriginal Peoples, vol. 4: Perspective and Realities (Ottawa: Minister of Supply and Services Canada, 1996) p. 33; Kroswenbrink-Gelissen, *Sexual Equality as an Aboriginal Right*, p. 111.

38 LAC, RG 22, Acc. 1998-01695-1, Box 7, File D1021-J1-1-2, vol. 9, draft DIAND discussion paper dated September 15, 1981; DIAND, Main Records Office, File D1021-J1-1-2, vol. 17, draft DIAND discussion paper prepared in ca. January 1982; LAC, RG 22, Acc. 1995-96/308, Box 37, File D1165-S1-6, vol. 2, DIAND briefing note dated November 13, 1981.

39 LAC, RG 22, Acc. 1995-96/308, Box 31, File D1165-S1-4, vol. 22, DIAND briefing paper dated August 26, 1983 entitled "Membership/Discrimination Against Indian Women." See also DIAND, Main Records Office, File D1021-J1-1-2, vol. 17, draft DIAND discussion paper prepared in ca. January 1982 and LAC, RG 22, Acc. 1998-01695-1, Box 7, File D1021-J1-1-2, vol. 10, parliamentary briefing card dated October 9, 1981.

40 LAC, RG 22, Acc. 1995-96/308, Box 23, File D1165-E1, vol. 5, Terms of Reference to Standing Committee on Indian Affairs and Northern Development prepared in ca. August 1982; DIAND Main Records Office, File E1021-J1-2, vol. 1, DIAND communiqué dated August 4, 1982 entitled "Committee to Review Issues facing Indians"; Canada, House of Commons, Minutes of the Subcommittee on Indian Women and the *Indian Act*, September 1 and September 8, 1982, no. 1, pp. 19–25; and LAC, RG 22, Acc. 1998-01695-1, Box 8, File D1021-J1-1-2, vol. 20, DIAND brief dated December 8, 1983 entitled "Removal of Sex Discrimination from the *Indian Act*."

41 DIAND, Main Records Office, File D1021-J1-1-2MBSHP, vol. 14, DIAND discussion paper published in August 1982 entitled "The Elimination of Sex Discrimination from The *Indian Act*."

42 DIAND, Main Records Office, File D1021-J1-1-2MBSHP, vol. 14, DIAND discussion paper published in August 1982 entitled "The Elimination of Sex Discrimination from The *Indian Act*."

43 LAC, RG 22, Acc. 1995-96/308, Box 23, File D1165-E1, vol. 5, Terms of Reference to Standing

Committee on Indian Affairs and Northern Development prepared in ca. August 1982; LAC, RG 14, Box 166, File 6050-321-I3, Wallet 1, Report of the Subcommittee on Indian Women and the *Indian Act*, prepared September 1982; LAC, RG 22, Acc. 1995-96/308, Box 31, File D1165-S1-3, vol. 2, memorandum to file dated September 1, 1982 by Ann Beauregard, [Corporate Policy], LAC, RG 22, Acc. 1995-96/308, Box 31, File D1165-S1-3, vol. 2, DIAND memo dated September 1, 1982; DIAND memorandum to file entitled "Standing Committee Meeting August 31, 1982"; LAC, RG 22, Acc. 1998-01695-1, Box 7, File D1021-J1-1-2, vol. 19, paper prepared by the Indian Consulting Group in January 1983 entitled "The Elimination of Sex Discrimination From the *Indian Act* and Related Issues"; Weaver, "First Nations Women and Government Policy," pp. 106–107.

44 Canada, House of Commons, Minutes of the Subcommittee on Indian Women and the *Indian Act*, September 1 and September 8, 1982, no. 1, pp. 19–32.

45 LAC, RG 14, Box 166, File 6050-321-I3, Wallet 1, Report of the Subcommittee on Indian Women and the *Indian Act*, prepared September 1982.

46 Canada, House of Commons, Minutes of the Subcommittee on Indian Women and the *Indian Act*, September 9, 1982, no. 2, pp. 39–76.

47 Canada, House of Commons, Minutes of the Subcommittee on Indian Women and the *Indian Act*, September 10, 1982, no. 3, pp. 6–59; Canada, House of Commons, Minutes of the Subcommittee on Indian Women and the *Indian Act*, September 13, 1982, no. 4, pp. 47–78.

48 LAC, RG 10, Acc. 1995-96/309, Box 7, File E1021-J1-8-2101, vol. 1, Indian Legislation Revision and Formulation Activities Report—January 1–September 30, 1982 prepared by the Assembly of First Nations in ca. October 1982; LAC, RG 22, Acc. 1995-96/308, Box 31, File D1165-S1-3, vol. 6, NWAC press statement dated September 1982; LAC, RG 14, Box 166, File 6050-321-I3, Wallet 1, Report of the Subcommittee on Indian Women and the *Indian Act*, prepared September 1982.

49 Canada, House of Commons, "Report of the Special Committee on Indian Self-Government," in Minutes of Proceedings of the Special Committee on Indian Self-Government, October 12 and 20, 1983, no. 40, pp. 54–56.

50 Canada, House of Commons, "Report of the Special Committee on Indian Self-Government" in Minutes of Proceedings of the Special Committee on Indian Self-Government, October 12 and 20, 1983, no. 40, pp. 54–56; PCO, File N-2-5(a), letter dated November 25, 1983 from Peter [Mark] for David Ahenakew, National Chief, AFN to Prime Minister Trudeau; PCO, File N-2-5 (a), letter dated November 17, 1983 from David Ahenakew, National Chief, AFN to Members of Parliament; newspaper article entitled "MP fears disaster if rights rejected," in *Winnipeg Free Press*, November 5, 1983, p. 10; DIAND, Main Records Office, File A1025-1-1, vol. 4, John Munro, Minister, DIAND, Response of the Government to the Report of the Special Committee on Indian Self-Government, March 5, 1984; Weaver, "Self-Government for Indians, 1980–1990," pp. 12–13.

51 LAC, RG 22, Acc. 1998-01695-1, Box 8, File D1021-J1-1-2, vol. 20, DIAND brief dated December 8, 1983 entitled "Removal of Sex Discrimination from the *Indian Act*"; Weaver, "First Nations Women and Government Policy 1970–1992," p. 111.

52 DIAND, Main Records Office, File A1025-1-1, vol. 4, John Munro, Minister of Indian Affairs and Northern Development, Response of the Government to the Report of the Special Committee on Indian Self-Government, March 5, 1984; LAC, RG 22, Acc. 1998-01695-1, Box 13, File D1021-J1-1-8, vol. 1, media transcript of CBC program "Our Native Land" dated March 17, 1984.

53 DIAND, Main Records Office, File E1021-J1-2-1, vol. 14, DIAND press release dated March 8, 1984, entitled "Government Announced Plans to Eliminate Discrimination Against Indian Women."

54 LAC, RG 22, Acc. 1998-01695-1, Box 13, File D1021-J1-1-8, vol. 1, media transcript of CBC program "Our Native Land" dated March 17, 1984; newspaper article entitled "Women follow men in traditional Indian society say chiefs," in *AMMSA*, May 25, 1984, p. 2; newspaper article entitled "Alberta chiefs walk out: Partial reinstatement accepted," in *AMMSA*, May 25, 1984, p. 3.

55 Newspaper article entitled "Judy riles the reserves,", *Alberta Report*, May 28, 1984, pp. 8–10; newspaper article entitled "Indian women's bill could be introduced early: Erola," in *The Ottawa*

Citizen, May 25, 1984, p. 5; Canada, House of Commons, Minutes of the Standing Committee on Indian Affairs and Northern Development, March 7, 1985, no. 12, p. 13; newspaper article entitled "Munro offers compromise over *Indian Act* changes," in *Globe and Mail*, May 19, 1984, p. 3.

56 LAC, RG 22, Acc. 1998-01695-1, Box 13, File D1021-J1-1-8, vol. 1, media transcript, CBC, May 17, 1984; Canada, House of Commons, Minutes of the Standing Committee on Indian Affairs and Northern Development, no. 12, March 7, 1985; newspaper article entitled "Munro offers compromise over *Indian Act* changes," in *Globe and Mail*, May 19, 1984, p. 3; newspaper article entitled "Alberta chiefs walk out: Partial reinstatement accepted," in *AMMSA*, May 25, 1984, p. 3.

57 Newspaper article entitled "Munro offers compromise over *Indian Act* changes," in *Globe and Mail*, May 19, 1984, p. 3; newspaper article entitled "Alberta chiefs walk out: Partial reinstatement accepted," in *AMMSA*, May 25, 1984, p. 3.

58 LAC, RG 22, Acc. 1998-01695-1, Box 13, File D1021-J1-1-8, vol. 1, media transcript, CBC, May 17, 1984; newspaper article entitled "Alberta chiefs walk out: Partial reinstatement accepted," in *AMMSA*, May 25, 1984, p. 3; newspaper article by Margaret Mironowicz entitled "The Indian women's fight to end double standard," in *Globe and Mail*, June 5, 1984, p. 7.

59 DIAND, Main Records Office, File E1021-J1-1, vol. 24, DIAND brief dated ca. June 1984; LAC, RG 22, Acc. 1998-01695-1, Box 13, File D1021-J1-1-9, vol. 1, DIAND brief sheet prepared in June 1984 entitled "Bill C-47"; Canada, Bill C-47, An Act to Amend the *Indian Act*, First Reading, June 18, 1984; DIAND, Main Records Office, File E1021-J1-1, vol. 24, "Speaking Notes for ... John C. Munro ... on Amendments to Remove Sex Discrimination from the *Indian Act*," dated June 18, 1984; DIAND, Main Records Office, File D1021-J1-1-8, vol. 1, transcript of press conference with John Munro, Minister of DIAND, dated June 18, 1984.

60 LAC, RG 10, Acc. 1997-98/374, Box 11, File E1021-J1-2-2, vol. 22, media transcript of CBC interview, dated June 23, 1984.

61 Newspaper article entitled "Parting thought," in *The Vancouver Sun*, June 26, 1984, p. A4; Canada, House of Commons, Minutes of the Standing Committee on Indian Affairs and Northern Development, June 26, 1984, no. 17, pp. 15–16.

62 Canada, House of Commons, Minutes of the Standing Committee on Indian Affairs and Northern Development, June 26, 1984, no.17, pp. 69, 70–71.

63 Canada, House of Commons, Minutes of the Standing Committee on Indian Affairs and Northern Development, June 27, 1984, no. 18, pp. 5–7.

64 DIAND, Main Records Office, File E1021-J1-8, vol. 5, DIAND communiqué dated June 27, 1984, entitled "Minister introduces Indian Self-Government Legislation"; LAC, RG 10, Acc. 1999-01284-4, Box 4, File N1021-J2, vol. 2, draft letter prepared ca. July 1984 from Douglas C. Frith, Minister, DIAND to Sheila Keet, Director, Women's Bureau, Department of Justice and Public Services, Government of the Northwest Territories.

65 Canada, Debates of the House of Commons, June 29, 1984, 5333-5334, 5336-5337; Canada, Debates of the Senate, June 29, 1984, p. 903; Canada, Debates of the House of Commons, June 29, 1984, pp. 5327–5341; Canada, House of Commons, Minutes of the Standing Committee on Indian Affairs and Northern Development, June 28, 1984, no. 19, pp. 87–88; Bill C-47, *An Act to amend the Indian Act*, June 18, 1984; Bill C-47, *An Act to amend the Indian Act*, June 29, 1984.

66 Newspaper article "Anti-discrimination law discriminates—Indians," in *Whitehorse Star*, September 17, 1984; newspaper article entitled "Coffee shop showdown: How the Indians halted the feminist cavalry," in *The Alberta Report*, July 23, 1984, p. 7; Canada, Debates of the Senate, June 29, 1984, p. 903; Canada, Debates of the House of Commons, June 29, 1984, pp. 5327–5341; newspaper article entitled "PC optimistic he can improve *Indian Act*," in *Winnipeg Free Press*, November 8, 1984, p. 58.

67 LAC, RG 22, Acc. 1998-01695-1, Box 13, File D1021-J1-1-8, vol. 1, DIAND media transcript dated December 16, 1984; newspaper article in the *Winnipeg Free Press* on March 13, 1985 entitled "Indian bands denounce bill"; PCO, File 1230-J1-3, vol. 3, letter dated January 21, 1985 from Chaviva Hosek, President of Action Committee on the Status of Women, to David Crombie, Minister of DIAND; LAC, RG 22, Acc. 1998-01695-1, Box 9, File D1021-J1-1-2, vol. 27, letter dated January 1, 1985 from Jenny Margetts, President, IRIW to Brian Mulroney, Prime Minster

of Canada; newspaper article by Susan Riley entitled "Indian woman split on how government should rule on discriminatory clause," in *The Ottawa Citizen*, December 4, 1984, p. A12; Article entitled "PC optimistic he can improve *Indian Act*," in *Winnipeg Free Press*, November 8, 1984, p. 58; DIAND, Main Records Office, File D1021-1-8, vol. 1, transcript of an interview with David Crombie, Minister of DIAND, on the CBC program *Morningside*, dated October 30, 1984; Weaver, "First Nations Women and Government Policy, 1970–92," p. 115.

68 DIAND, Main Records Office, File D1021-1-8, vol. 1, transcript of an interview with David Crombie, Minister of DIAND, on the CBC program *Morningside*, dated October 30, 1984; Canada, House of Commons, Minutes of the Standing Committee on Indian Affairs and Northern Development, no. 3, December 4, 1984, pp. 4–13.

69 DIAND, Main Records Office, File D1021-J1-1, vol. 7, transcript of remarks by David Crombie, Minister of DIAND, during a Press Conference on *Indian Act* Amendments, dated February 28, 1985.

70 DIAND, Main Records Office, File D1021-J1-1, vol. 7, transcript of remarks by David Crombie, Minister of DIAND, during a Press Conference on *Indian Act* Amendments, dated February 28, 1985.

71 LAC, RG 22, Acc. 1995-96/308, Box 7, File D1021-33-1-C-31, vol. 1, DIAND presentation prepared ca. February 1985; LAC, RG 10, Acc. 1999-01284-4, Box 4, File N1021-J2, vol. 2, DIAND paper prepared in ca. July 1985 entitled "Key Amendments to the *Indian Act*—A Summary"; DIAND, Main Records Office, File D1021-J1-1-11, vol. 1 DIAND paper prepared in ca. February 1985 and entitled "Background Notes: Removal of Discrimination from the *Indian Act*."

72 LAC, RG 10, Acc. 1999-01284-4, Box 4, File N1021-J2, vol. 2, DIAND paper prepared in ca. July 1985 entitled "Key Amendments to the *Indian Act*—A Summary"; DIAND, Main Records Office, File D1021-J1-1-11, vol. 1, DIAND paper prepared in ca. February 1985 entitled "Background Notes: Removal of Discrimination from the *Indian Act*."

73 DIAND, Main Records Office, File D1021-J1-1, vol. 7, transcript of remarks by David Crombie, Minister of DIAND, during a Press Conference on *Indian Act* Amendments, dated February 28, 1985; DIAND, Main Records Office, File D1021-J1-1-11, vol. 1, DIAND paper prepared in ca. February 1985 entitled "Background Notes: Removal of Discrimination from the *Indian Act*"; LAC, RG 22, Acc. 1995-96/308, Box 7, File D1021-33-1-C-31, vol. 1, DIAND presentation prepared in ca. February 1985.

74 DIAND, Main Records Office, File D1021-J1-1, vol. 7, transcript of remarks by David Crombie, Minister of DIAND, during a Press Conference on *Indian Act* Amendments, dated February 28, 1985.

75 Canada, House of Commons, Minutes of the Standing Committee on Indian Affairs and Northern Development, March 7, 1985, no. 12, pp. 6–11; newspaper article entitled "Parting thought," in *The Sun*, June 26, 1984, p. A4.

76 Canada, House of Commons, Minutes of the Standing Committee on Indian Affairs and Northern Development, March 26, 1985, no. 24, pp. 11–13, 32–34, 42–43; LAC, RG 14, Accession 1996-97/193, Box 80, File 5900-331-I1, P 33, Wallet 3, submission on Bill C-31 dated March 14, 1985 prepared by the Women of the Tobique Reserve for the Standing Committee on Indian Affairs and Northern Development; Affairs and Northern Development, March 27, 1985, no. 25, pp. 7–11.

77 Canada, House of Commons, Minutes of the Standing Committee on Indian Affairs and Northern Development, 1985, March 28, no. 28, pp. 56–70, 94–96.

78 Canada, House of Commons, Minutes of the Standing Committee on Indian Affairs and Northern Development, March 28, 1985, no. 28, pp. 96–100. For example, for views of Quebec Native Women's Association and Native Okanagan Women's League, see Canada, House of Commons, Minutes of the Standing Committee on Indian Affairs and Northern Development, no. 24, March 26, 1985, p. 14; Canada, House of Commons, Minutes of the Standing Committee on Indian Affairs and Northern Development, March 27, 1985, no. 26, p. 7.

79 Canada, House of Commons, Minutes of the Standing Committee on Indian Affairs and Northern Development, March 14, 1985, no. 16, pp. 5–10.

80 Canada, House of Commons, Minutes of the Standing Committee on Indian Affairs and Northern Development, March 12, 1985, no. 13, p. 35; Canada, House of Commons, Minutes of the Standing Committee on Indian Affairs and Northern Development, March 18, 1985, no. 17, p. 12.

81 Canada, House of Commons, Minutes of the Standing Committee on Indian Affairs and Northern Development, March 21, 1985, no. 22, p. 17; Canada, House of Commons, Minutes of the

Standing Committee on Indian Affairs and Northern Development, March 20, 1985, no. 21, pp. 8–9; Canada, House of Commons, Minutes of the Standing Committee on Indian Affairs and Northern Development, March 21, 1985, no. 22, p. 35.

82 Canada, House of Commons, Minutes of the Standing Committee on Indian Affairs and Northern Development, March 21, 1985, no. 22, p. 59. For the views of other Alberta bands see Canada, House of Commons, Minutes of the Standing Committee on Indian Affairs and Northern Development, March 21, 1985, no. 22, p. 42 and; Canada, House of Commons, Minutes of the Standing Committee on Indian Affairs and Northern Development, March 28, 1985, no. 28, p. 40.

83 Canada, Debates of the House of Commons, June 12, 1985, pp. 5686–5687; DIAND Library, Press Release Binder, 1985, DIAND communiqué dated June 28, 1985.

84 Canada, Debates of the House of Commons, June 12, 1985, pp. 5686–5687; DIAND Library, Press Release Binder, 1985, DIAND communiqué dated June 28, 1985.

2

Revisiting Histories of Legal Assimilation, Racialized Injustice, and the Future of Indian Status in Canada

Martin Cannon

Introduction

This paper is concerned with the history of injustice surrounding the 1985 *Indian Act* amendments. Demographers suggest these amendments will lead eventually to the legal assimilation of Status Indians in Canada (Clatworthy, 2003a, 2005). These predictions present governments with a number of issues involving citizenship and Aboriginal identity. The future of reserve-based lands also requires attention by governments, especially if the *Indian Act* is contributing to the extinction of the Registered Indian population who are entitled to live on them.

I wish to reflect on matters of citizenship and Aboriginal identity in this paper as well as the history of "involuntary enfranchisement" as this relates to Status Indians and Canadian Indian policy. I hope to invigorate the thinking toward histories of policy-based enfranchisement, racialized injustice, and gender-based exclusion. My discussion also draws from my qualitative research concerning issues of Indian status, the accommodation of Indian policy, and the accessibility of legal knowledge in Status Indian communities (Cannon, 2005).

This research is ongoing, but in this paper I focus on a series of interviews I conducted between February and March of 2006.[1] During this time, I spoke with ten individuals in Saskatchewan and Ontario who are registered as Status Indians under Canada's *Indian Act*. Their views reflect a diversity of experiences based on age, gender, spirituality, and political orientation. They suggest that a series of knowledges and attitudes exist in Canada about Indian status. This paper is an exploration of these views using qualitative methodology.

The 1985 *Indian Act* Amendments: Wherein Lies The (In)justice?

On June 28, 1985, Bill C-31: *An Act to Amend the Indian Act* was given royal assent in Canadian Parliament. It promised to end years of blatant sex discrimination directed toward Aboriginal women under section 12(1)(b) of the 1951 amend-ments. I have sought to develop a critical understanding of Bill C-31 (Cannon, 2006b), and I have shared in that criticism with other academics, Aboriginal people, and non-Aboriginal individuals (Lawrence, 2004; Holmes, 1987; Indian and Northern Affairs Canada, 1990).

The 1985 amendments are now over twenty years old, but they have not received widespread attention from federal policy makers. Discrimination is still made possible under Bill C-31, but it is not always clear or obvious. Under the new legislation, three new types of discrimination were made possible. These include inequalities of Indian status (Holmes, 1987), discrimination toward unmarried or unwed women (Clatworthy, 2003b; Mann, 2005), and the development of Canadian case law concerning Aboriginal citizenship rights (Issac, 1995; Moss, 1990).

Those who register as Status Indians now do so under one of seven different sections of the *Indian Act* (1985). The major difference lies between sections 6(1) and 6(2). These sections reproduce legal inequalities because the children of women who married non-Indians before 1985 cannot pass along Indian status under section 6(2) (Holmes, 1987). The children of men do not face this same restriction as they are registered under section 6(1). The inequality I am describing has been referred to as the second-generation cut-off rule (Huntley et al.,1999: 74).

The "second generation cut-off" clause is something that affects people who are related as cousins. This refers to a current generation of Status Indians that is being treated differently in law because of their grandmother's choice to marry a non-Indian. For example, my mother's grandchildren are not eligible for Indian status even though my uncle's grandchildren (their second cousins) are registered under section 6(2). His children maintained Indian status under section 6(1)(a) of the amendments, and his grandchildren therefore inherited section 6(2) status by birthright. My siblings and I reacquired Indian status under section 6(2) of the 1985 amendments and cannot therefore pass status on to our children unless we marry Status Indians.[2] This is an example of the inequality created by Bill C-31 between the second and subsequent generations of men and women marrying non-Indians.[3]

With the exception of Lawrence (2004), the community-based impact of *An Act to Amend the Indian Act* (1985) has been under-studied from a qualitative perspective in academic literature (but see Huntley et al, 1999; Public History Inc, 2004; Fiske and George, 2006). This is unusual, especially since the *Act* has created a series of complexities for many communities—and for individuals— in terms of identity (Cannon, 2005). I have employed in-depth interviews as a method of addressing the question of policy-based exclusion and its accommodation by individuals (Cannon, 2005). I will highlight some of this research as a way of illustrating histories of assimilation and the current injustices surrounding "out-marriage" and the loss of legal entitlements.

It is the children born to women—but not to men—before 1985 who face ongoing legal assimilation under section 6(2). If they marry non-Indians, these people are unable to pass along Indian status like those that are registered under section 6(1). The Canadian Advisory Council on the Status of Women describes this matter as a human rights issue. "Sections 6(1) and 6(2) together with band membership criteria, perpetuate the unequal treatment of Indian men and Indian women," they suggest, "by giving fewer rights to the grandchildren of women who married out" (quoted in Holmes, 1987: 16).

The *Indian Act* produces legal inequalities for the entire Status Indian collective, and therefore represents an injustice for every Status Indian (Cannon, 2006a and b). But these issues have not always been framed in racialized terms by governments. Instead, the issues involving Indian status have been understood only to involve sex discrimination (Cannon, 1995). But sex discrimination is a misnomer when it comes to describing legal inequalities produced by Indian status provisions. The children of women who continue to marry non-Indians are both male and female Indians. A great deal is riding on their so-called choice to marry non-Indians, or individuals whose "race" is different than that described in the *Indian Act*.

Exogamous marriage (marriages outside of one's group) is now an important question to raise in qualitative research. Demographers predict that the *Indian Act*, including section 6(2), will lead to eventual legal assimilation of Status Indians and their lands in Canada (Clatworthy, 2003a, 2005). High rates of unstated paternity, especially in Manitoba, Saskatchewan, and the NWT are also being reported (Clatworthy, 2003b; Mann, 2005). Are people aware of the consequences of their choice to marry non-Indians? Why do people refuse to state paternity? What are their reasons and are any of them nation-based or cultural?

These are questions that need to be raised in the context of public policy research, and that require further qualitative analysis. If section 6(2) furthers the loss of Indian status, how well is this knowledge being transferred to Status Indian communities? How familiar are people with the consequences of marrying non-Indians and how do they feel about legal assimilation in general? Before exploring these questions, it is important to revisit the history of enfranchisement in Canadian policy and law.

Revisiting Histories of Enfranchisement in Indian Policy

[Bill C-31] ... aimed to shrink the number of "Indians" in Canadian society in order to reduce the government's obligations and liabilities to the status community (Miller, 2004: 45).

The injustice of section 6(2) of the *Indian Act* cannot be appreciated until one revisits the history of Indian policy aimed at assimilation and gender-based exclusion. Indian policy aimed at assimilating Status Indians has had a long history in Canada. As an ideology, it refers to something that is entrenched in the law, and has been since the early 19th century (Dickinson & Wotherspooon, 1992; Henry and Tator, 2006: 347).

Assimilation has always had a cultural and legal component in Canadian Indian policy. Cultural assimilation refers to "the loss, by an individual, of the markers that served to distinguish him or her as a member of one social group" (Jackson, 2002: 74). The schooling of Aboriginal children in residential schools until 1969 is an example of the kinds of policy aimed at cultural assimilation. These were policies aimed at cultivating Euro-Christian behaviours, appearances, and values. They were intended to re-socialize Aboriginal peoples into productive members of an emerging capitalist economy.

Legal assimilation is the word that is used to describe the act of losing Indian status in Canada. This started in 1850 when Canada introduced *An Act for the Protection of the Indians in Upper Canada from Imposition, and the Property Occupied or Enjoyed by them From Trespass and Injury*. It was also a part of policy in 1857 to encourage the "gradual civilization" of the Indian tribes (Miller, 2004: 17). These two statutes introduced two new racialized categories of Aboriginal peoples: Indian and non-Indian. It was assumed (and expected) that band council governments would administer these new categories of people.

Sociologists refer to this process, whereby a heterogenous, linguistically diverse population is singled out for different (and often unequal) treatment in Canada, as racialization (Li, 1990: 7). But racialization, as it is often defined, does not refer to the act of taking up or realizing racial categories, however conscious a person might be of that process. Aboriginal peoples did not play a part in creating the "racial" category Indian, but policy has had the effect of institutionalizing the category as a system of relations among Status Indians in Canada. This is what is meant by racialization.

The history I am describing is etched in the memory of some, but not all, Status Indians. I include myself as one of these individuals, because I am a Status Indian and I have personally witnessed what the *Indian Act* is capable of doing legally, especially section 6(2). The *Indian Act* has been just as concerned with constructing the legal category "Indian" as it has been on getting rid of Status Indians. Legal assimilation must therefore refer to the process of becoming a Non-Status Indian—whether an Aboriginal person is made aware of it or not.

Legal assimilation was one of the motivations behind enfranchisement policy. Enfranchisement emerged in 1857 with the explicit and avowed purpose of assimilating Status Indians. The premise behind this policy was simple: upon meeting certain criteria, Indian men who were literate, free of debt and of good moral character could (along with their "dependents"), give up legal status and become non-Indians. Enfranchisement was re-established in three subsequent pieces of legislation, but it was not always voluntary in the way I have described.

In 1918, Indian men (along with their wives and children) could become voluntarily enfranchised if they lived away from their communities (*Indian Act*

[S.C. 1918, c.26, s.6(122A)(1)] reprinted in Venne, 1981: 220; Indian and Northern Affairs Canada, 1991: 10–11). The policy of enfranchisement was not only racialized, it was therefore simultaneously patriarchal (Cannon, 1995; Stevenson, 1999: 57). Enfranchisement policy assumed that, like other women, Indian women were to be legally subject to their husbands (Jamieson, 1978). This was a foreign notion to my own nation of peoples, the Six Nations of Grand River Territory (Cannon, 2004).[4]

Enfranchisement continued well into the 20th century. In 1951, enfranchisement was made possible for individuals meeting the variety of criteria established in sections 12, 15, and 108 (*Indian Act* [S.C., 1951, c.29] reprinted in Venne, 1981: 319, 348–349; Indian and Northern Affairs Canada, 1991: 15–17). These sections included a) the involuntary enfranchisement of women marrying non-Indians and b) the voluntary enfranchisement of entire bands of people who so desired upon approval of the Minister of Indian Affairs (ibid). The children of women born prior to a woman's marriage to a non-Indian also became involuntarily enfranchised under an amendment to the *Indian Act* in 1956 (*Indian Act* [S.C., 1956, c.40, s.26] reprinted in Venne, 1981: 398, Indian and Northern Affairs Canada, 1991: 19].

The very concept of voluntary enfranchisement (or voluntarily becoming a Non-Status Indian) did not end in Canada until June 28, 1985 with the passing of section 6(1)(d) of *An Act to Amend the Indian Act* (*Indian Act*, R.S.C. 1985 (1st Supp.), c.32, s.6(1)(d)). In a manual on registration and entitlements legislation, Indian and Northern Affairs Canada proclaimed that section 6(1)(d) had "abolished" the practice of enfranchisement under the *Indian Act* (1991: 21). However, there is reason to believe that involuntary enfranchisement survives the 1985 amendments to the *Indian Act*.

Involuntary Enfranchisement in Demographic Perspective

Enfranchisement, voluntary and involuntary, was not achieved, and by 1985 Canada had to abandon the policy after close to 130 years of frustration. (Miller, 2004: 271)

Involuntary enfranchisement takes place in Canada whenever a Status Indian (registered under section 6(2) of the *Indian Act*), marries and has children with a non-Indian person. This act of exogamy or "out-marriage" may seem a relatively neutral one, but section 6(2) works to disenfranchise the grandchildren of women who married non-Indians before 1985. These individuals represent a new class of "involuntarily enfranchised" Indians: the children of section 6(2) intermarriages.[5] These children lose their parents' birthright to be registered as Status Indians in Canada. The loss of legal entitlements is brought on by their parent's choice to marry non-Indians.

Individuals often marry non-Indians in the process of migrating to cities. Their choices are sometimes influenced by the depletion of resources and the lack of economic opportunities on reserves in Canada (Frideres, 2005: 164–170). These decisions lead to a loss of inheritance for the children born of section 6(2) inter-marriages. As I will demonstrate, it is superficial to assume that all Status Indians are aware of this process, or that it leads to their children's losing status. However conscious Status Indians may be of it, the children of section 6(2) intermarriages are not legally entitled to *Indian Act* status like the children of section 6(1) inter-marriages.[6]

Section 6(2) of the *Indian Act* (R.S.C 1985 (1st Supp.), c. 32, s. 6(2)) is little different in effect than section 12(1)(b) of the *Indian Act* (S.C. 1951, c. 29, s. 12(1)(b)). Both sections furthered the loss of Indian status by those who marry non-Indians. The only difference is that now men also involuntarily enfranchise their children and grandchildren when marrying non-Indians. The choices facing these *male and female* Indians of the Status Indian population registered under section 6(2) of the *Indian Act* are therefore not any different than those facing women from 1850–1985.

Despite the passage of Bill C-31, intermarriage is still not a neutral act for Status Indians in Canada. It is the children of those who are registered under section 6(2) and who marry non-Indians that are now being disinherited. These are the grandchildren of women who married non-Indians prior to 1985, as well as the grandchildren of men and women who married non-Indians after 1985. They are, collectively, a class of Indians that stand to alter and change the composi-tion of Status Indian populations in Canada. Clatworthy (2003a, 2005) has placed these trends into demographic perspective by providing a series of population forecasts.

Clatworthy (2005: 32, and in this volume) predicts that the Registered Indian population will witness a dramatic decline because of section 6(2) and other changes stemming from the 1985 *Indian Act* amendments. He projects that on- and off-reserve populations entitled to membership and Indian registration will witness a population of 914,300 by the year 2077, a dramatic drop from the projected 987,600 in 2052 (ibid).

As Clatworthy (2003a: 86–87) explains:

> Within two generations, most of the children born to First Nations populations are not expected to qualify for registration under the new rules. Within four generations, only one of every six children born to First Nations populations is expected to qualify for registration. Unlike the rules of the old *Act,* which guaranteed registration to nearly all of the descendants of Registered Indian males, Bill C-31's rules have the potential to result in the extinction of the Registered Indian population.

These forecasts raise a series of concerns about the future of Indian status in Canada. They suggest that policies of legal enfranchisement, including the long term effects of section 6(2), will result in the eventual legal assimilation of Status Indians and their lands in Canada. Several factors will influence the rate at which this takes place, including the frequency of exogamous marriage. But legal assimilation also depends on a people's familiarity with, and knowledge about, section 6(2) of the *Indian Act*. In general, what do Status Indians think about the *Indian Act*, and about the prospect of legal assimilation? Are people aware of the potential effects of section 6(2)? These questions require ongoing qualitative inquiry (Lawrence, 2004; Cannon, 2005).

Revisiting Histories of Legal Assimilation in Indian Policy

Legal assimilation is something that takes place in law whenever Indians registered under section 6(2) intermarry and have children with a person outside of the racialized collective. This "choice" creates a new generation of legally enfranchised grandchildren. These children do not have Indian status because their parents (registered under section 6(2) of the *Indian Act*) married non-Indians. They may also include the grandchildren of women who refuse to state the "race" of fathers at the time of registration (Mann, 2005).

The children I am describing are a new generation of Aboriginal peoples. Their ages range from 0–22, and they are not currently entitled to register as Status Indians. They have been placed in unequal relation to the status collective, and to the children of persons registered under section 6(1) of the *Indian Act*. These include, for example, the grandchildren of men who married non-Indians prior to the 1985 amendments.

As previously detailed, the injustice I am describing is known as the second-generation cut-off rule (Huntley et al, 1999: 74). It refers to the legal inequality facing the grandchildren of men and women who married non-Indians before 1985. This generation of Aboriginal peoples inherits the historic weight of racialized and gender-exclusionary discrimination. They are the second-generation of descendants to experience inequalities in the law. They are placed in the same unequal relationship to one another as their grandparents were before 1985.

Twenty-two years ago, it was possible for an Indian man to marry a non-Indian woman and remain a Status Indian. Because he never lost Indian status, he was able to make his wife and children Status Indians prior to 1985. His children were entitled to registration under section 6(1)(a) following the 1985 amendments.[7] The children of out-marrying women, on the other hand, could only register under section 6(2) of Bill C-31. Those who are registered under section 6(2) cannot pass along Indian status. Only those with section 6(1) status are able to pass status on to their children.

It is important to ask how legal inequalities created by sections 6(1) and 6(2) are playing themselves out among status populations today. In fact, some of these inequalities have yet to be fully articulated in political, judicial, and social forums. This occurred to me in ongoing research where I asked a group of Status Indians, aged 19–35, what it meant to be registered under section 6(2) of the *Indian Act*.

In one interview, I asked one of my study participants if she knew of the consequences of being registered under section 6(2) of the *Indian Act*. She responded:

> I'm just categorized under section 6(2), what can I do? It's like, I just fall under that status under what their requirements are, you know? And so, I'm just another person basically categorized into a spot. That's about it. (Interview Transcript #7: 4).

In other interviews, people were very aware of the inequality produced by section 6(2) of the *Indian Act*, but these individuals expressed cynicism where finding a resolution to them is concerned. As one person explained:

> I can't see the government telling me "Well, if you go and do this, your children won't have status." I think they'd rather me just go and do it without my knowing and then my children would be screwed over. That is an issue for me, I'd like my children to be Status Indians, not for any reason in particular, it's just cause I feel like that's a right that every Native person in Canada should have ... Having to worry about who you marry shouldn't be an issue, but it is, you know?... (Interview Transcript #3: 4).

Another person I interviewed for the purposes of this paper expressed confusion where understanding Indian registration is concerned. As she explained:

> [W]hen they gave me my status, they basically sent me a letter saying I was approved with my status number but it had nothing on there stating what I was considered to be like, you know, Bill C-31 or whatever. My parents are Bill C-31s, but I have no idea what that makes me, and I have no idea what that is gonna make my children. Like, I think that's a big problem. I haven't actually gone out and tried to figure it out on my own, but I've asked a lot of people, you know teachers, profs, and everything, to see if they can explain it to me ... (Interview Transcript #4: 3).

There exists both apathy and criticism about Indian status and citizenship injustices. Issues of knowledge, accessibility, and sharing create some of this apathy. Injustices must be therefore placed into terms that "the general Native public" understands, particularly before individuals can take action (Huntley et al, 1999: 74). But issues of knowledge, accessibility, and dissemination will not alone eliminate the apathy that is expressed toward the 1985 amendments.

Apathy is also expressed because of some people's preference to talk of identity in terms of nations, territories, or a community of people to which they belong. This is common at Six Nations of Grand River Territory, the nation where I am a band member and an Oneida citizen (Monture-Angus, 1995; Cannon, 2004).[7] I have also heard these ideas expressed by Status Indians in other parts of Canada as well.

According to one of the individuals I interviewed for this paper:

> Having a status card doesn't make you any more Indian. I definitely think it has a lot to do with your culture and how much of it you actually connect with, you know? ... I've always enjoyed anything that has to do with my culture, like powwows, round dances, and feasts. My family has always been involved in a lot of that stuff. So I think being Native has to do with how much you connect with your culture ... (Interview Transcript #8: 2).

Another Status Indian identified herself as belonging to a community of people. This is what mattered in defining herself as an Aboriginal person. As she explained:

> I guess I've never even concerned myself with things like status. I see my children as Indians because I've raised them as such, and for me, what makes them Indians is the values, which is why the traditions and the ceremonies are important to me. Being part of a larger Indian community is really important to me, it's not about blood or what the government says (Interview Transcript #5: 1).

Despite the imposition of status boundaries, identities are being realized outside of racialized status provisions, and in nation-specific terms (also see Lawrence, 2004). These identities are tied to communities, nation-to-nation agreements, and to historic treaties (Henderson, 2002). The capacity of liberal pluralism to acknowledge and grasp these identities is an outstanding matter of colonial injustice in Canada (Kymlicka, 2000; Green, 2001; Schouls, 2003).

Rethinking Indian Status and Engaging With Citizenship

The interviews I conducted with Status Indians concerning the 1985 *Indian Act* amendments permit three major conclusions. First and foremost, that legal assimilation is furthered by the inability of governments (deliberate or inadvertent) to transfer knowledge concerning legal inequality to Status Indian communities. Second, that many people prefer to talk of identity and citizenship in nation-specific terms. Third and finally, that it is necessary to scrutinize the political and legal contexts that prevent "identification approaches" to identity and citizenship from happening (Schouls, 2003: 35, 166).

According to my research, there is variable knowledge possessed by a new and emerging generation of individuals registered under section 6(2) of the *Indian Act*. Some of these individuals know what it means to be a Non-Status Indian while identifying as an Aboriginal person. Some of them endeavour to establish, or maintain, a connection with their own and other communities. But others know very little about status injustices. This is something that actually works in the interest of legally assimilating the Registered Indian populations of Canada.

If section 6(2) contributes to the loss of Indian status as demographers predict, then this knowledge must somehow be transmitted to each and every Status Indian. Aboriginal peoples are entitled to know about status inequalities, especially within the broader context of history aimed at their racialization, legal assimilation, and enfranchisement. The sharing of this knowledge ensures the right of Aboriginal peoples to revisit and decide on a more equitable system of defining Indian status—or of resisting this system altogether.

People have been made unequal to each other because of the *Indian Act*. To pretend that Indian status is inconsequential is to therefore undermine the importance of legal distinctions, and how these affect the relationship between Status Indians, both male and female. But the people I interviewed also suggested a way of thinking about identity outside of Indian status provisions. These issues of citizenship and belonging are of immediate importance to Aboriginal populations. The question is, how do we get around to debating them and where ought they to be debated?

Section 6(2) injustices invite the people who want to challenge them to become even more deeply drawn into the colonial frameworks that have been used to define and sometimes divide them (Lawrence, 2004: 42). Seeing women and men in state-constructed terms often conceals historic events which imposed racialized distinctions on all Aboriginal nations, and that later required people to be legislated outside of them. It also detracts from the kinds of conversations that governments could be having where Aboriginal identity and citizenship is concerned.

Correcting Historic Wrongs or Racialized Injustice?

Freedom from colonization is the sense of an unbounded self and the ability to live fully in a wide and open world. It is to feel and live large! Being "Indian" and being "Aboriginal" is accepting a small self, imprisonment in the small space created for us by the white man: reserves, Aboriginal rights, *Indian Act* entitlements, etc. (Alfred, 2005: 165)

A major change in thinking is required before issues of Indian status can be fully understood or rejuvenated in Canada. I believe the future is now being realized—and can be realized—by refusing to acknowledge the *Indian Act* as the source of determining Aboriginal citizenship. Legal assimilation is less threatening to individuals who are mindful of Aboriginal identity and community in all of its infinite capacities. But I have intended to show in this paper how even these individuals are unable to prevent the legal assimilation of Status Indians and their reserve lands in Canada.[9]

Indian status or status inequalities will require the ongoing attention of federal and band-based governments. Several issues will emerge out of these discussions involving citizenship and Indian status. Before meaningful discussion can take place around any one of them, it will be necessary to move beyond the *Indian Act*. This will require legally acknowledging a sense of belonging based on real or assumed bonds between people, their shared knowledge of traditional stories or history, original nation-to-nation agreements, common beliefs, and a tie to some specific territory—including urban areas (see Green, 2001; Lawrence, 2004; Schouls, 2003: 177).

It is also necessary to begin the process of *affirming* the nations of Aboriginal peoples in law and politics, including who it is that we define as our citizens (Denis, 2002: 115–117). Only after these issues are addressed are Aboriginal peoples able to become truly self-determining. Phil Fontaine, Grand Chief of the Assembly of First Nations, recently noted:

> It is morally, politically and legally wrong for one government to tell another government who its citizens are, and we are calling for a process to move citizenship to the jurisdiction where it properly belongs, and that is with First Nations governments (*Prince Albert Grand Council Tribune*, 2005).

By focusing on "intercultural identification" or "intercultural belonging" (Henderson, 2002: 432), the *Indian Act* remains ineffective as a tool for regulating identity (Lawrence, 2004: 230). But this does not mean that Canada is prepared to acknowledge the people who no longer "qualify" for Indian status and registration. It does not even require that nation-to-nation agreements, urban-based individuals, territories, or nation-specific understandings of citizenship be acknowledged (Anderson and Denis, 2003: 382–388). Nor does it justify the kinds of ongoing legal inequalities created under section 6(2) of the *Indian Act*. These things require the attention of governments, policy makers, and those most affected by citizenship injustices.

A change in the way of thinking about Indian status is required in Canada. Citizenship injustices have their origins in the racialized and sexist understandings that were introduced historically and that remain a part of colonial policy. It follows that historical analysis (or "liberating strategies") be committed to realizing—and addressing—both types of discrimination (Cannon, 1995). The loss of Indian status—and Indian status in general—is not something that belongs to women or "individuals." The loss of Indian status is something that belongs to the Aboriginal collective because of the potential of section 6(2) to disinherit them, and because of complex injustices that exist at the intersection of racialization and patriarchy (ibid). Indeed, many men are now included among individuals experiencing discrimination at the "intersection" of race and gender.

A new politics of identity is forming in Canada, and it includes a generation of men and women who are disqualified from Indian status, even though they are Aboriginal peoples. Some of these individuals were registered under section 6(2) of the *Indian Act* and face the same choices available to their mothers as "Indians." For the generations affected by it, section 6(2) brings about a different way of thinking about "Indianess." It could even bring forward a new way of thinking about historical discrimination, preferably leading many of us to realize that citizenship injustices were never really about women. They were about state-inspired definitions, and the act of becoming (or not) a member of the racialized collective.

Endnotes

1   I would like to acknowledge the Strategic Research and Analysis Directorate at the Department of Indian and Northern Development for funding this research.

2   The details I am describing here about Indian status and the way it defines people differently within my own immediate family is but one example of how the *Indian Act* has complicated the lives of Status Indians in Canada. Many people share entirely different experiences where Indian status is concerned. In current research, I am seeking to better document these histories through the use of qualitative research methodology.

3   Section 6(1)(a) of *An Act to Amend the Indian Act* (1985) read: "6(1) a person is entitled to be registered if (a) that person was registered or entitled to be registered immediately prior to April 17, 1985."

4   For an analysis of the matrilineal and matrilocal kinship organization of the Haudenosaunee or "Iroquois," see Randle, 1951; Richards, 1967; Druke, 1986; Brown, 1975; and Eastlack-Shafer, 1990. For an analysis of social change and cultural continuity with respect to matrilineal and matrilocal kinship structure, see Shoemaker, 1991 and Doxtator, 1996. Also see Fiske & George, 2006 and Native Women's Association of Canada, 1992.

5   This new generation of individuals also includes the children of women registered under section 6(2) who do not state paternity at the time of registration.

6   For a description of the process see Clatworthy this volume. For graphical representation of the process see Clatworthy, S. "Impacts of the 1985 Amendments to the *Indian Act* on First Nations Populations" in Jerry White et al. *Aboriginal Conditions: Research as a Foundation for Public Policy*. Vancouver: UBC Press. (2003)

7   See footnote 2.

8   Monture-Angus writes: When I was growing up, the word I learned to describe who I was, was "Indian." Since then, I have learned that it is not a good way to name myself. I have been learning how these constructs and processes support racism. The meaning of the word "Indian" is a purely legal definition. An Indian is a person who is entitled to be registered under the definitions in the *Indian Act*. It is not a good way to describe ourselves because it is a definition that has been forced on us by the federal government (30–31).

9   These individuals also face what Denis (2002: 115) calls the "heavy burden of historical proof." This refers to a set of expectations that have been placed upon Aboriginal peoples in legal arenas to demonstrate an unbroken and timeless connection with the past or face charges of being inauthentic or no longer entitled to rights-based claims (also see Garroutte, 2003).

References

Alfred, Taiaiake. 2005. *Wasase: Indigenous Pathways of Action and Freedom*. Peterborough: Broadview Press.

Anderson, Chris and Claude Denis. 2003. "Urban Natives and the Nation: Before and After the Royal Commission on Aboriginal Peoples." *Canadian Review of Sociology and Anthropology*. Vol. 40, no. 4: 373–390.

Brown, Judith K. 1975. "Iroquois Women: An Ethnographic Note." In Rayna Reiter (ed.), *Towards and Anthropology of Women*. New York: Monthly Review Press, 235–251.

Cannon, Martin J. 2006a. "First Nations Citizenship: An Act to Amend the *Indian Act* (1985) and the Accommodation of Sex Discriminatory Policy" *Canadian Review of Social Policy*, no. 56: 40–71.

Cannon, Martin J. 2006b. Revisiting Histories of Gender-Based Exclusion and the New Politics of Indian Identity. Unpublished Paper Written for the National Centre for First Nations Governance.

Cannon, Martin J. 2005. "Bill C-31—*An Act to Amend the Indian Act*: Notes Toward a Qualitative Analysis of Legislated Injustice." The Canadian Journal of Native Studies. Vol. 25, no 1: 153–167.

Cannon, Martin J. 2004. A History of Politics and Women's Status at Six Nations of the Grand River Territory: A Study of Continuity and Social Change Among the Iroquois. Unpublished Doctoral Dissertation. York University, Toronto.

Cannon, Martin J. 1995. Demarginalizing the Intersection of 'Race' and Gender in First Nations Politics and the Law. Unpublished Master of Arts Thesis. Queen's University, Kingston.

Clatworthy, Stewart. 2005. *Indian Registration, Membership and Population Change in First Nations Communities*. Ottawa: DIAND Strategic Research and Analysis Directorate.

Clatworthy, Stewart. 2003a. "Impacts of the 1985 Amendments to the *Indian Act* on First Nations Populations." In Jerry P. White, Paul S. Maxim, and Dan Beavon (eds.), *Aboriginal Conditions: Research as a Foundation for Public Policy*. Vancouver: UBC Press,. 63–90.

Clatworthy, Stewart. 2003b. *Factors Contributing to Unstated Paternity*. Ottawa: DIAND Strategic Research and Analysis Directorate.

Denis, Claude. 2002. "Indigenous Citizenship and History in Canada: Between Denial and Imposition." In R. Adamoski, D.E. Chunn and R. Menzies (eds.), *Contesting Canadian Citizenship: Historical Readings*. Peterborough: Broadview Press, 113–126.

Dickinson, Harley and Terry Wotherspoon. 1992. "From Assimilation to Self-Government: Towards a Political Economy of Canada's Aboriginal Policies. In Vic Satzewich (ed.), *Deconstructing a Nation: Immigration, Multiculturalism and Racism in '90s Canada*. Halifax: Fernwood Publishing, 405–421.

Doxtator, Deborah. 1996. What Happened to the Iroquois Clans?: A Study of Clans in Three Nineteenth Century Rotinonhsyonni Communities. Unpublished PhD Dissertation. University of Western Ontario, London.

Druke, Mary. 1986. "Iroquois and Iroquoian in Canada." In R. Bruce Morrison and Roderick Wilson (eds.), *Native Peoples: The Canadian Experience*. Toronto: McClelland and Stewart, 302–324 .

Eastlack-Shafer, Ann. 1990. "The Status of Iroquois Women" [1941]. In W.G. Spittal (ed.), *Iroquois Women: An Anthology*. Ohsweken, Ontario: Iroquois Publishing and Craft Supplies, 71–135.

Fiske, Jo-Anne and Evelyn George. 2006. *Seeking Alternatives to Bill C-31: From Cultural Trauma to Cultural Revitalization through Customary Law*. Ottawa: Status of Women Canada.

Frideres, James and René Gadacz. 2005. *Aboriginal Peoples in Canada*, 7th Edition. Toronto: Pearson Education Canada.

Garroutte, Eva Marie. 2003. *Real Indians: Identity and the Survival of Native America*. Berkeley: University of California Press.

Green, Joyce. 2001. "Canaries in the Mines of Citizenship." *Canadian Journal of Political Science*. Vol. 34, no. 4: 715–739.

Henderson, James (Sákéj) Youngblood. 2002. "Sui Generis and Treaty Citizenship." *Citizenship Studies*. Vol. 6, no. 4: 415–440.

Henry, Frances and Carol Tator. 2006. *The Colour of Democracy: Racism in Canadian Society*, 3rd Edition. Toronto: Thompson Nelson.

Holmes, Joan. 1987. *Bill C-31: Equality or Disparity?* Ottawa: Canadian Advisory Council on the Status of Women.

Huntley, Audrey, et al. 1999. *Bill C-31: Its Impact, Implications and Recommendations for Change in British Columbia—Final Report*. Vancouver: Aboriginal Women's Action Network (AWAN).

Indian and Northern Affairs Canada. 1991. *The* Indian Act *Past and Present: A Manual on Registration and Entitlement Legislation*. Ottawa: Indian Registration and Band Lists Directorate.

Indian and Northern Affairs Canada. 1990. *Correcting Historic Wrongs? Report of the Aboriginal Inquiry on the Impacts of Bill C-31*. [Impacts of the 1985 Amendments to the Indian Act (Bill C-31)] vol. 1. Ottawa: Indian and Northern Affairs Canada.

Interview Transcript #3. Conducted by Martin J. Cannon. March 1, 2006. Saskatoon, SK.

Interview Transcript #4. Conducted by Martin J. Cannon. March 3, 2006. Saskatoon, SK.

Interview Transcript #5. Conducted by Martin J. Cannon. March 4, 2006. Saskatoon, SK.

Interview Transcript #7. Conducted by Martin J. Cannon. March 6, 2006. Saskatoon, SK.

Interview Transcript #8. Conducted by Martin J. Cannon. March 10, 2006. Saskatoon, SK.

Issac, Thomas. 1995. "Case Commentary. Self-Government, Indian Women and their Rights of Reinstatement under the *Indian Act*: A Comment on Sawridge Band v. Canada." *Canadian Native Law Reporter*, vol. 4: 1–13.

Jackson, Deborah Davis. 2002. *Our Elders Lived It: American Indian Identity in the City*. DeKalb, IL: Northern Illinois University Press.

Jamieson, Kathleen. 1978. *Indian Women and the Law in Canada: Citizens Minus*. Ottawa: Status of Women Canada.

Kymlicka, Will and Wayne Norman (eds.) 2000. *Citizenship in Culturally Diverse Societies: Issues, Contexts, Concepts*. Oxford: Oxford University Press.

Lawrence, Bonita. 2004. *'Real' Indians and Others: Mixed Blood Urban Native Peoples and Indigenous Nationhood*. Vancouver: UBC Press.

Li, P. S. (ed.). 1990. *Race and Ethnic Relations in Canada*. Toronto: Oxford University Press.

Mann, Michelle. 2005. *Indian Registration: Unrecognized and Unstated Paternity*. Ottawa: Status of Women Canada.

Miller, J.R. *Lethal Legacy: Current Native Controversies in Canada*. Toronto: McClelland & Stewart.

Monture-Angus, Patricia. 2004. *Thunder in My Soul: A Mohawk Woman Speaks*. Halifax: Fernwood Publishing.

Moss, Wendy. 1990. "Indigenous Self-Government and Sexual Equality under the *Indian Act*: Resolving Conflicts between Collective and Individual Rights." *Queen's Law Review*, vol. 15: 279–305.

Native Women's Association of Canada. 1992. *Matriarchy and the Canadian Charter: A Discussion Paper*. Ottawa: Native Women's Association of Canada.

Prince Albert Grand Council Tribune. 2005. "AFN Calls for Control of First Nations Citizenship 20 Years After Bill C-31: Population of Status Indians Will Decline Because of Bill C-31" *Prince Albert Grand Council Tribune*. August, 2005. <**www.pagc.sk.ca/tribune/page14.php**>.

Randle, Martha Champion. 1951. "No. 8: Iroquois Women, Then and Now." In William N. Fenton (ed.), *Bulletin no. 149: Symposium on local diversity in Iroquois culture*. Washington, D.C.: Smithsonian Institution Bureau of American Ethnology, 169–180.

Richards, Cara E. 1967. "Huron and Iroquois Residence Patterns, 1600–1650." In Elizabeth Tooker (ed.), *Iroquois Culture, History and Prehistory: Proceedings of the 1965 Conference on Iroquois Research*. Albany: University of the State of New York, State Education Dept., New York State Museum and Science Service.

Schouls, Tim. 2003. *Shifting Boundaries: Aboriginal Identity, Pluralist Theory and the Politics of Self-Government*. Vancouver: UBC Press.

Venne, Sharon H. 1981. *Indian Acts and Amendments, 1868–1975: An Indexed Collection*. Saskatoon: Native Law Centre, University of Saskatchewan .

White, Jerry, Paul Maxim, and Nicholas Spence. 2004. *Permission to Develop: Aboriginal Treaties, Case Law and Regulations*. Toronto: Thompson Educational Publishing, Inc.

Winona Stevenson. 1999. "Colonialism and First Nations Women in Canada." In Enakshi Dua and Angela Robertson (eds.), *Scratching the Surface: Canadian Anti-Racist Feminist Thought*. Women's Press, 55–57.

Shirley Clarke

Shirley Clarke was born August 23, 1952. She is the daughter of Joseph B. Peters and Doris Mary Brooks; both parents were registered. Shirley lost her Indian status through marriage to a non-native. At that time Shirley was on the Annapolis Valley Band. She did not receive anything from her band stating that she was no longer a band member but she knew she was no longer considered Indian. She never asked her band for assistance because she knew she didn't qualify for any type of assistance. Although Shirley and her husband could of used assistance for housing, they made out as best as they could. Ms. Clarke felt that the men should have also lost their Indian status for marrying non-natives; she said she was discriminated against for being a native woman. For years Shirley and her family lived off the reserve. She said that there was a stigma against native women because they were treated differently and still are. For years native women were treated differently, did not have equality, and no one cared.

Shirley gained her Indian status in 1985. She says it was a step forward for native women. Bill C-31 didn't correct all the injustice that was inflicted on native women. Nothing has really changed for the better for First Nation women and no one seems to care. Shirley stated that we need the support from the Chiefs, if we are to get justice. Shirley is now Chief of the Glooscap First Nation. She has been the Chief for eighteen years. She stated that the majority of the Chiefs felt that 12(1)(b) and Bill C-31 was a women's problem; and they don't accept native women as equals. These Chiefs really have a problem with the women bringing non-native men on the reserves but didn't have a problem with non-native women on the reserves. Chief Clarke stated that the native women who lost their Indian status were denied their birthrights for generations and they should be compensated.

Part Two:
Community Impacts

3

Bill C-31:
A Study of Cultural Trauma[1]

Jo-Anne Fiske and Evelyn George

Introduction

In 1985 Canada amended the *Indian Act* in respect to the criteria regulating registration under the *Act*. Among other provisions, the amendments allowed women formerly stripped of Indian status due to marrying non-Indians to be restored to the Indian Register and to membership in their natal First Nation.[2] Known as Bill C-31, these amendments created new classes of registration: section 6(1) designates individuals who have two parents with Indian status, while section 6(2) lists individuals with only one registered parent. Children with two parents registered under either 6(1) or 6(2) are registered under section 6(1) and can transmit status to their children. The denial of status to children of a single parent with 6(2) registration is commonly referred to as the second-generation cut-off rule.

In order for women to register their children they are now required to disclose the father's identity and to prove his Indian status. Mothers who fail to do so cannot register their children under the same section as to which they themselves are entitled to. That is, the child of a mother registered under 6(1) but whose father is not identified as a Registered Indian is designated 6(2), while a child of a mother registered under 6(2) whose father is not proven to be registered is excluded from the Registry and becomes known as a Non-Registered or Non-Status Indian. Without status the child cannot share in the rights and privileges protected by the *Indian Act* and enjoyed by her/his mother and her registered kin. Across Canada, Indian women have protested Canada's policy demanding disclosure of paternity. They object on a number of grounds, not the least of which is the state's intrusion into their personal lives. Disclosure of paternity can place them in social jeopardy, perhaps endanger them, and at the very least cause social conflicts where a man either denies paternity or refuses to acknowledge it to authorities.

While section 4 (1) of the *Indian Act* does allow some exceptions, these are not guaranteed for everyone in this situation. If a band takes control of its membership it can include members who do not have status. Under these terms, section 4.1 permits these members to be deemed "Indian" for specified sections of the *Act*. For example, such members could receive an individual allotment of reserve land from the band council.

In 2003, Stewart Clatworthy reviewed the demographic outcome of this policy for Indian and Northern Affairs Canada (INAC). Clatworthy (2003a) reported high levels of non compliance with the policy pressure to disclose paternity. Overall Clatworthy found that from 1985–1999, 37,300 births to women holding 6(1) status were registered with unstated paternity. Young mothers in particular do not disclose paternity. Thirty percent of births with unreported paternity were born to this age group, with the highest percentage to mothers under fifteen. Smaller First Nations feel the greatest effects of this practice; out-marrying is more common because in communities of fewer than 100, residents are too closely related to permit high rates of endogamy (marriage within the community). Out-marrying, or exogamous parenting as Clatworthy terms it, threatens the future of First Nations as fewer individuals are registered under the *Indian Act* and increasing numbers of families experience disruption through generations as non-status children and grandchildren lose ties with their cultural community.

Although Bill C-31 was designed to repair the harm done to women and their communities when women lost status upon marriage to a non-Indian or lost membership upon marriage to a member of another First Nation, the repercussions of Bill C-31 have been painful and contradictory because the amendments also offered First Nations some control over their membership while requiring them to recognize certain "acquired rights" to membership. This has placed some women in conflict with those First Nations that deny them membership rights provided by the Act, limit or refuse access to housing and other services, and marginalize them in social life. In light of these conflicts and the effects of the second generation cut-off, studies of Bill C-31 have traditionally focused on three issues: gender conflicts arising from the reinstatement of women who lost status through out-marriage to their natal community (Bear 1991;Green 1985, 2000, 2001), issues of conflict between individual and collective rights (Macklem 2001, Schouls 2003), and questions of identity arising from distinctions made between Status and Non-Status Indians (Lawrence 2004; Miskimmim 1996). In this paper, we shift the focus from these established discourses to consider Bill C-31 and the attendant policy requiring disclosure of paternity as cultural trauma.

Embedded in the late-twentieth-century discourse of trauma, new perspectives on disruption of intergenerational cultural continuity came to be construed within the metaphor of wounding. The idea of cultural trauma is not used uniformly. Anthropologists and sociologists use the idea of cultural trauma to speak to slow, insidious disruptions of well-being that are collectively claimed although individually experienced. By labelling these insidious interruptions of cultural trauma, human experience is exposed in terms of immediate and delayed suffering and located within specific historical and social contexts. Alexander (2004, 44) asserts cultural trauma constitutes a threat to collective identity and exists within a context of continuous and recurrent struggle. Responses to cultural trauma include a multiplicity of defenses and coping mechanisms, such as contested responses within the membership group, denial, scapegoating (projection), and rationalizing (46–47).

Here we apply the notion to three different processes: trauma to culture, collective stigmatization or rejection by one's own culture, and historic trauma. Trauma to a culture is experienced collectively. Sztompka (2000) suggests trauma to a culture occurs when social change results in disruption of "the very central assumptions of a culture, or more precisely is interpreted as fundamentally incongruent with the core values, bases of identity, foundations of collective pride etc." (2000, 453). He includes in his example "delegalization of traditional family forms" (453). Thus, Bill C-31 generally, and most specifically through its imposition of patrilineal identity with respect to children of reinstated women and the unstated paternity policy and its discontinuity of intergenerational membership, constitutes trauma to a culture, and radically so to matrilineal cultures. The trauma generated by Bill C-31 arises not from an unexpected event of horrific consequences but rather from a persistent destruction of individual well-being and collective continuity. Bill C-31 is experienced as traumatic within a cultural process shaped by continuing fragmentation of First Nations identity and sovereignty resulting from colonization. Fragmentation continues today in new and often subtle ways. Current power hierarchies exist within an historic legacy that is marked by paternalism and patriarchal assumptions that are imposed upon First Nations women without regard to cultural differences.[3]

The Context

Bill C-31 entered the lives of First Nations women after centuries of colonial displacement and historic traumas. These included patriarchal and sexist practices that disrupted family relations, diminished women's economic autonomy, and eroded community well-being and collective identity. In addition, First Nations people mark the residential school as an experience that wounded their societies more deeply than any other colonial intrusion in their collective memories. Traumatic consequences of a schooling regime that led to the deaths of children in institutional epidemics, estrangement of grandchildren from grandparents, and immeasurable losses to language, cultural knowledge, spiritual wellbeing, and social cohesion are now conceded by Canada to have left legacies "of personal pain and distress that continue to reverberate in Aboriginal communities to this day." (IRSRC 2007). The social disruption and family suffering from loss of children nurtured in First Nations' cultures were exacerbated by the "sixties scoop," a period during the 1960s when children were apprehended by the state and placed in residential schools, adopted by non-Aboriginal families, and even shipped to foreign countries (Johnston 1983). The frustrations wrought by the failure of Euro-Canadian society to meet the needs of First Nations families and to honour Aboriginal rights have led to emotional despair and abiding mistrust that continue to shape perceptions of the *Indian Act* in all its manifestations.

The first point of reference of colonialism for many women was imposed gendered concepts of Indian identity, which date from 1857. From 1876–1985 the federal *Indian Act* discriminated against women by denying them rights to Indian status by virtue of marriage to a non-Indian. Insofar as the law constitutes family, as Cott (1995) has argued, the *Indian Act* has displaced the core social structures of First Nations—kin, corporate, and extended family groups—with the patriarchal, patrilocal nuclear family. By legally constituting women as "Non-Status" upon marriage to non-Indians, Canada asserted its control over an entire population through delegitimization (and non-recognition) of customary kin relations. With this assault on First Nation concepts of kin relations the very essence of the imaginary construct of family in First Nations terms was denigrated. Imposed patriarchy carried with it dualistic conventions of the public/private divide that privilege men as men, not as kinsmen, and subordinate women as kinswomen to men and as citizens (cf Pateman 1988). Women acquired and lost citizenship through men; at birth through their father at marriage through their husband. Bill C-31 locates women who married-out prior to 1985 in an inferior position to men who did the same by allowing these men to retain their Indian status and extending full Indian status to their non-Indian wives and their children. Under the 1985 amendments to the *Indian Act*, the descendants of Indian men who married-out are deemed to have two Indian parents regardless of the "race" of the mother, thus constituting the children as 6(1), a benefit denied children whose mothers married-out. Subordination of such women within their kin networks seeps into their subordination within the public realm, as they and their descendants are marked as different in terms of the *Act*. Women and children whose status was reinstated have come to be known as "C-31s" or "C-31ers" and viewed as outsiders to a community of authentic members (Fiske and George 2006; Lawrence 2004; Macklem 2001). Subordination of women through state imposed concepts of family and identity, we will now argue, constitutes a wounding of individuals and communities that shapes not only personal identity but contextualizes the impact of the policy demanding disclosure of paternity.

Trauma to the Culture

In a study we conducted in 2004, women of three First Nations with traditional matrilineal organization gave voice to the pain of subordination and their helplessness in the face of Bill C-31.[4] They addressed questions of geographic and cultural alienation from their home communities, tensions within their families, fear of the second-generation cut-off rule, and discriminatory practices within their communities. The imposition of patrilineal rules for transferring Indian status and/or band membership essentially delegitimizes traditional family structures grounded in kin corporate status. The women identified this as the most compelling evidence of trauma to their cultures. Historically, matrilineal descent in these nations conferred membership in clans, that is to say a social group sharing economic rights, obligations, land, and other privileges. Through the clan system, children were never dependant solely upon a nuclear family for nurture and sustenance. All children would have two clans active in their lives—the mother's and the father's clans—each bearing particular obligations to nurture and provide for the child. If a father was outside of the community or unknown, the mother's father's clan assumed the paternal obligations to the child. For a girl, this meant women of the father's clan would take an especially close interest in her development and well-being, not only in youth but as she matured and became a mother. Boys also turned to the paternal clan for care and guidance. The roles of the father's clan were formalized in rites of passage and clearly defined obligations reciprocated with the mother's clan. Reciprocal obligations were, and continue to be, acknowledged through feasting and gift exchanges known as the balhats. Today the state's focus on nuclear two-parent family denies the traditional roots of identity and the matrilineal kin structures that locate each child as a community member. Although social and cultural engagement in the community through the clan system remains vibrant at a personal level, because traditional kin authorities have been delegitimized, only the state can transmit full membership and attendant privileges defined within the *Indian Act*.

Women frame their experiences of Bill C-31 in terms of collective loss and ensuing community and kin tensions. They describe how their communities suffer, as they, their children, and their female kin are forced to live away from the home community. Language knowledge is lost. Highly skilled and capable individuals migrate to urban centres. Traditional forms of governance are weakened and matrilineal lines of succession disrupted. The desire to "be Indian" intensifies as government regulation of personal life leads to resentment that erupts into retaliation. As tensions ripple through families and communities, traditional principles of respect and generosity are undermined. Children are cast adrift from their culture when alienated by distance or status identity. A woman who had experienced this in her childhood stated,

> I believe it takes a community to raise a child and without the support and help of the community the child does not learn the culture and the language. As a result these children are lost, confused and end up on the streets.

Another described the long-term cultural impact when traditions of respect are not taught to the young. In response to being asked if traditions are meaningful today, a young woman responded with the following:

> I think the traditions still work for us especially for those who follow them strictly. These are the ones who do not get into trouble because our traditions are based on respect. Respect includes everything from animals to plants. If we base everything on respect then there would not be anyone feeling they don't belong. All people will belong where they were meant to be. We need to get back to our traditional ways and no government.

In the words of one woman, a leader in her community,

> there has been a lot of mistrust, lack of respect, manage[ment] and control issues. There is loss of historical identity, language and cultural traditions. Confusion between the Western way of doing things and the Indian way, and at times those two clash, and leaves unnecessary wounds.

She goes on to say that while the matrilineal traditions endure for residents or those living sufficiently close to learn the ways of their people through participation in the balhats,

> the indirect impact is for individuals coming back from outside the community not prepared and/or having lost touch with their teachings whereby [they try] to introduce protocols and/or principles that do not fit the traditional ways.

Her experience in administration and governance has led her to realize that

> there seems to be a lot of misconceptions as to their entitlements. They seem to think that as leaders, previous leaders, we were responsible for the choices their parents made. Show how they feel that we as a Nation owe them for any possible wrong doing that happened at the hands of the government.

Her observations are supported by personal experiences of leaders and office workers in a second of the communities. Here the elders are just now feeling the effects of Bill C-31 in their own families and coming to recognize the implications for a nation with fewer than 300 members. Elders pressure their First Nation to include non-registered children in services and to provide homes for reinstated women and their families. Office workers and elected councillors feel the impact as they explain,

> members who fall under Bill C-31 become ... lost in space because they don't have any benefits. So we are losing our numbers because of Bill C-31 and the ones that we are losing don't understand why and get pretty upset with us because we have no choice but to refuse them services.

Women's experiences substantiate observations of elected leaders and officer workers. Individuals' narratives illustrate the depth of trauma the cultures have experienced as families are divided by the regulations of Bill C-31. Women describe the pain of being raised outside of the community and the conflicts between cousins as young children in extended families become aware that some of them will have rights to inherit family property while others will not. Within families, some of the women who are cultural leaders either do not have status or are listed as 6(2) and their children do not have status. This creates uncertainty for the future of the community. A young girl of a large family whose members are fluent speakers of their language and are skilled in the traditional economic cycle described her anxieties.

> As I said my aunties are Bill C-31. There are not in my community but we go out to our summer village where we are from, it is there that they are in the community. I think they belong to that community and it is there that they practice their traditional skill and their cultural ways. This is good because they pass the tradition to us. It is in the community that they were taught this tradition. Our traditional ways are being lost and if these women are willing to be in our community and pass these traditional skills on then this is a good thing.

Her cousin, whose adoptive mother lost and then regained status, shares her fears for the future. This young girl is raised with a brother who is registered 6(2) while she is 6(1). She realizes all too well the possibility that her family will be further torn asunder by the second-generation cut-off rule and the demand for disclosure of paternity.

> I would like to go to my summer home and not worry that some day that house would be taken away from me or even the following generation of my family. I fear ... the effects of Bill C-31. [for] my children's children or any of my following generations ... and wonder if they may not get their education because of C-31. I would like for every native in the Act of Bill C-31 to be able to live on their homeland despite that they did not choose a native person to be their partner.

Others in this large extended family are torn with emotion as the aunties come to recognize that their grandchildren are not registered and under the current rules will be unable to inherit property or engage in traditional economic practices such as netting salmon.[5] Under the rules of the *Indian Act*, customary laws that establish resource use rights through clan membership offer no protection for individuals denied Indian status, in consequence non-status family members are vulnerable to federal laws regulating First Nations access to and use of natural resources.

Exogamous parenting is perceived to be the greatest threat small First Nations face. A number of participants spoke of the conflict between Bill C-31 and local patterns of marriage in remote communities where most residents are related. Generations have been taught that out-marriage is necessary to avoid violating social rules governing incest within clans and marriage to close relatives. In consequence, women were often encouraged to marry non-Indians in customary marriages. Communities were unaware of the implications of the *Indian Act* for matrilineal First Nations. As long as the married couple maintained harmonious relations with the community and the Indian Agent failed to intervene, children were registered and integrated fully in their natal community. In some cases, the children were raised by a non-biological father from the community, a practice that placed them beyond intervention by the Indian Agent. With this practice matrilineal descent remained undisrupted and children's birthright in the community unquestioned. In small communities, this is extraordinarily significant. Out-marrying is a necessity to avoid marrying kin relations or clan members. As Clatworthy and others have indicated, out-marriage and potential loss of future members is highest in communities under 100 members.

Bill C-31 is particularly felt as an assault on customary law and is experienced as a contraction to more progressive policy gestures whose purpose is to strengthen the extended family and bridge generations. Adoption and foster care within extended families is now encouraged by Canada and the province, a stance compatible with matrilineal practice. In the cultural tradition of the three First Nations we are studying here, a grandmother routinely adopts children. Elderly women are the source of wisdom. A child raised by a grandmother is viewed as special, in the eyes of some a child gifted by the spirits. As adults these children will be primary caregivers to their aging kin members. If they are denied access to First Nations land and resources, they will not be able to fulfill their traditional obligations in a meaningful way. Without sufficient support from federal funding, small First Nations are currently unable to provide for their citizens. Denial of status to the third generation in the small communities means the First Nations will not have funds to support children who in the future would be supporting the elders. Whatever customs of reciprocity and obligation may have prevailed in the past, adherence to legal custom of care for adoptive parents within kin and clan networks is not now constituted as legal grounds for granting status. The very basis of customary law—reciprocal obligations—has been delegitimized and in consequence the foundation of social relations disrupted.

This rupture of family is seen as a most serious violation of Aboriginal rights. Community members recall the 1993 court decision, *Casimel v. ICBC* that upheld the rights of First Nations to follow customary adoption.[6] However, insofar as customary adoption by grandmothers is recognized under Bill C-31, children adopted by widowed grandmothers and/or unmarried grandmothers are denied 6(1) status even when this is the category of the adopting mother, and adoptions by grandmothers registered as 6(2) have not conferred status in all instances. Participants were unable to explain why this was occurring but they worry that adoption by a widowed grandmother is viewed as a one-parent family if no father is registered in these circumstances. In the words of one grandmother, "They [INAC] just don't want our clan system." When probed she reiterated that under customary law the child would be adopted into a father's clan and "doesn't need to say anything more."

Women, in particular elders and hereditary chiefs, do not view Bill C-31 in isolation but in the context of other government interventions into family life. Apprehension of grandchildren by social services is particularly problematic and this issue dominated all the discussions we had with interviewees in the three communities. When daughters and granddaughters do not disclose paternity, the rift within communities intensifies when elders beseech their elected governing councils and administrative staff to intervene. In these communities the full impact of Bill C-31 comes as a shock as elders struggle to comprehend the reality that is facing their families. With their new understanding of government policy comes the recognition that grandchildren and great grandchildren are not eligible to inherit lands and cannot pass inheritance rights to future generations. "What is to become of us?" asked one distraught grandmother, a sentiment commonly shared by young and old alike.

Bill C-31 constitutes a trauma to culture as it threatens to drastically reduce the future status population (Clatworthy 2003b). As women came to recognize their personal grief over the exclusion of their grandchildren they turned to the question: How many of our nation's babies are not registered? They asked: "Why is the government doing this to us?" And they answered their own question in terms of racialized gender discrimination. As they live with the repercussions of Bill C-31 and the administrative policy that requires disclosure of paternity they recognize that the state intrudes into their private lives and sense of identity in a way that no other women in Canada face.

When asked how they would like to deal with the crises caused by Bill C-31, the participants were at a loss for words. Bill C-31 is but one of several assaults on their culture that has left First Nations powerless to control their destiny. In keeping with customary law, the women emphatically repeated that the answer must lie in matrilineal membership: time honoured recognition of women as family leaders and grandmothers' customary practices of adoption were raised repeatedly as the solution to cultural continuity and family strength.

Collective Trauma: Stigmatization and Rejection

Collective stigmatization or rejection by one's own culture forces individuals away from cultural foundations that should offer coherent expressions of identity. By its very nature, the *Indian Act* sets the terms of this stigmatization. Socio-legal distinctions give rise to social disparities: C-31 has become a state of being. INAC commonly refers to persons as "C-31s." In their daily talk[7] Aboriginal people ask such questions as "Who *is* C-31?" Indeed in our own research this was a continuous expression as researchers and participants alike signaled social distinctions by labelling who was and was not C-31, which communities had residents who were C-31, who had C-31 mothers, etc. Stigmatization and rejection are insidious forms of trauma; they reflect the internalization of colonial biases and create marginalized minorities within minorities. In this way, a collective trauma is felt; a shared suffering emerges to mark a common purpose with others who have endured moral and social violation. Identity, contrary to liberal notions of choice and multiple identities, is coercively imposed in negative terms: to *be* C-31 is to be outside full community membership. It is to be displaced to community margins without relocation in any community as a fully belonging member.

Reinstated women related common experiences of reinstatement. Whether returning home for a short period, seasonally or permanently, they found themselves stigmatized and often rejected. Few have had the opportunity to move onto the reserve and become permanent community members living in their own homes. Because the region is sparsely settled and long distances separate off-reserve "white" communities, reinstated women find it difficult to live near their home communities. Isolation from reserve communities compounds stigma. Financial and geographical barriers block regular participation in community events. In the words of one young woman whose father is registered and whose mother is non-native, "You really don't consider yourself Indian ... It is easier to live in urban areas because on-reserve you are discriminated from those that live there." Echoing her experience, a second woman from the same community described what she had lost in her childhood as a consequence of not having status in her mother's nation.

> Because of Bill C-31 I did not gain status until my early teens, so I lost out on many things. I lost out on many benefits because of the patrilineal ways of thinking. I also experienced racism from those who were status who thought that as a Bill C-31 I—we—were infringing on their rights.

A son of a woman who lost status through marriage was fortunate to spend his summers in the fishing village with his extended family. However, he recalls the difficulties his parents faced from the economic burdens of medical and dental costs others did not have to carry. Despite these differences he is now a resident band member—registered as 6(2)—and defends the cultural rights defined by the matrilineal lineage against government intrusion. He points out that by marriage to a registered band member his children are protected under 6(1) registration. The irony that his children have "full status," as many refer to 6(1) registration, as a consequence of their mother being 6(1) does not escape him. "That's the matrilineal way," he smiles, "they are 6(1) just like their mom and I'm only 6(2)."

Community members express a range of conflicting views over the residential choices of reinstated women. Some felt that rules and resources were needed to aid the women in reestablishing themselves in First Nations lands, others thought reinstated women and young adults registered as 6(2)

> prefer not to live on the reserve, because I know the ones who fall under Bill C-31, rather than move to the reserve, move to large urban cities or Prince George, or they move to other provinces and try to find work. They may even find it easer to survive over there with the mainstream, rather than they do at home ... everyone knows who's who and they might lose out on fishing and hunting. They don't get to have hands on, but they do receive fish and moose ... they request it.

These views conflicted with personal experiences of young adults who grew up away from their home communities. Young adults expressed a sense of frustration and social loss, caught between their own desire for community membership and a felt need to build social ties outside reserve communities in the interests of their children.

Stigmatization and conflicting needs of mothers and children did not deter all the participants in their quest to return home. The desire to live in their home community led these women to endure the ongoing struggle for acceptance. They were "willing to face any situation just to be home." However, the failure of the government to provide the necessary resources, in particular housing, left the women feeling cheated. Government discrimination had set them apart from their families and communities and compounded the insult by denying them benefits that they felt were a right.

Socio-legal divisions that have been created between mothers and children are a constant source of personal and collective trauma. Women who have fought the stigma of not belonging must now guide their children through the same maze of humiliating experiences. In small communities that are marked by tensions between Aboriginal and non-Aboriginal residents, this is no easy task. Mothers face the dilemma of teaching their children to be proud of their First Nations culture even as the children come to know that they are different than their on-reserve family and friends.

Just as the residential schools were constituted as an assault on Aboriginal identity and were meant to remold the First Nations people in the image of Euro-Canadians, denial of status to women marrying-out was intended to reconstitute their identity. And like the residential schools, the *Indian Act* failed.

Clinical psychologists disagree with sociologists and political scientists who see identity as adaptable to changing public definitions and interpersonal relations. In their eyes identity is neither as discursively malleable as some would claim, nor as easily reconstituted through positive cultural praxis as many hope. Rather, clinical psychologists have found that developmental traumas not only emerge from childhood sexual trauma but also arise from "the abuses of a racist, sexist, heterosexist society" (Layton 1995,120; also see Brown 1991). The participants in this study narrate their own and their families experiences of these abuses. A woman from Lake Babine Nation has observed the stresses her relatives suffer because Bill C-31 categorizes family members differently.

> I want to be able to live on the reserve and have what rightfully belongs to me. I do not want to be classed differently. Everyone always segregates the First Nations people. This is another example of segregation. We have always wanted to just belong where we come from and the government is always trying to change us.

Another woman who lost status and her right to reserve residency describes the devastation felt by her entire family.

> At the time I was enfranchised my mom and dad were very upset that I would not be considered henceforth. Undue stress and misery I'm sure was felt by my whole family. It was bad enough to my family that I was marrying a non-native (in those days it was almost taboo to marry out of our race), but to lose my status over him was completely devastating to my whole immediate family … As you are aware I am living on the reserve now, but when I was not and considered non-Indian I felt very alone in that old non-Native world. I felt like I did not belong anywhere and yet I had historical roots in the Lake Babine Nation. It was a very disconcerting time for me. I used to long to be able to return home and live next to Mom and Dad.

The impact of disrupted social and cultural relations and imposed notions of changing identity are felt strongly by women who experience rejection in their First Nation community and in the mainstream society. Before her reinstatement, a woman recalls that her family

> had to live off the reserve in town. Therefore I grew up across the tracks away from the reserve. We dealt with racism from both non-Natives and Natives. The non-Natives did not like us because we were Natives and the Natives did not like us because they thought that we were acting better than them just because we grew up off the reserve … I know a few that are Bill C-31 and yes I do think this affects them in a major way. They are not able to learn the culture and the language.

The desire for acceptance is very strong among women and their children who struggle to integrate into cultural life after reinstatement. When they do not feel accepted they find it hard to practice their tradition. A young woman explained that "to participate in the balhats they need to feel they are accepted" by the entire community.

Questions of identity and the experiences of fragmentation arise as well from government bureaucratic processes that assign numbers on the register and place names in vital statistics records. The son of an out-marrying woman experienced stress at finding he has been registered under two different family names: the non-native father's surname and his mother's surname. He uses humour to deal with his feelings, "So I got two birth certificates so maybe you have a split personality you don't know about." However, his pain surfaces as he reflects on the implications of this. He continues saying, "That could be white on the outside and native inside, half and half. Half and half is better than nothing." Thus, he reiterates stereotypes that reflect concerns over fragmented identity. He speaks within the perspective shared by other participants who use terms "full status" and "half status" to label community members whose identity has been defined after registering under section 6. As this man listens to the researcher who is interviewing him he comes to recognize the broad significance of C-31 and the struggles women are having with respect to their children and grandchildren.

> Holy! I didn't know that! Bill C-31 is a lot bigger than just women marrying a white man. It is bigger, it's just what we've been told … when we come into problems with our children is where women are starting to stand up and look into the bill especially when we're told that oh yeah, your child is not going to have any part of the status. Your grandchildren, that's when it hurts.

To fully understand this process as traumatic, one must appreciate the conflicting constructions of identity that emerge as individuals and communities struggle against internalizing racial distinctions foisted upon them. Bill C-31 exacerbates tensions of identity that arise from intermarriage as children of mixed parentage are cast into denigrating categories, C-31ers or "half status," that are articulated within state discourses and personal conversation. Racial stereotyping implicit in the term C-31 is explicitly raised within stigmatizing labels. One young man's experience exemplifies this. Although others in his family are registered, he is not. Because he "looks white" he is taunted as "white wash" and "puppy face white wash." In these circumstances, government-imposed definitions of identity do not offer coherence or stability but situate children and adults as victims of culturally imposed trauma that shatters identity, and reflect back to individuals and communities negative, fragmented images of identity and social well-being. The above speaker sees the solution as the government creating a new situation where

> everything [is] equal. Like just 'cause a woman marries a white guy you know that doesn't give the government the okay to say "Well you're no longer Native." You were born Native. How could the government … come and say "Well you got to be white now 'cause you got married."

Perhaps more damaging than any other disruption of identity was the act of stripping women of their cultural identity upon marriage. As Sandra Lovelace proved before the international courts, women and their children were alienated from their ethnic and cultural rights (Silman 1987).[8] In the process there is no doubt that they and their children were stripped of the cultural coherence that is the foundation of stable, healthy identity formation and maintenance. For one family participating in this study, fragmented identity of their mother led to multiple traumas for the entire family. The speaker was born to a mother whose status was reinstated under Bill C-31 and to a non-status father. In this circumstance the speaker would normally be registered as 6(2). However, she was adopted by a father with status and thus achieved registration as 6(1). Through adoption the speaker feels she is entitled to live in her mother's natal community and as a result has achieved a higher quality of living than any of her sisters. Because her sisters were not adopted by a status father they did not achieve parity in being registered. Without a father on the reserve they did not feel they could make their home there. During the mother's period of not being registered, she disassociated herself from her Nation because she was ineligible for benefits. When her status was restored there was no housing on the reserve and she could not return. In her daughters' words:

> I think my mother kinda found out her benefits were gone ... she slowly stopped being dependent on the ... Nation for anything, like to the point where she was disability and she was on white welfare instead of coming home to her native nation to be happier. She stayed in Vancouver and stayed on her disability and I think that the result of her alcoholism causing her death. So because she was Bill C-31 she was unable to come home. Well, theoretically, she would of come home but she wouldn't have got the benefits the white government was able to provide her because of her status ... Eventually we [the speaker and her sisters] followed mom to Vancouver and we all didn't survive...I got two sisters with HIV and I've got two sisters that died of overdosing along with my mother drinking and overdosing, she died herself ... I've got two nieces and a nephew in foster care ... they have heart conditions so they are considered disability....

Clearly the social and cultural alienation of this family led to oppressive situations in which sustaining good mental health became impossible. In crisis, the family members become entrapped in negative stereotypes in a complex situation that has been termed "ethnostress." This occurs

> when the cultural beliefs or joyful identity of a people are disrupted. It is the negative experience they feel when interacting with members of different cultural groups and themselves. The stress within the individual centres around the self-image and sense of place in the world. Beginning on an individual basis, the effects of the ethnostress phenomena are analyzed and then applied to the collective groups of family, community and nation. (Antone, Miller and Myers 1986, 7).

Ethnostress carries with it a sense of helplessness and powerlessness, what women describe as "having their hands tied behind their back" as they confront the pain of their families and the future impacts of the second generation cut-off and unstated paternity. Having suffered themselves and watched their children suffer, they worry about the grandchildren to come. The disclosure of paternity mandate will inevitably alienate more of their grandchildren. Stresses of identity, alienation from family and community, and mixed messages of racialization and marginalization are bound to affect the future generations in the same ways as the women and children initially alienated by section 12(1)(b) of the old act and by section 6 of the current act.

Women and men alike express a sense of helplessness that spills over from personal anguish to shared feelings. They share the view that their lives are not theirs to live freely. Through seeking to control intimate relations and reproduction, they see the government as not only telling women with whom they should have children but also constraining communities in how and to whom they pass down tangible and intangible resources and teachings. The impact of the cultural and collective trauma will continue to be felt through the generations as children of today are forced to cope with disruptions in identity in the future. In this way, Bill C-31 will come to resonate as an historic trauma as the direct experiences of racist, sexist, and cultural oppression today come to shape the meaning of personal experiences and identity in the future.

Historic Trauma

Historic trauma is initially experienced directly. Over time it is experienced indirectly by subsequent generations in consequence of the meaning the traumatic event carries in historic narratives. Maria Yellowstone Braveheart defines the term as "collective and compounding emotional and psychic wounding over time … [it is] multi-generational and is not limited to [an individual's] life span" (1996, 6). Historic trauma is experienced across wide networks of people and is transferred through generations just as lived experiences of descendents of the original trauma victims are shaped by the past. The complexity of historic trauma lies in relations of power; identities constituted through the dominating powers' view of the traumatized community force themselves into identity formation. Bill C-31 emerges from colonial distortion of identity and belonging, and exists within current cultural disruption that denies individuals access to a coherent culture from which the wisdom and skills necessary for community survival are drawn. Within this context to *be* C-31 can erode self-esteem and cause a depression of estrangement whereby one feels alienated and pushed to the margins of community.

Community members are well aware of the historical prejudices against them because of their matrilineal organization. They see state imposed patrilineal laws as a deliberate attack on matrilineal peoples that has humiliated women and has left First Nations governments powerless to control their destinies and women powerless in their personal lives. They do not view the impact of the *Indian Act* over the past century in isolation but within the historical context of colonization by church and government. Categorization of First Nations individuals under Bill C-31 is understood as being interwoven with the traumatic consequences of the residential schools and the ongoing dilemma of child apprehension. Participants' narratives speak to three themes of historic trauma: colonially imposed arranged marriages that stigmatized and forced young women from their families, forced removal of women who married out, and disruption of family ties through the generations as women and men were treated differently upon marriage.

From the time of contact with Europeans through to the present, colonial biases have stigmatized matrilineal traditions and the women who asserted their autonomy and individuality. In the early fur trade years, customary marriages with European men took women from their home communities. All too often, the foreign men did not hold their wives in high regard. Traders are known to have abandoned the women or to have passed the women among themselves as property (Fiske and Patrick, 2000, 148–49). While Catholic missionaries were critical of individual abuses by European men, they justified government interventions into family life as a means of undermining matrilineal family formations and the balhats and clan system. They chastised women whose sexual behaviours and personal actions differed from Catholic expectations of female subordination and chastity and stigmatized women who refused to abide by missionaries' rules against marital separation. Catholic missionaries and Indian agents also objected to customary forms of adoption and the strategies used by families to ensure collective well-being in ways that may now stigmatize families for their forebears' actions (Fiske and Patrick 2000, 153–155).

These sexist and racist sentiments have influenced present day perceptions of family histories. One family's history illustrates the impact of racist attitudes toward historic marriage practices, as these become shaped by meanings arising from Bill C-31. Up until the mid-twentieth century, families arranged marriages for young women. Families sometimes did so in order to meet economic needs, such as alleviating debts or bringing into an extended family men who could earn wages and/or provide by hunting and other unpaid labour. Several decades ago, when this family faced an economic and social crisis, they followed tradition and arranged a marriage between a daughter and a non-Indian. Following Bill C-31, the children of this marriage were able to regain status in the 6(2) category. But, today their own children and grandchildren have been denied status. Through four generations this family is doubly traumatized: Family members fight to override the Euro-Canadian social stigma associated with the "forced marriage" of their mother/grandmother and the perception that the bride was "sold" either out of heartless action or from desperate poverty. Currently, the generations denied status seek to assert their cultural identity through social and economic affiliation within the feasting system and other community ties of reciprocal obligation. However, they carry the sense of being outside and remain anxious for the social and cultural future of their grandchildren.

Under the 1951 amendments to the *Indian Act*, the forced removal of out-marrying women left communities feeling helpless in the face of government actions. By denying out-marrying women community membership and cultural identity, the *Indian Act* has continuously signaled to First Nations peoples—and matrilineal peoples in particular—disregard, if not contempt, for cultural practices that differ from Euro-Canadian sentiments and values. To the extent that these views have been internalized, they are reflected in community practices and individual sentiments. Thus community members may hold individual women responsible for their decisions to marry-out. And under the legislation, the First Nations themselves have no power to redress the current situation. The result is the alienation of out-marrying women's descendants who now feel "punished" for the mothers' personal choices as they find themselves unwelcome in the community and denied the benefits their close kin enjoy.

Families suffer from a complex of having been "divided and conquered." Some participants in this research, for example, spoke of family turmoil and personal pain resulting from the sexist biases of Bill C-31. A sister and brother born to unwed parents, Status Indian father and non-Indian mother, now have different entitlements. The brother is 6(1) because his entitlement comes from being registered prior to 1985 when patrilineal rights were bestowed on "illegitimate" sons. The sister is categorized 6(2) because she could only be registered after 1985 and can claim only one registered parent.[9] Imposed sexist biases leave female kin vulnerable to low esteem and mistrust as they witness their male kin benefiting while they endure feelings of isolation and rejection.

The traumatic impact of Bill C-31 is felt most strongly in the demands for disclosing paternity. Few participants wished to discuss this issue, and those who did were not mothers directly affected by the policy. Grandmothers wept and trembled as they learnt for the first time that grandchildren and great grandchildren were not, and apparently could not be, registered. Many, however, would only speak privately. In the presence of each other, their grief consumed them. Younger women were often too stressed to address the issue in focus groups.

Most troubling is the lack of awareness regarding rules for stating paternity. Some community members shared views reported by Clatworthy (2003a) that naivety, ignorance, and the complication of registering babies can explain why young mothers are not identifying fathers. But older women were far more concerned about young mothers, who they thought were remaining silent for important reasons of safety. One woman pointed out that when she was young women did not speak out and name the father if they were not married. She described teenage mothers raising their babies in an extended family setting, where customary adoption was never questioned. Grandmothers simply took in the baby and "everyone knew" the child was being adopted. To her, disclosing the father's name breached rules of respect and personal dignity. Silence, not disclosure, she suggested, is the way to respect everyone where naming a father could shame others.

Speaking quietly after one focus group, an elder raised a troubling violation of her culture. Like many others, she accepts principles of reincarnation. She sees the demand to reveal a father as a misunderstanding of life. People "come back" she explained, and we can never be sure that the babies the government refuses are not ones who have "come back" to be with their families. By not registering babies because their fathers are not named, communities lose continuity through generations.

The impact of unstated paternity constitutes historical trauma. It is shaped by colonial history and shapes the future. The policy implicitly reintroduces the historic Euro-Canadian repugnance for matrilineal societies and moral judgments against "illegitimate" births. It reinforces the very biases against "mixed heritage" that resonate in the multiple categorizations listed in section 6 of the *Indian Act*. More specifically, by enforcing patrilineal notions of descent, and implied measures of blood quantum, this rule disregards the very essence of cultural difference: The sacred social and psychological meanings of birth are swept aside by imposing a universal means by which to construct identity and to constrain defining characteristics of First Nations membership. By dividing families at the time of birth, it inflicts trauma on mothers whose children will be alienated in the future. If carried into the future it will place burdens of proof on the children whose paternity is unstated, creating social distress for those who cannot determine their fathers' identities, and for those who can and cannot register in consequence. Knowing the depth of misery felt today as a result of the *Indian Act*, it is impossible to view a coherent and stable future for children and families divided by unstated paternity. Concern for the future creates genuine and deep anguish across communities of First Nations.

Like families, communities also struggle with a sense of having been "divided and conquered" as they confront the emotional conflicts resulting from Bill C-31 and individuals' demands that First Nations leaders take action. A member of the Nee Tahi Buhn First Nation described the continuing impact of the *Indian Act* as a "silent crime." Community fractures from the initial discrimination of 12(1)(b) in the 1951 Act through to the impact of C-31 on extended family today, she says, have not been addressed publicly by either the government or First Nations leaders. In her eyes there has been no accountability and without public apologies the community will remain divided. She describes the situation today as one in which the Nee Tahi Buhn First Nation is "like two separate bands ... Bill C-31 feel separate. Nee Tahi bun is a small band of 128 and we shall see the impacts very heavy in the future generation." Similarly, a member of the much larger Lake Babine Nation calls for healing of historic wrongs. She contextualizes her criticism of the *Act* within the need to "decolonize people." In her view,

> some people are conditioned to this new [*Indian Act* regime] era ...We need to heal from the impacts of colonization, the residential school and child welfare system and look at things holistically, where by we can make informed decisions and move our nations forward in a progressive manner.

She also views the need to heal in historical context: First Nations must move beyond the history of government control to a point where they can take their destiny in their own hands and act on their responsibility for future generations. In sum, the *Indian Act*, and Bill C-31 in particular, must be understood as historic trauma.

Conclusion

Any understanding of Bill C-31 needs to be placed within the colonial circumstances that have wrought historic trauma on First Nations women, families and kin networks. The historic, multilayered impact of state-imposed identity constructs is the root of contemporary experience of Bill C-31. Women experience Bill C-31 within their collective articulation of what has happened to women and children in the past, in the present and within their shared apprehension of the future, as fewer and fewer children carrying 6(1) status are born into their First Nations communities.

Bearing in mind the axiom "laws make persons," it follows that where law and force of the state delegitimizes established forms of family, kin, and identity, law remakes identity. To the extent that this imposes cultural discontinuity and social disruption, the ensuing process is one of multilayered trauma that encapsulates individuals and communities. With respect to Bill C-31 and the demands for disclosure of paternity, the trauma has and will continue to reverberate through kin relations as communities are depleted of registered members and grandmothers struggle with the loss of grandchildren whom they can never know on their own terms.

Endnotes

1   This study is funded by Policy Research Directorate, Status of Women Canada. A fuller account of this research can be found in the report *Seeking Alternatives to Bill C-31: An investigation of matrilineal models of First Nations citizenship and community membership policies*, published by Status of Women Canada (2006).

2   Sexist discrimination in the *Indian Act* has been documented in numerous studies. Under Section 12(1)(b), a woman who married a man who was not a Registered Indian was stripped of her Indian status, removed from Indian band registration and denied all the privileges and protections of the *Indian Act* including rights to residency, inheritance of property on the reserve, burial on the reserve, and access to traditional resources through fishing and hunting. Efforts to eliminate these stipulations and achieve equality with Indian men led to protracted political and legal struggles that continue to this day. For histories of the struggles in the 1970s that led up to the 1985 amendments see Jamieson (1978), Silman (1987) and Hartley, this volume.

3   A number of terms are used to describe families organized around male authority and social and economic privileges. The patriarchal nuclear family is the conventional family form of Europe: a married couple and dependent children with the husband/father carrying privileges of authority and rights denied to the wife/mother. In keeping with preferences for patriarchal family organization, colonial authorities enforced patrilineal rules, or descent through the father, to determine Indian status. Married women were expected to reside in the home community of their husbands, a practice known as patrilocal residence. Paternalism is the assumption that male authorities within the family and state are best able to define the needs of others. All of these practices undermined traditional membership in extended groups of kin who shared property and resource rights. These groups, known as kin corporate groups, protected women's access to resources through descent and through marriage.

4   This study was conducted with three First Nations of central British Columbia: Cheslatta Carrier First Nation, Lake Babine First Nation and the Nee Tahi Buhn First Nation. In this work, three community researchers, each familiar with the communities, held focus groups and individual interviews. Seventy-five participants were involved. Community researchers who are well known in the First Nations communities conducted the interviews and focus groups. The researchers have personal experiences with Bill C-31 either through their own marital relationships or through the splintering impact of the Bill on members of their families. The meetings were held on-reserve where possible and where not possible in meeting halls the communities regularly use. The meetings were tape-recorded. Throughout, notes were placed on flip charts for the participants' reference. Private interviews were held at a location of the participant's choice. Some agreed to be tape-recorded, others did not. Family narratives are intensely personal; none can be told without spilling into the narratives of other families with whom the storyteller is linked. The sensitive nature of asking questions about the impact of Bill C-31 and the division of family and community through the distinctions of 6(1), and 6(2) led researchers to adopt flexible approaches to interviewing in order to best serve the individual participant's needs.

   A detailed account of the Lake Babine Nation's social organization and complex system of customary law is provided in *Cis Dideen Kat: When the Plumes Rise, The Way of the Lake Babine Nation*. (Fiske and Patrick 2000).

5   The speaker is from a First Nation that has followed the *Indian Act* rules and excludes non-status individuals from its membership code. The First Nation is engaged in debate on membership but is reluctant to alter membership codes at the present time.

6   This case arose in the neigbouring Stellate'n First Nation, whose laws and social practices are grounded in principles of matrilineality and reciprocal obligations. In this case a young man had been adopted by his maternal grandparents, Francis and Louise Casimel. When he was killed in a vehicle accident the parents anticipated receiving the dependent parent allowance from the Insurance Company of British Columbia. The company denied them benefits and the Casimels turned to the courts for redress. In 1993, the Appeal Court of British Columbia ruled in their favour and upheld customary family law. The case was not appealed to the Supreme Court.

7   We have recorded use of "C-31" as a term of identity at public talks, at conferences, and in meetings between INAC officials and First Nations.

8   Sandra Lovelace took the issue of discrimination to the United Nations Human Rights Committee. In 1981 it declared the *Indian Act* provision discriminatory with respect to the alienation of women from the culture and natal community. This brought international embarrassment for Canada and helped to pave the way for Bill C-31.

9   Section 11(1)(c) of the *Indian Act* provided status to male persons in direct descent of the male line. The issue of illegitimate children was raised in the Martin Case heard by the Supreme Court in 1983; the court ruled that because section 11(1)(d) dealt with legitimate children, section 11(1)(c) applied to male descendants in general. As a result of the Martin case, male children of entitled Indian males were eligible for registration whether or not they were legitimate. The legitimate male and female children of Indian men and non-Indian women were registered under section 11(1)(d).

References

Alexander, Jeffery C. 2004. "Toward a theory of cultural trauma." In *Cultural Trauma and Collective Identity*. Jeffery C. Alexander, Ron Eyerman, Bernhard Giesen, Neil J. Smelser, and Piotr Sztompka (eds). Berkeley: University of California Press. 1–30.

Antone, Robert, Diane Miller, and Brian Myers. 1986. *The Power within People*. Deseranto: Peace Tree Technologies.

Bayefsky, Anne F. 1982. "The Human Rights Committee and the case of Sandra Lovelace." *Canadian Yearbook of International Law*. 20: 244–265.

Bear, Shirley. 1991. "You can't change the *Indian Act*?" In *Women and Social Change: Feminist Activism in Canada*. Jeri Dawn Wine and Janice L. Ristock (eds). Toronto: James Lorimer and Company. 98–220.

Braveheart, Maria Yellowhorse. 1995. *The Return to the Sacred Path: Healing from Historical Unresolved Grief among the Lakota and Dakota*. PhD Dissertation. Smith College, Northampton, Mass.

Casimel v. I.C.B.C. (1993), 82 B.C.L.R. (2d) 387 at 394– 95, 18 C.C.L.I. (2d) 161 (C.A.).

Clatworthy, Stewart. 2003a. *Factors Contributing to Unstated Paternity*. Ottawa: Indian and Northern Affairs Canada.

Clatworthy, Stewart. 2003b. "Impacts of the 1985 amendments to the *Indian Act* on First Nations populations." In *Aboriginal Conditions*. Jerry White, Paul S. Maxim, and Dan Beavon (eds). Vancouver: UBC Press. 3–90.

Cott, Nancy. 1995. "Giving character to our whole civil polity: Marriage and the public order in the late nineteenth century." *United States History as Women's History: New Feminist Essays*. Linda Kerber, Alice Kessler-Harris, and Kathryn Kish Sklar (eds). Chapel Hill: UNC Press. 107–24.

Fiske, Jo-Anne and Evelyn George. 2006. Seeking Alternatives to Bill C-31: An investigation of matrilineal models of First Nations citizenship and community membership policies. Ottawa: Status of Women Canada.

Fiske, Jo-Anne and Betty Patrick. 2000. *Cis Dideen Kat: When the Plumes Rise, The Way of the Lake Babine Nation*. Vancouver: UBC Press.

Green, Joyce. 1985. "Sexual equality and Indian government: An analysis of Bill C-31 amendments to the *Indian Act*." *Native Studies Review* 1(2): 81–95.

Green, Joyce. 2000. "Constitutionalizing the patriarchy: Aboriginal women and Aboriginal government." *Expressions in Canadian Native Studies*. Ron F. Laliberte, Priscilla Settee, James B. Waldram, Rob Innes, Brenda Macdougall, Lesley McBain, and F. Laurie Barron (eds). Saskatoon: University of Saskatchewan Extension Press. 28–354.

Green, Joyce. 2001. "Canaries in the mines of citizenship: Indian women in Canada." *Canadian Journal of Political Science*. 34: 715–738.

Indian Residential Schools Resolution Canada. 2007.Statement of Reconciliation, 1998. Ottawa: Indian Residential Schools Solution Canada. <**www.irsr-rqpi.gc.ca/english/reconciliation.html**> Date accessed: April 11, 2007.

Jamieson, Kathleen. 1978. *Indian Women and the Law in Canada: Citizens Minus*. Ottawa: Minister of Supply and Services.

Johnston, Patrick. 1983. *Native Children and the Child Welfare System*. Ottawa: Canadian Council on Social Development.

Lawrence, Bonita. 2004. *"Real" Indians and Others: Mixed-Blood Urban Native Peoples and Indigenous Nationhood*. Lincoln: University of Nebraska Press.

Layton, Lynne. 1995. "Trauma, gender identity and sexuality: Discourses of fragmentation." *American Imago*. 52(1): 107–125.

Macklem, Peter. 2001. *Indigenous Difference and the Constitution of Canada*. Toronto: University of Toronto Press.

Miskimmin, Susanne E. 1996. "'Nobody took the Indian blood out of me": An analysis of Algonquian and Iroquoian discourse concerning Bill C-31. PhD Dissertation. University of Western Ontario, London.

Pateman, Carole. 1988. *The Sexual Contract*. Stanford: Stanford University Press.

Schouls, Timothy A. 2003. *Shifting Boundaries: Aboriginal Identity, Pluralist Theory, and the Politics of Self-government*. Vancouver: UBC Press.

Silman, Janet. (1987). *Enough is Enough: Aboriginal Women Speak Out*. Toronto: The Women's Press.

Sztompka, Piotr. (2000). "Cultural trauma: The other face of social change." *European Journal of Social Theory*. 3(4): 449–466.

within the boundaries of the Winnipeg Census Metropolitan Area (CMA), the community remains essentially rural in character. According to the 2002 Indian Register, the Registered Indian population of Brokenhead totalled 1,423. At that time, about 30% of the population (429 individuals) lived on-reserve. Although data concerning the location of the off-reserve component of the population are limited, most are believed to reside in the City of Winnipeg or in small communities located within the Winnipeg region.

Brokenhead is governed by a Chief and a four member Council elected by band members. The community maintains its own membership list (pursuant to section 10 of the 1985 *Indian Act*).[3] Members may reside either on- or off-reserve. Brokenhead assumes responsibility for the provision of a wide range of services, including governance, housing and community infrastructure, elementary and secondary education, employment and training, social services, and health services. Most of these services relate to the population living on-reserve, although specific services, (e.g. employment and training) are also administered for the off-reserve population. Other services and programs available to Brokenhead members living on-reserve, (e.g. economic development, community futures) are administered by the Southeast Resources Development Council (SERDC), of which Brokenhead is a member.

Study Approach and Data Sources

Research undertaken for this case study involved three main components. The initial component focused on estimating the role of the 1985 amendments to the *Indian Act* in contributing to changes in the size and composition of the Brokenhead population. This aspect of the study examined population changes that have occurred from the time of enactment of the 1985 *Indian Act* (in April of 1985) to December 31, 2002. In addition to documenting existing population impacts, this study component also explored future population changes over the course of the next 75 years (roughly three generations). A custom population projection was developed to explore these longer-term changes in relation to the populations entitled to Indian registration and eligible for membership with Brokenhead Ojibway Nation. Data used for the population impact components of the case study were obtained from the Indian Register and the Brokenhead membership list.

A second research component involved examining administrative data and records concerning changes in program and service usage, as well as conducting interviews with key staff and council members responsible for administering or overseeing programs and services delivered by Brokenhead. These interviews were designed to obtain views and opinions of staff and management concerning policies related to service provision and the impacts of Bill C-31 registrants on program and service demand and usage. In addition to records maintained by Brokenhead, this aspect of the study also examined data provided by Health Canada concerning Bill C-31 usage of the Non-Insured Health Benefits Program.

Figure 4.1: Historic Estimates of the Registered Indian Population by Location of Residence, Brokenhead Ojibway Nation, 1985–2002

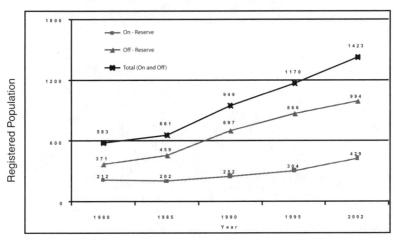

Source: Indian Register, 1980–2002 (Unadjusted)

The third component of the research involved a survey designed to capture perceptions and opinions concerning Bill C-31 from the members of Brokenhead Ojibway Nation. The survey of members addressed a wide variety of issues, including:

- Views and opinions about Bill C-31's impacts on themselves, their families, and the community
- Knowledge of and concerns about Brokenhead's rules governing membership
- Experiences and perceptions of equality in terms of accessing various programs and services administered by Brokenhead
- Concerns about potential future impacts of Bill C-31

The survey was administered using in-person or telephone interviews and included members residing both on- and off-reserve, as well as members who (re)acquired registration under Bill C-31 (i.e., Bill C-31 registrants) and those who were members prior to Bill C-31 (i.e., pre-Bill C-31 members).[4] A total of 170 individuals completed the survey, including 101 living on-reserve and 69 living off-reserve.[5] Thirty-six survey respondents (or about 21% of all) were registered under the reinstatement/registration provisions of Bill C-31.[6]

Growth of the Brokenhead Ojibway Nation Population

Historic data from the Indian Register were used to identify changes in the size of the Brokenhead Registered Indian population over the 1980–2002 time period

Figure 4.2: Cumulative Number of Bill C-31 Registrations, Brokenhead Ojibway Nation, 1985–2002

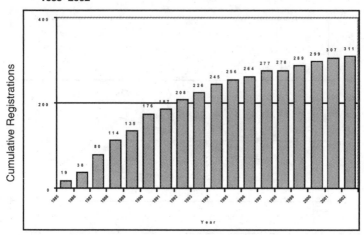

Source: Indian Register as of December 31, 2002 (Unadjusted)

(See **Figure 4.1** – page 75). Between 1980 and 2002, the population increased by about 144% from 583 to 1,423. Most of this population growth has occurred since 1985, suggesting that changes introduced by the 1985 *Indian Act* have played a significant role in population growth.

Estimating the Contribution of the 1985 Indian Act *Amendments*

In order to understand the role played by the 1985 *Indian Act* amendments in promoting the population growth observed for Brokenhead, it is necessary to understand some specifics of the changes that were introduced by the *Act*. Prior to the 1985 amendments, Indian registration could be gained or lost through marriage or other events. Section 12 of the 1951/56 *Indian Act* excluded or authorized the removal from the Register of:

- Women who married non-Indian men (and any children born to such women prior to the marriage)[7]
- The descendants of these marriages
- "Illegitimate" children of Indian women and non-Indian men (through successful protest within 12 months of the child's registration)
- Persons whose mother, and father's mother, were non-Indian (the "double mother" clause).

Section 11 of the 1951/56 *Indian Act* allowed:

- Indian men (subject to the "double mother" clause) to transmit registration entitlement to any of their children, regardless of the child's mother and without the consideration of marriage[8]
- Non-Indian women who married Indian men to gain Indian registration.

Table 4.1: Distribution of Children by Parent Registration and Bill C-31 Registration Status, Brokenhead Ojibway Nation, April 17,1985 to December 31, 2002

Father's Registry Status		Mother's Registry Status				Total
		Pre-Bill C-31	Bill C-31		Not Registered	
		6(1)	6(1)	6(2)		
Pre-Bill C-31	6(1)	86	8	4	84	182
Bill C-31	6(1)	13	3	1	4	21
	6(2)	12	5	2	n/a	19
Not Registered		81	8	n/a	n/a	89
Paternity Not Stated		85	8	n/a	n/a	93
Total		277	32	7	88	404

Source: Indian Register as of December 31, 2002 (Unadjusted)

In addition to removing the provisions of previous *Indian Act*'s that resulted in the loss of registration, the 1985 *Indian Act*:

- Allowed for the reinstatement of Indian registration to those who lost their registration under prior versions of the Act, as well as the "first-time" registration of their children
- Established new rules governing entitlement to Indian registration for all children born on or after April 17, 1985.

The revised rules governing Indian registration are contained in section 6 of the 1985 *Indian Act*, and provide for registration under one of two sub-sections:

- **Section 6(1)**, where both of the individual's parents are (or are entitled to be) registered
- **Section 6(2)**, where one of the individual's parents is (or is entitled to be) registered under Section 6(1) and the other parent is not registered

Unlike the previous rules governing registration entitlement, which were subject to widespread allegations and claims of gender discrimination, the revised rules are *gender-neutral,* meaning that they apply to children born to both males and females.

In relation to the prior *Act*, the 1985 *Indian Act* created four new sources of growth in the Registered Indian population. These sources of growth include:

- Bill C-31 reinstatements and registrations
- Children born to Bill C-31 and pre-Bill C-31 parents after April 16, 1985 who would not have qualified for registration under the prior rules
- Indian women who have not been removed from the Register after April 16,1985 as a result of marriage to a non-Indian male

As non-Indian women cannot acquire registration through marriage under the 1985 *Indian Act*, this source of growth no longer applies.

Bill C-31 Reinstatements and Registrations

Figure 4.2 (page 78) illustrates the cumulative number of additions to the Registered Indian population of Brokenhead through Bill C-31's reinstatement and registration provisions. As revealed in the figure, the cumulative number of Bill C-31 registrants, as of December 31, 2002, was identified to be 311. The figure also reveals that growth in the number of Bill C-31 additions to the population has slowed dramatically since the mid-1990's. For the 1999–2002 portion of the period, new Bill C-31 registrants have averaged about seven annually, a level roughly one-quarter of that recorded annually at the outset of the 1990s.

As of December 31, 2002, the surviving population of Bill C-31 registrants (i.e., those still alive) numbered 298 individuals and represented about 21% of the total Registered Indian population of Brokenhead.

Other Population Growth Impacts of Bill C-31

Although reinstatements and registrations form the largest component of incremental growth in the Registered Indian population attributable to Bill C-31, other changes made to the rules governing Indian registration have also contributed to significant incremental growth of the Brokenhead population during the 1985–2002 time period.

Children Born After April 16, 1985

A custom data file linking children with their parents was created for this study. This file allows one to identify the parenting patterns of males and females and for the Bill C-31 and pre-Bill C-31 populations. Data on parenting patterns have been compiled for the parents of all children born and registered with Brokenhead since the adoption of Bill C-31 (April 17, 1985) to December 31, 2002.[9] These patterns, which are summarized in **Table 4.1** (page 79), provide a basis for estimating the scale of the secondary components of population growth associated with Bill C-31. Of particular interest in this regard, are children who qualify for Indian registration under the rules of the 1985 *Indian Act*, but who would not have qualified had the rules of the previous *Indian Act* remained in force during the period. These children include:

- Children born to two Bill C-31 parents
- Children born to a Bill C-31 parent registered under Section 6(1) and whose other parent is not registered
- Children born to a pre-Bill C-31 woman and non-Indian male
- Children born to a pre-Bill C-31 woman and a male registered under Bill C-31

The numbers of children born to these specific combinations of parents are identified in the shaded areas of **Table 4.1**. As of December 31, 2002, an estimated 137 children have been recorded on the Register who would not have qualified for registration under the pre-1985. About 59% of these children (81 in total) result

Table 4.2: Incremental Growth Associated with the 1985 Indian Act by Component, Brokenhead Ojibway Nation, 1985–2002

Component of Growth	Population Increase	% of Increase
Reinstatements and Registrations	298	67.4
Incremental Births	137	31.0
Net Women Retained	7	1.6
All Components	442	100

Source: Based on analysis of data contained in the December 31, 2002, Indian Register

from parenting between pre-Bill C-31 women and males who would not have qualified for registration under either Bill C-31 or the rules of the previous *Indian Act*. The remaining 41% (56 children) result from parenting by individuals who acquired or reacquired Indian registration under Bill C-31.

Retention of Women Who Married Non-Indians After April 16, 1985

As Bill C-31 no longer allows for the removal of women from the Indian Register for marriage to a non-Indian, some portion of the growth in the Registered Indian population after April 16, 1985, derives from the retention (on the Register) of pre-Bill C-31 women who intermarried. Data concerning the actual marriage patterns of Registered Indians are not available for this time period and precise or *direct* estimates of the number of Indian women who would have been removed from the Register in the absence of Bill C-31 cannot be obtained. An approximation of this number, however, can be obtained by applying estimates of the total fertility rate (TFR) of Registered Indian females to the number of children born to pre-Bill C-31 women and non-registered (or Bill C-31) males.[10] Application of the TFR to the (106) children born to pre-Bill C-31 women (and non-Indian men) resulted in an estimate of 35 women who were not removed from the Indian Register during the 1985–2002 period through marriage to non-Indian males.

Women Not Added Through Marriage to Indian Males after April 16, 1985

As noted previously, Bill C-31 also removed the provisions of the previous *Indian Act* which allowed non-Indian females to acquire Indian registration through marriage to Indian males. As recent marriage data were also unavailable on this topic, the total fertility rate procedure described above has also been used to provide a rough estimate of the number of women who did not gain registration during the study period. Application of the total fertility rate to the number of children (84) born to pre-Bill C-31 males and non-registered females, results in an estimate of 28 women who did not gain registration through marriage during the study period.

Summary of Total Incremental Population Growth Attributable to Bill C-31

An estimate of the total incremental growth in the Registered Indian population can be obtained by aggregating the individual components discussed above. **Table 4.2**, which provides a summary of results of the analysis, reveals that the total growth in the Registered Indian population of Brokenhead attributable to the changes introduced by the 1985 Indian Act is roughly 442 individuals, including 298 Bill C-31 registrants, 137 children (who would not have qualified under the previous rules) and 7 (35–28) women (resulting from Bill C-31's changes to the marriage provisions).

The incremental population attributable to Bill C-31's changes represents about 31.1% of the total registered Indian population of Brokenhead in 2002 and an increase in the Registered Indian population of about 45.1% over that expected, had the provisions of the previous *Indian Act* remained in force throughout the April 17, 1985 to December 31, 2002 time period.[11] Analysis conducted by location of residence indicates that Bill C-31 accounted for the majority of population growth reported during the period both on- and off-reserve (52.4% and 60.4% respectively).

Implications of Bill C-31 Population Growth

Given the sizable increases in Brokenhead's population identified above, the possibility clearly exists that the 1985 *Indian Act* has contributed to significant changes in the demand for and use of programs and services administered by Brokenhead, as well as changes in the political and social fabric of the community.

As noted previously, these issues were examined through analysis of administrative data, interviews with program staff and management and the survey of members. In reporting the findings of the research, the discussion focuses initially on the topic of program and service impacts. Observations concerning impacts on the social and political fabric of the community are discussed later.

Impacts on Demand for Programs and Services

The case study's examination of the impacts of Bill C-31 population growth on programs and services administered by Brokenhead included eight service areas: social assistance, housing, elementary and secondary education, post-secondary education, community health service, non-insured health benefits, child and family services, and training and employment. A brief summary of the main findings of the research for each of these service areas is provided below.

Social Assistance

Social assistance support is provided on the basis of need and is available to all reserve residents, regardless of registration or membership status. Administrative records maintained by Brokenhead do not distinguish between Bill C-31 and pre-Bill C-31 recipients.[12] Brokenhead has established a relationship with the province for the recovery of expenditures for non-registered recipients of benefits. Resources for Registered Indians are provided by Indian and Northern Affairs Canada (INAC). Although the social assistance caseload on reserve has increased steadily in recent years, this increase is attributed by staff to changes in local and regional employment opportunities and changes in the values or work ethics of those who maintain young families. Bill C-31 population growth was not viewed as a factor in the recently observed increase in the caseload.

Housing On-Reserve

Brokenhead's policy concerning allocation of reserve housing restricts access to band-owned housing to those who are members. Applicants are evaluated based on the time of application and needs in relation to housing availability. Historically, Bill C-31 status was believed to be a factor affecting access (i.e. in practice pre-Bill C-31 members were given preferential access), but this policy is no longer applied.

Brokenhead did receive a special INAC allocation in the late 1980s to provide incremental housing for Bill C-31 members. Administrative records concerning this allocation and occupants of Bill C-31 housing were unavailable to the study.

Population growth associated with Bill C-31 is believed by staff to have increased the demand for band housing resources during the late 1980s period. The current impact of Bill C-31 population growth on increases in housing demand is not documented and remains unknown.

Elementary and Secondary Education

All reserve residents are eligible for education services subject to school capacity restrictions. Brokenhead provides education service directly for grades kindergarten to eight. Junior to senior high school services are provided by off-reserve schools. Capital, operations and maintenance (O&M), and program resources for elementary and secondary education services are provided by INAC to the schools located on-reserve. No special resources were provided to Brokenhead following the enactment of the 1985 *Indian Act*, although educational program resources associated with any incremental demands associated with Bill C-31 students would have been funded by INAC based on nominal roll counts.

Elementary and secondary education enrolment has been growing steadily and the community requires more classroom space and resources for the elementary programs. This situation is not viewed by staff as an impact of Bill C-31 population growth.

Post-Secondary Education Support

Financial support for post-secondary education is available to members residing both on- and off-reserve subject to the availability of resources. Brokenhead does not have any specific policy concerning Bill C-31 members and did not receive any special allocations for this segment of the member population. The demand for post-secondary education funding has been growing steadily and more quickly than available resources. Population growth associated with Bill C-31 may have contributed to increased demand, but the extent of any impact cannot be documented from available records and remains unknown.

Community Health Services and Non-Insured Health Benefits

Basic community health services are available to all reserve residents, regardless of registration or membership status. The Non-Insured Health Benefits Program is available to those who are registered, regardless of residency. Community health services and the non-insured health benefits are resourced by Health Canada. Brokenhead did not receive any special allocation for the Bill C-31 population.

Demand for community health services has been growing rapidly on reserve. Although some portion of this growth may relate to the Bill C-31 population, staff believes that increases in service demand derive from increased incidence of substance abuse and diabetes among community residents.

Statistical data supplied to this study by Health Canada for the Non-Insured Health Benefits Program allow one to distinguish beneficiaries (and program service costs) on the basis of Bill C-31 status. Analyses of these data for the 1996 and 2001 time periods reveal rates of program usage and service costs to be quite similar for the Bill C-31 and pre-Bill C-31 components of the population. This finding implies that population growth associated with Bill C-31 has likely resulted in significant increases in the demand for and resources required to provide non-insured health benefits.

Child and Family Services

Child and family services are provided by the Southeast Resources Development Council (SERDC) and include some services to both on- and off-reserve residents. SERDC is mandated to provide a full range of services, including child protection and apprehension, to all reserve residents. Services off-reserve exclude child protection and apprehension.

Resources to support child and family services are provided by INAC, although some resources are also supplied by the province. Services being provided presently to members off-reserve are not currently funded by INAC.

According to SERDC staff, demand for child and family services is increasing both on- and off-reserve, and is outpacing available resources, resulting in growing waiting lists for some services. This situation is not viewed by staff as an impact of Bill C-31 population growth, but rather the increasing complexity of clients needs.

Training and Employment Services

Until recently, employment and training services to Brokenhead members residing on- and off-reserve were provided by SERDC. All members, regardless of location are now serviced by Brokenhead, which has received additional resources from Human Resources and Social Development Canada (HRSDC).

The employment and training program operated by Brokenhead is relatively small. Demand for services on reserve has been growing steadily on-reserve (now about 36 trainees per year), and more rapidly off-reserve (now about 14 trainees per year).

As the program does not differentiate trainees on the basis of Bill C-31 registration status, the extent of Bill C-31 participation in the program remains undocumented. Population growth associated with Bill C-31 may have contributed to increased demand for employment and training services, but the extent of any impact remains unknown.

Community Perspectives Concerning Bill C-31 Impacts

The survey of members conducted for this study attempted to address a broad range of potential impacts associated with Bill C-31 population growth. Issues explored included perceptions concerning equality of access to services, the use of specific programs and services, and perceptions concerning changes in the social and political fabric of the community. Some of the key findings of the member survey are highlighted below.

Results from the on-reserve component of the member survey provide additional evidence of the role played by Bill C-31 in promoting growth among the population living on-reserve. All of the on-reserve Bill C-31 members interviewed reported that they had moved to the community since (re)acquiring Indian registration under the 1985 *Indian Act*. Migration to the reserve of sizable numbers of Bill C-31 registrants appears to have played a significant role in the population increase observed on-reserve following Bill C-31.[13]

Roughly one-half of the on-reserve members interviewed for this study expressed the view that Bill C-31 had resulted in changes within their community. Among those who reported changes, most noted increased population growth. Many—although still a minority—of the on-reserve respondents also perceived some negative impacts of Bill C-31, including: increased levels of prejudice and discrimination (13%), housing shortages (12%), reduced access to other programs and services (6%) and greater difficulties obtaining employment (4%).[14]

Survey responses among members living both on- and off-reserve provide little evidence of inequality in access to or receipt of programs and services based on Bill C-31 registration status. Bill C-31 members were slightly more likely than pre-Bill C-31 members to report that they had applied for programs and services administered by Brokenhead. Among those who did apply for services, no differences were identified between Bill C-31 and pre-Bill C-31 respondents in terms of the proportion reporting receipt of services. With the exception of post-secondary education—and to a lesser extent, children's education services—a large majority of Bill C-31 members believed that they had the same level of access to services administered by Brokenhead as other (i.e. pre-Bill C-31) members. Of the small number of on-reserve respondents (23) who reported difficulties obtaining services, only 3 (or 13%) reported Bill C-31 status as the reason for not being able to obtain services.

The member survey results also provided very little evidence that profound changes have occurred in the social and political fabric of the community as a consequence of Bill C-31. Less than 5% of all on-reserve respondents believed that Bill C-31 had resulted in increased friction among members of the community.

First Nations Membership

As noted earlier, the 1985 *Indian Act* also introduced changes affecting membership. Under section 10 of the *Act*, First Nations were permitted to develop and apply their own rules governing membership. In cases where the rules for membership differ from the rules governing registration, the registered and member populations can differ.

As permitted under section 10, Brokenhead elected to adopt its own membership rule. The rule admitted into initial membership all individuals contained on the band list as of June 25, 1987, including all those who regained their registration under the reinstatement provisions of the 1985 *Indian Act*. Individuals who were not on the band list or born after June 25, 1987, are eligible to apply for membership if they are sponsored by a member and are entitled to Indian registration. This includes not only descendants of members but other Registered Indians as well (e.g. Indian spouses of members).

The membership rule also contains additional criteria which are used to evaluate adult applicants. These criteria include:

- The band's financial and housing capabilities
- The applicant's character and lifestyle
- Kinship and other community ties

The membership rule also contains residency provisions, although individuals living off-reserve can also apply for and be admitted into membership.

Decisions concerning applicants are made by a membership committee and in the case of adults, decisions require ratification by Chief and Council. Until recently, Brokenhead's membership rule was administered by the SERDC. According to Brokenhead staff now involved with membership, under SERDC's administration virtually everyone who applied for membership and met the Indian registration criterion, was approved for membership. Administration of the membership rule was assumed by Brokenhead in 2001 in response to a desire to exert more control over the applicant screening and approval process.[15]

As noted above, the membership rule requires that eligible individuals apply for membership and many individuals who are eligible for membership have not applied to become members. As of March 2002, the member population of Brokenhead numbered approximately 730 individuals, representing about 52% of the total registered Indian population. Although nearly all of those who were registered but not members, resided off-reserve, off-reserve members formed about 41% of the total population of members.

Community Perspectives on Membership

Based on the responses to the survey of members, issues surrounding membership do not appear to be well understood among those living either on- or off-reserve. Only 35% of respondents to the survey were aware that Brokenhead had adopted its own rule governing membership. Less than 25% reported that they had some knowledge of the details of the rule. Awareness and knowledge of the rule were especially low among off-reserve respondents (less than 8%).

Among those who reported some knowledge of the details of the rule, nearly one-half expressed concerns about the rule or its implementation. Concerns identified most frequently included lack of consistency in application of the rule (23%) and the rule's potential to deny membership in the future to descendants who do not qualify for Indian registration (19%). This latter issue (i.e. loss of registration entitlement and membership eligibility among descendants) was also noted by more than 25% of all survey respondents as a concern in relation to the future impacts of the 1985 *Indian Act* rules governing Indian registration and Brokenhead's membership rule.

Longer-Term Impacts on Population and Membership

As discussed above, Indian registration represents one of the main criteria for membership in Brokenhead Ojibway Nation. As such, the future population eligible for membership with Brokenhead will be affected by the 1985 *Indian Act*'s rules governing Indian registration. As noted by Clatworthy and Smith (1992), in concert with intermarriage these rules have the potential to result in loss of registration entitlement among large and growing numbers of descendants. Responses to the survey conducted for this study suggest that many members are concerned about the future impacts of the registration rules of the 1985 *Indian Act* on their families and the community of Brokenhead.

As part of this case study, custom population projections were developed to explore the longer-term impacts of the 1985 *Indian Act* and Brokenhead's membership rule on the populations eligible for Indian registration and membership with Brokenhead Ojibway Nation.[16] Clatworthy and Smith (1992) have demonstrated that the rate of intermarriage (i.e. parenting between Registered Indians and non-Indians) is a critical factor affecting the future population entitled to Indian registration.

Estimates of intermarriage (i.e. Indian/non-Indian parenting) rates for the Brokenhead population were constructed using data contained on the 2002 Indian Register and are presented in **Figure 4.3** (page 88). As indicated in the figure, Indian/non-Indian parenting accounts for about 67% of all children born to Brokenhead Registered Indians during the 1985–2002 time period, a level considerably higher than the national average (48%). Rates of Indian/non-Indian parenting during this period, were considerably higher among females (59%) than

Figure 4.3: Estimated Rate of Indian/Non-Indian Parenting by Gender and Location, Brokenhead Ojibway Nation, 1985–2002

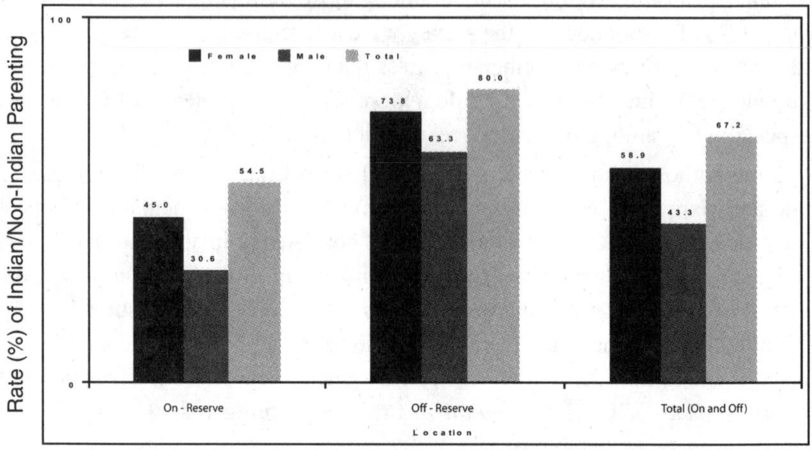

Source: Analysis of data contained on the December 31, 2002, Indian Register

males (43%) and also considerably higher among those living off-reserve than those living on-reserve (80% versus 55%).

The high rates of Indian/non-Indian parenting which characterize the Brokenhead population imply that quite significant composition changes can be expected to occur among the populations residing both on- and off-reserve, as many descendants of the current population are likely to lack eligibility for Indian registration and consequently membership.

Projection Results

Figure 4.4 illustrates the projected population of Brokenhead survivors and descendants by Indian registration and membership eligibility status, assuming the rates of Indian/non-Indian parenting as observed for the 1985–2002 time period remain stable in the future.[17] The projection spans a 75-year period, which can be roughly interpreted as three generations into the future.

As illustrated in the figure, the population entitled to Indian registration (and eligible for membership) is projected to rise for roughly one generation (25 years) from about 1,488 (adjusted for late reporting) in 2002 to 1,943 in 2027. Throughout the remainder of the period, this segment of the population is projected to decline at an accelerating pace and number 1,472 after three generations. Further declines in this population would be expected in the longer term. The population of survivors and descendants who do not qualify for Indian registration, and consequently will be ineligible for nation membership, is projected to increase rapidly throughout the period from just 77 individuals in 2002 to 1,639 after three generations. At that time, non-entitled individuals are expected to form a majority of the Brokenhead population.

Figure 4.4: Projected Population of Brokenhead Ojibway Nation by Indian Registration and Membership Status, 2002–2077

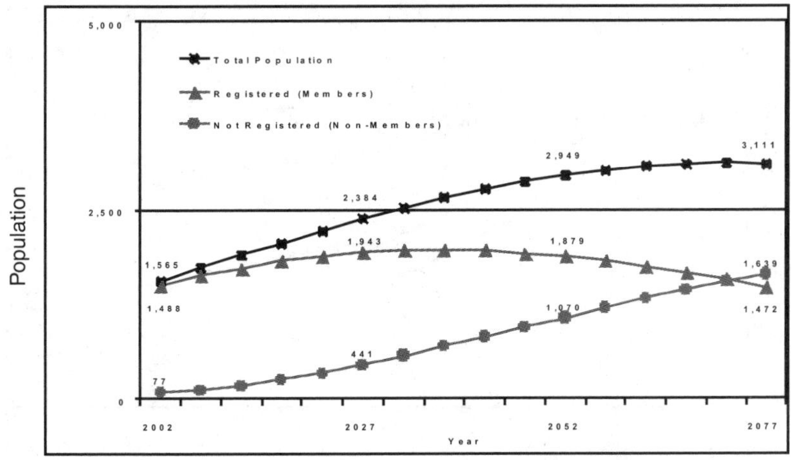

Source: Projection based on the December 31, 2002 Indian Register

Loss of entitlement to Indian registration and membership is projected to affect large and growing numbers of descendants both on- and off-reserve. As illustrated in **Figure 4.5** (page 90), within one generation (25 years), about one in every four children born on-reserve is expected to lack registration entitlement and eligibility for membership. Within three generations, children who qualify for registration and membership are expected to form a minority. The figure also reveals that the process of loss of registration entitlement and membership eligibility is expected to occur much more rapidly off-reserve where rates of Indian/non-Indian parenting are considerably higher. Off-reserve children who are projected to qualify for registration and be eligible for membership are expected to form a minority within about 20 years. Within three generations (75 years), the projections suggest that only about one in every eight children off-reserve will qualify for registration and be eligible for membership.[18]

Conclusion

The results of this analysis clearly suggest that the 1985 *Indian Act* amendments have had quite significant impacts on the size of the Brokenhead's Registered Indian population. In fact, the analysis reveals the changes introduced by the 1985 *Indian Act* have been the most important factors affecting growth both on- and off-reserve during the 1985–2002 period.

A significant minority of Brokenhead members believe that the population growth associated with the 1985 *Indian Act* has resulted in changes to their community, including population growth, greater competition for programs and services, and more competition for jobs. A much smaller minority (about 8%)

Figure 4.5: Projected Proportion of Children Entitled to Indian Registration and Eligibility for Membership by Location, Brokenhead Ojibway Nation, 2002–2077

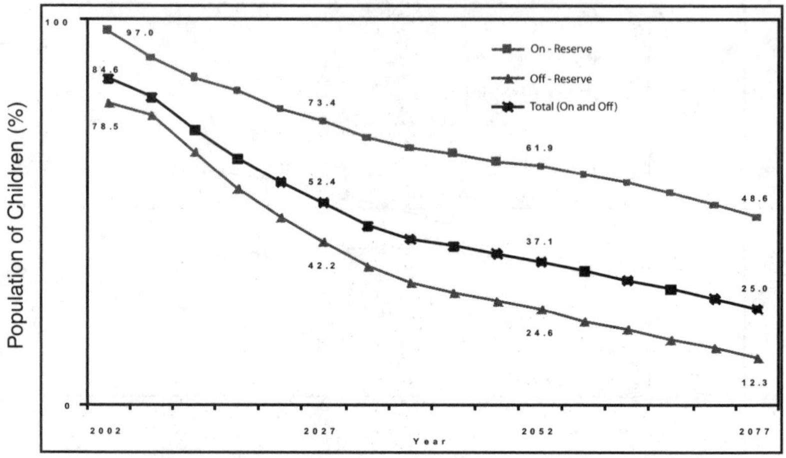

Source: Projection based on the December 31, 2002, Indian Register

believe that the population changes associated with the 1985 *Act* have also contributed to erosion of social cohesion within the community.

There is very little evidence (statistical or otherwise) to suggest that inequality exists with respect to access to band-administered programs and services on the basis of Bill C-31 status. Rates of application for services and rates of receipt of services do not differ greatly between Bill C-31 and other members. Moreover, only a very small minority of members attribute difficulties in obtaining services to Bill C-31 residents or Bill C-31 status.

A significant minority (more than one-quarter) of the Brokenhead population expressed concerns about the future impacts of the 1985 *Indian Act*. These concerns relate to the potential impacts of the rules governing Indian registration and membership eligibility on descendants. Longer-term population projections developed for this study suggest that these concerns are well-founded, as high rates of intermarriage are expected to result in growing numbers of descendants who lack entitlement to Indian registration and consequently to membership under Brokenhead's current membership rule.

The transformation of Brokenhead's population from one which is almost entirely comprised of those who are both registered and eligible for membership to one in which a majority lacks both registration entitlement and eligibility for membership clearly presents a number of challenges to Brokenhead's population and leadership. Although Brokenhead also faced (and based on the findings of this research, responded constructively to) challenges associated with population growth and change during the 1985–2002 period, the challenges emerging in the future appear to be of significantly greater magnitude and complexity. Issues related to membership, maintaining and promoting political and social equality, ensuring equality of access to needed programs and services, and responding to the differential rights and entitlements of different classes of citizens are likely to require the community's attention in the near future. These issues should also be an important part of the research agenda so that we can develop a better understanding of how these issues affect communities.

Endnotes

1 The term intermarriage is used to refer to the process of exogamous parenting (i.e. parenting between someone who is a Registered Indian and someone who is not entitled to registration). Under the rules of the 1985 *Indian Act* governing registration, two successive generations of exogamous parenting results in descendants of the second generation lacking registration entitlement.

2 This research was undertaken as part of a broader examination of the 1985 amendments of the *Indian Act* supported by the Southern Chiefs Organization, Inc. of Manitoba and the Strategic Research and Analysis Directorate of Indian and Northern Affairs Canada (INAC).

3 One of the changes introduced by the 1985 *Indian Act* was the opportunity for individual First Nations to control their own membership. These provisions are found in section 10 of the 1985 *Indian Act*.

4 The term "pre-Bill C-31" is used to refer to those individuals who were entitled to Indian registration and membership prior to the enactment of Bill C-31 in April of 1985. This population is also frequently referred to as "original" members.

5 The on-reserve segment of the survey was administered to a sample of 101 individuals aged 16 or more years of age selected randomly from the membership list maintained by Brokenhead. The off-reserve sample for the survey was initially designed to survey a random sample of 160 individuals. More than one-half of the off-reserve sample could not be located or contacted.

6 The proportion of Bill C-31 respondents in the sample (21.2%) is roughly equal to the Bill C-31 share of the total Registered Indian population (20.9%) of Brokenhead.

7 The provision of the 1951/56 *Indian Act* that allowed for the removal from the Register of children born prior to a woman's marriage to a non-Indian was successfully challenged in the courts with the 1979 the Ranville case.

8 In the case of "illegitimate" births to Indian males and non-Indian females, only the male children were permitted to register. The status rights of illegitimate male children was confirmed in the 1983 Martin Case ruling on section 11(1)(c). See Chapter 3 (endnote 9).

9 The Indian Register does not contain a complete record of all children born to registered Indian parents. Specifically, those children who have only one Indian parent registered under Section 6(2) are not in the Register, as they do not qualify for registration under the provisions of Bill C-31.

10 The total fertility rate estimate used in this study derives from recent research undertaken by Statistics Canada as part of the 2001-based projections of Canada's Registered Indian population (prepared for Indian and Northern Affairs Canada). Fertility rate estimates for Registered Indian females in Manitoba were applied to estimate the number of women involved in child-bearing during the study period.

11 The estimated incremental impact of Bill C-31 on growth of the Brokenhead population (about 45%) is considerably larger than the national average, which was recently estimated by Clatworthy (2005a) to be about 33%.

12 As social assistance and some other administrative records maintained by Brokenhead identify the band number of program/service beneficiaries, Bill C-31 service users could be identified by linking the administrative data with the Indian Register. Requests to Indian Affairs to carry out such a linkage for purposes of this project could not be accommodated within the study time frame.

13 Some movement from on- to off-reserve was also identified by the off-reserve component of the member survey. About 22% of the off-reserve Bill C-31 members interviewed reported that they had moved from the reserve after the enactment of Bill C-31.

14 It is interesting to note that several respondents to the on-reserve component of the survey believed that although Bill C-31 population growth had contributed to increased competition for services, it also had the positive effect of increasing the incentive for some members to seek employment as an alternative to relying upon band resources for financial support.

15 Brokenhead's reasons for assuming direct control of membership approval could not be clearly determined. Part of the motivation may be linked to the Supreme Court ruling on Corbière, (1999) which extended voting rights for First Nations elections to members living off-reserve.

16   As the Brokenhead membership rule contains discretionary provisions which cannot be reasonably included in the projections, the projections examine only the population that is eligible to apply to membership. It should be recognized that the actual number of future members is likely to be considerably smaller than the number who are eligible to apply, as some may not apply and some who do apply may not be approved for membership.

17   The projection uses a model developed by Clatworthy for the specific purpose of exploring the longer-term impacts of the 1985 *Indian Act* rules governing Indian registration entitlement and membership. For this study, the model was configured to reflect the fertility rate trends of the Brokenhead population and the mortality rate trends of Registered Indians in Manitoba. In addition to fertility and mortality, the projection model explicitly incorporates rates of Indian/ non-Indian parenting and the rules governing entitlement to Indian registration. Readers interested in the specifics of the projection approach are encouraged to review Clatworthy (2005a) and Norris et al. (2001).

18   Projections developed to explore scenarios of increasing rates of Indian/non-Indian parenting reveal much more rapid rates of loss of registration and membership eligibility both on- and off-reserve. In the on-reserve context, for example, a 20% increase in rates of Indian/non-Indian parenting would result in a minority of children being eligible for registration and membership within 45 years.

References

Clatworthy, S. J. 1991. *Modeling the Future Population Eligible for Indian Registration and Band Membership: Selected Communities of the Meadow Lake Tribal Council.* Meadow Lake Tribal Council, Saskatchewan.

Clatworthy, S. J. and A. H. Smith. 1992. *Population Implications of the 1985 Amendments to the* Indian Act. Ottawa: Assembly of First Nations.

Clatworthy, S. J. 1994. *Revised Projection Scenarios Concerning the Population Implications of Section 6 of the* Indian Act. Ottawa: INAC.

Clatworthy, S. J. 1998. *Population and Membership Projections: Mohawks of Kahnawake.* Intergovernmental Relations Team, Mohawk Council of Kahnawake, Mohawk Territory of Kahnawake.

Clatworthy, S. J. 1999. *Population Implications of Proposed Revisions to the Blood Tribe Membership Code.* Blood Tribe Membership Review Committee, Blood Tribe, Alberta.

Clatworthy, S. J. 2001a. *Re-Assessing the Population Impacts of Bill C-31.* Strategic Research and Analysis Directorate. Ottawa: INAC.

Clatworthy, S. J. 2001b. *First Nations Membership and Registered Indian Status.* Winnipeg: Southern Chiefs Organization, Inc.

Clatworthy, S. J. 2002a. *Implications of First Nations Demography: Recent Trends and Projected Population Changes*, prepared for the Strategic Research and Analysis Directorate. Ottawa: INAC.

Clatworthy, S. J. 2002b. *Population Implications of Proposed Revisions to the Peigan Nation Membership Code.* Brocket, Alberta: Peigan Nation Membership Review Committee.

Clatworthy, S. J. 2005a. *Indian Registration, Membership and Population Change in First Nations Communities,* prepared for Strategic Research and Analysis Directorate. Ottawa: INAC.

Clatworthy, S. J. 2005b. *Membership and Registration: Population Impacts of Bill C-31 on First Nations in Northern Manitoba*, prepared for the Assembly of Manitoba Chiefs, Winnipeg, Manitoba.

Norris, M.J., S. Clatworthy, and E. Guimond. 2001. *Demography, Legislation and Ethnic Mobility: Considerations and Implications for Projections of Canada's Aboriginal Population.* Washington, D.C.: Population Association of America.

United Anishnaabeg Councils. 1999. *Impacts of the Authority to Determine Band Membership*, prepared for Strategic Research and Analysis Directorate. Ottawa: INAC.

Smith, A. H. 1991. *Bill C-31 Impact Study: Meadow Lake First Nations.* Meadow Lake, Saskatchewan.

Ethelyne Peck

Ethelyne Peck was born July 10, 1951, in Baddeck, Nova Scotia. Her parents were James and Elizabeth Peck. She lived in Wagmatcook until 1971. At twenty-one years of age she married a non-native and moved to Lunenburg, Nova Scotia and resided there for fifteen years. She had three children. She couldn't get any assistance from her Band. She remembers receiving a letter from her band, but she never signed the letter; however, circumstances didn't changed. She and her husband struggled with day-to-day expenses. Ethelyne lived in an abusive relationship for twenty years and just couldn't put up with the abuse anymore, so she moved back to her community.

Ethelyne had five children when she moved back to Wagmatcook. The Band refused to assist her. Her mother and sister helped her. She moved into her mother's tiny two-bedroom house and lived there for several years. She was treated like an outsider in her community and she suffered emotionally from the loss of her two children. She struggled to survive. The Chief at that time told her to marry an Indian and she would get a house but Ethelyne didn't want to have to do that; especially having been through such an abusive marriage. She eventually got a house from the Native Council of Nova Scotia. She received training as an early childhood development worker and was able to feed her family and care for them.

Today Ethelyne said things are somewhat better but the strain and struggle through the years took its toll on her. She stated that not only was she denied assistance from her band, she missed her community and family and nothing could bring her comfort for the difficult times that she endured. She stated that even today there is as negative stigma attached to being a victim of Bill C-31; you are never really regarded as a community member again, you are referred to as a Bill C-31.

Ethelyne stated that all First Nations that were affected by discriminatory legislation through the Indian Act *should be rightfully compensated.*

Part Three:
Demographic Impacts

5

Indian Registration, Membership, and Population Change in First Nations Communities

Stewart Clatworthy

Introduction

The 1985 amendments to the *Indian Act* (commonly referred to as Bill C-31) introduced three key changes, including:

- The reinstatement of Registered Indian status to those individuals who had lost their registration through provisions of earlier versions of the *Indian Act*, and the first-time registration of many of their children
- New rules governing entitlement to Indian registration for all children born after April 16, 1985 (section 6)
- The opportunity for individual First Nations to develop and apply their own rules governing First Nations membership (section 10)

Until recently, most of the attention concerning the impacts of the 1985 changes to the *Indian Act* has focused on the reinstatement and registration provisions, which have resulted in substantial increases to the Registered Indian populations of many First Nations.[1] While the short-term impacts associated with Bill C-31's reinstatement and registration provisions have clearly been substantial, the latter two changes have the potential for more significant impacts on First Nations populations and communities in the medium- and longer-terms. These impacts emerge from the interplay of the new rules for determining entitlement to Indian registration, the rules adopted by First Nations for determining membership, and the parenting patterns of First Nations populations.

Prior to the 1985 *Indian Act*, the concepts of Registered Indian status and First Nation or band membership were equivalent. "Band members" were defined as individuals contained on the Indian Register (or Treaty List) for a given First Nation. Since the adoption of Bill C-31, the Indian Register continues to determine membership only in cases where a First Nation has *not* adopted its own membership rule.[2] For First Nations that have adopted membership rules under section 10 of the 1985 *Indian Act*, the "Band List" is maintained by the First Nation and is distinct from the Indian Register.[3] For many First Nations, the population eligible for membership can differ from that entitled to Indian registration.

The distinction between Indian registration and First Nation membership is important, as registration and membership convey different sets of rights, entitlements and benefits. For example, Indian registration guarantees freedom from taxation on-reserve, eligibility for post-secondary education support, and access to a broad range of health care services provided under Health Canada's Non-Insured Health Benefits (NIHB) Program. The Registered Indian population is also the basis for determining financial allocations to First Nations for some programs and services. For some Registered status may mean recognition of being an Indian. Membership, however, imparts a sense of belonging to a particular community. It also conveys political rights (including the right to vote in First Nation elections and run for Council), and in many First Nations is a defining criterion for access to a wide range of programs and services administered by the First Nation (see Clatworthy "Brokenhead" this volume).

As Clatworthy and Smith (1992) have noted, the separation of Indian registration from First Nation membership can result in the fragmentation of First Nations populations into "classes of citizens" with differing rights and entitlements. They also suggest that inequalities related to these class distinctions may serve as a source of conflict in First Nations communities[4] and lead to legal challenges and jurisdictional squabbles among governments over responsibilities for providing and funding services to various segments of First Nations populations.

Although clearly important to the future well-being of First Nations communities and populations, the interplay of parenting patterns, the rules governing Indian registration, and First Nation membership rules have received little attention in prior research. The most comprehensive previous analysis in this regard remains that of Clatworthy and Smith (1992). Their study examined and classified all of the membership rules adopted by First Nations as of April 1992 and explored, via a series of case studies and hypothetical projections, the nature and scale of the longer-term population changes which are expected to occur among First Nations that apply various types of membership rules.[5]

This study seeks to both revise and extend upon the earlier work of Clatworthy and Smith by:

- Examining and classifying First Nations membership codes adopted subsequent to their research
- Identifying the nature of any changes to First Nations membership rules that have occurred since the time of initial adoption and reclassifying these rules in light of these changes
- Providing current (i.e., 2002) and projected estimates of the populations eligible for First Nations membership and for Indian registration
- Assessing the implications of expected population changes for service provision to First Nations populations

The study concludes that there are several important issues arising from the continuing operation of Bill C-31. For example, First Nations and other governments are likely to experience growing pressures to provide services to people who lack Indian registration and/or membership. The populations are changing and we find a movement toward more and more individuals who do not meet the requirements for both Indian registration and First Nations membership. This is more pronounced off-reserve but that may shift in many reserve communities. There is going to be a period where jurisdictional and financial responsibilities for program and service provision to the various classes of residents that are created by the *Act* are unclear. If present policy is maintained, there may be many groups of citizens who lack access to needed services where allocation is restricted to those who qualify as band members. This may be magnified by the lack of appropriate funding levels under current intergovernmental transfer agreements which do not recognize the service needs of all subgroups or classes of citizens residing in First Nations communities. This could result in an increase of inequalities that, in turn, may result in community conflict and legal challenges.

A Review of First Nations Membership Rules

In their 1992 review, Clatworthy and Smith examined many features of the membership rules adopted by 236 First Nations as of April, 1992. These features included:

- Definition of the initial member population (i.e. those who qualify for membership at the time of adoption of the rule)
- The "descent or inheritance rules" by which descendants of the initial member population inherit or qualify for membership in the future
- Additional criteria (limitations or tests) applied to individuals who otherwise qualify based on kinship or descent
- Provisions and conditions related to extending membership to other individuals who do *not* qualify for initial membership or do *not* qualify on the basis of descent (e.g. spouses, adopted children, transfers from other First Nations)
- The mechanics associated with implementing the rules, including the nature and responsibilities of decision-making bodies involved in the review and approval/rejection of membership applicants

Using information concerning the population eligible for initial membership and the descent (or inheritance) rules which determine how membership eligibility is transferred to future generations, Clatworthy and Smith identified four main types of membership rules adopted under section 10 of the 1985 *Indian Act*.[6] These rules included:

- **Limited One Parent (or Act Equivalent) rules**, where eligibility for membership requires that a person have at least one parent who is a member and that the person also be entitled to Indian registration
- **Unlimited One Parent rules**, where eligibility for membership requires that a person have at least one parent who is a member, regardless of the person's entitlement to Indian registration

- **Two Parent rules**, where eligibility for membership requires that both parents of the person be members
- **Blood Quantum rules**, where a person's eligibility for membership is determined on the basis of the amount of "Indian blood" that person possesses in relation to a minimum standard

The four main types of membership rules were further divided into subgroups (22 in total) based on the definition of the population admitted into initial membership (i.e., the rules for determining who qualifies to be part of the original member population). This latter factor (i.e. the population admitted into initial membership) is important as First Nations that adopted membership rules prior to June 28, 1987, were allowed to exclude from membership certain groups of individuals whose (acquired) rights to membership were not protected under the 1985 *Indian Act*.[7]

In practice, the largest group of individuals excluded from initial membership included the children of women who lost Indian registration status (under the previous *Indian Act*) as a consequence of marriages to non-Indians and who were born subsequent to those marriages.[8] The exclusion of this group of individuals from membership also has important implications for their descendants. Under the terms of most First Nations membership rules, the descendants of these individuals will also not qualify for membership. The failure of the revised *Act* to guarantee rights to membership for the children of women who were removed from the Indian Register as a consequence of intermarriage has given rise to claims of residual gender discrimination in the 1985 *Indian Act* and is the basis for several on-going legal challenges.

Revising the Clatworth and Smith Typology

As the information compiled by Clatworthy and Smith is now somewhat dated, efforts were undertaken to extend and revise the results of their study. This involved two main activities including:

- Identifying and classifying membership rules adopted subsequent to the time of their initial study
- Identifying any amendments or revisions which have occurred since the time of initial adoption of the membership rules

Status of Membership Rules

All First Nations that propose to establish membership rules under section 10 of the 1985 *Indian Act* are required to submit the rules to Indian and Northern Affairs Canada for review and approval. As of December 31, 2002, department records indicate that 311 First Nations had submitted membership rules. Of these, 241 rules (about 77%) were identified to have received approval by the department. Of the 70 non-approved rules, only eight were currently under review by the department.[9]

Table 5.1: Summary of First Nations Membership Rules Adopted Since the 1992 Clatworthy/Smith Review

First Nation	Type of Membership Rule (Clatworthy/Smith Typology)
Loon River Cree Nation	One parent rule limited to Indians and including all Registered Indian descendants of members
Cheslatta T'en First Nation	Unlimited one parent rule open to all descendants of original members
Tsawataineuk Indian Band	Unlimited one parent rule open to all descendants of original members
Adams Lake Indian Band	One parent rule limited to Indians and including all Registered Indian descendants of members
Williams Lake Indian Band	One parent rule limited to Indians and including all Registered Indian descendants of members

Source: INAC Administrative Data

Nine of the 241 First Nations who were identified with approved section 10 membership rules were no longer applying these rules. Eight of these First Nations now determine membership under alternative (self-government) legislation. The remaining First Nations now base membership on the rules governing Indian registration (section 6 of the *Indian Act*).

Membership Rules Adopted Since April 1992

The department's records revealed that only five First Nations had submitted membership rules that were approved since the time of the original review by Clatworth and Smith in 1992. Membership rules for these First Nations were reviewed and classified using the same criteria developed by Clatworthy and Smith. The results of the review are summarized in **Table 5.1**.

Application, Amendments, and Revisions

There is no requirement under the 1985 *Indian Act* for First Nations that have adopted membership rules to inform or notify the department of subsequent changes or amendments. As a result, a survey of all First Nations that had adopted membership rules under section 10 of the *Indian Act* was undertaken to determine whether approved rules were actually being applied and to obtain information concerning the nature of any approved or planned amendments to the original rules.[10] Information concerning changes to the status or nature of First Nations membership rules collected via the survey was then used to update the original classification of First Nations by type of membership rule, as presented by Clatworthy and Smith (1992).

The main findings of the survey are summarized below:

- A large majority of First Nations that adopted section 10 rules are applying these rules to determine membership. Of the 212 First Nations for which interviews were completed, only 18 (about 8.5%) reported that they are presently not using a membership rule.

Table 5.2: Distribution of First Nations by Type of Membership Rule and INAC Region, 2002

Region	Section 10 First Nations				Indian Act	All Types
	Unlimited One Parent	Act Equivalent	Blood Quantum	Two Parent		
Atlantic Region	4	2	0	5	22	33
Quebec	2	1	0	0	27	30
Ontario	18	12	13	10	85	138
Manitoba	8	10	2	0	42	62
Saskatchewan	6	0	1	23	40	70
Alberta	9	13	6	3	15	46
British Columbia	34	19	3	23	115	194
Yukon	2	1	1	0	6	10
Northwest Territories	1	0	0	0	25	26
All Regions	84	58	26	64	377	609
% of First Nations	13.8	9.5	4.3	10.5	61.9	100.0

Note: The total of 609 First Nations excludes 19 First Nations whose membership is determined through (self-government) legislation other than the Indian Act. These 19 First Natioins have not been included in this study.

Source: Clatworthy and Smith (1992) revised on the basis of the study's survey

- Among the 18 First Nations not applying their membership rule, seven reported that they were currently using the *Indian Act* rules (section 6) for determining membership in their First Nations. Four First Nations reported that all decisions concerning membership were being made by Chief and Council. Another four First Nations reported that a moratorium was in place concerning membership. Two First Nations indicated that membership was being based on family or community sponsorship. One First Nation did not reveal the current basis for determining membership.

- Thirty-one First Nations reported that they had made amendments to their original membership rule. Respondents for six of these First Nations either refused to specify or were unsure of the nature of changes made. Rule amendments for all but six of the remaining 25 First Nations dealt with minor aspects of the rules and would appear to have little impact on membership eligibility.

- More substantive amendments were reported for six First Nations, including two that had made changes to the underlying descent provisions of the rule (i.e., the type of code). Both of these First Nations were originally identified to be using restrictive two-parent rules. One reported a change to the descent provisions governing Indian registration (i.e., section 6 of the 1985 *Indian Act*). The other reported a change to the

Table 5.3: First Nations Registered Indian Population by Type of Membership Rule and INAC Region, 2002

Region	Section 10 First Nations				Indian Act	All Types
	Unlimited One Parent	Act Equivalent	Blood Quantum	Two Parent		
Atlantic Region	2,598	566	0	6,111	20,261	29,536
Quebec	986	506	0	0	51,601	53,093
Ontario	25,080	12,149	13,058	9,068	109,745	169,100
Manitoba	18,471	15,345	12,604	0	70,244	116,664
Saskatchewan	7,748	0	925	30,430	76,147	115,250
Alberta	10,086	20,232	22,717	5,142	34,461	92,638
British Columbia	22,174	8,577	5,067	11,953	65,032	112,803
Yukon	1,229	139	379	0	3,255	5,002
Northwest Territories	1,316	0	0	0	14,499	15,815
All Regions	89,688	57,514	54,750	62,704	445,245	709,901
% of First Nations	12.6	8.1	7.7	8.8	62.7	100.0

Source: Derived from the December 31, 2002, Indian Register

more inclusive descent provisions of a one parent rule. In both cases, the expected effects of these changes would be to allow for a larger segment of future descendants to qualify for membership.

- Two other First Nations that had initially adopted rules which excluded the descendants of women who intermarried prior to the 1985 *Indian Act* amendments, reported changes that extended initial membership eligibility to all Bill C-31 registrants, including this group of descendants. In the future membership eligibility would also be extended to some of the descendants of this group.[11]

Revised Summary of First Nations by Type of Membership Rule

Based on the findings of this component of the study, it is possible to reassign First Nations which have made changes to their membership rules according to the membership rule categories developed by Clatworthy and Smith. **Table 5.2** identifies the revised distribution of First Nations by membership rule type and province or region. As revealed in the table, membership in most First Nations (377 or about 62%) is determined by the rules governing Indian registration (Section 6 of the 1985 *Indian Act*). In addition to these First Nations that did not adopt their own membership rules, 58 First Nations are currently applying rules which are equivalent to the *Indian Act* rules. These First Nations account for about 10% of all First Nations. The remaining 174 First Nations are applying rules which differ significantly from the rules governing Indian registration. These include 84

First Nations (about 14%) using unlimited one parent rules, 64 First Nations (about 11%) using two parent rules, and 26 First Nations (about 4%) using blood quantum rules. A summary of the Registered Indian populations associated with First Nations using the various types of membership rules is provided in **Table 5.3** (page 105).

Projecting the Populations Eligible for Indian Registration and First Nation Membership

As noted in the introduction, the Clatworthy and Smith study contained a series of hypothetical and case study projections which were intended to illustrate the nature and scale of the impacts of various types of membership rules on the future populations of First Nations. This section of the report discusses the results from a new series of projections which estimate the future population *eligible* for First Nation membership and for Indian registration. The projections span a 75-year period (2003–2077), which can be roughly interpreted as three generations into the future.

It should be noted that the projections reported in this study focus on the population that is eligible for membership by virtue of satisfying the descent or inheritance requirements of First Nation membership rules and (if applicable) other limiting conditions such as entitlement to Indian registration. As noted earlier, other discretionary factors may also be applied to some groups of individuals and be important in determining the population that actually acquires membership. As these discretionary provisions generally have the ability to exclude some individuals from membership, the actual population of First Nation members is likely to be smaller than the population eligible for membership.[12]

Approach and Methodology

The projections developed for this study focus on the populations of 593 First Nations, including the 232 First Nations that adopted their own membership rules under Section 10 of the *Indian Act* and 377 First Nations that did not adopt their own rules and where membership continues to be determined by the rules governing Indian registration (section 6 of the 1985 *Indian Act*).

As the study's resources did not allow for projections to be constructed for each of the 593 First Nations, individual First Nations were aggregated into reasonably small groups on the basis of three key factors which are expected to influence their future populations. These factors include the type of membership rule in use, the rate of exogamous (i.e. Indian/non-Indian) parenting, and regional location. A total of 93 discrete First Nations groups were constructed. For each group, custom population projections were developed.

The projections were carried out using cohort-survival models that were customized to incorporate not only the standard features of fertility, aging, and mortality, but also the membership and Indian registration composition of the

Table 5.4: Estimated 2002 First Nations Populations by Membership Eligibility, Indian Registration Entitlement, and Type of Membership Rule, Canada, 2002

Type of Membership Rule	Population (thousands)				
	Reg. Member	Reg. Non-Member	Non-Reg. Member	Non-Reg. Non-Member	Total Population
Indian Act or Equivalent	348.7	0.0	0.0	19.2	507.9
Act Equivalent but excluding those without acquired rights as of June 28, 1987	4.7	1.0	0.0	0.3	6.0
Unlimited One Parent	74.6	0.0	2.8	0.0	77.4
One parent but excluding those without acquired rights as of June 28, 1987	10.6	1.9	0.0	0.6	13.1
Two Parent	45.2	17.5	0.0	2.1	64.8
50% Blood Quantum	45.8	0.6	0.0	1.6	47.9
25% Blood Quantum	8.4	0.0	0.2	0.0	8.6
All Types of Rules	**678.1**	**20.8**	**3.0**	**23.7**	**725.7**

Note: Totals may not sum due to rounding

Source: Estimated from the December 31, 2002, Indian Register (adjusted for late reporting of births and deaths)

Totals may not sum due to rounding.

population, future population additions through the reinstatement provisions of the 1985 *Indian Act*, rates of exogamous (Indian/non-Indian) parenting, and assignment rules for allocating children born in the future to membership, Indian registration, and blood quantum categories (in the case of blood quantum rule). The baseline populations and key parameters of the projections (i.e. fertility, mortality, future Bill C-31 additions, rates of exogamous parenting, and assignment rules) were configured to reflect the specific circumstances of each of the 93 groups of First Nations. Separate projection models were also configured for the populations residing on- and off-reserve.

Depending upon the type of membership rule in use, four population subgroups are projected within the models. These subgroups include:

- Individuals entitled to Indian registration and also eligible for membership (**registered members**)
- Individuals entitled to Indian registration but *not* eligible for membership (**registered non-members**)
- Individuals not entitled to Indian registration but eligible for membership (**non-registered members**)
- Individuals neither entitled to Indian registration nor eligible for membership (**non-registered non-members**)

Table 5.4 presents estimates of the composition of the baseline (2002) population associated with First Nations that use various types of membership rules. As

Figure 5.1: Projected Population of Survivors and Descendants by Membership Eligibility and Indian Registration Entitlement, Canada, 2002–2077

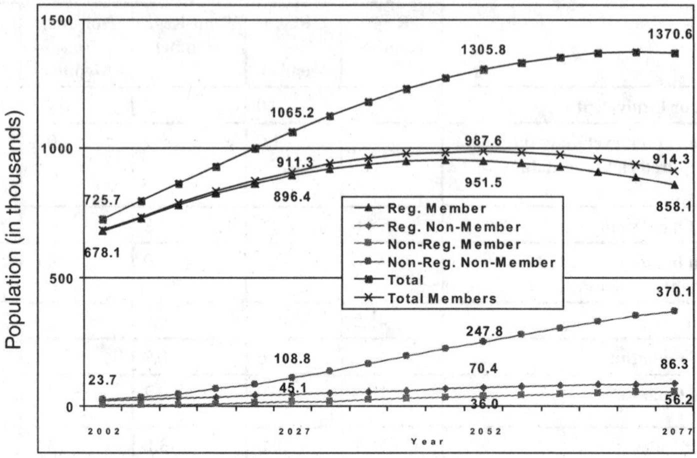

Source: Custom projections based on the December 31, 2002 Indian Register

revealed in the table, registered members form the largest component of the First Nations population associated with each of the main groups of membership rules.

Significant numbers of individuals who were entitled to Indian registration but ineligible for First Nations membership (i.e. registered non-members), were common only among First Nations using two parent rules and one parent rules that excluded from initial membership individuals whose rights to membership were not protected under the *Indian Act* prior to June 28, 1987. Non-registered descendants who also lacked eligibility for membership (i.e., non-registered non-members) were common among First Nations using all types of rules except unlimited one parent and 25% blood quantum rules. Individuals who lacked entitlement to Indian registration but who met the conditions for First Nations membership (i.e., non-registered members) were common only among First Nations using unlimited one parent membership rules.

Most of the roughly 45,000 individuals who were ineligible for First Nations membership form one of two subgroups: the section 6(2) children born to women who intermarried (and lost their registration status under the prior *Indian Act*) and the descendants of these children.

Data aggregated to the national level mask quite large variations in the population composition of First Nations that use the same type of membership rule. In general, First Nations which experience higher rates of exogamous parenting have populations where those who are entitled to Indian registration and eligible for membership (i.e. registered members) form a smaller segment of the population.

Figure 5.2: Projected Population of Survivors and Descendants On-Reserve by Membership Eligibility and Indian Registration Entitlement, Canada, 2002–2077

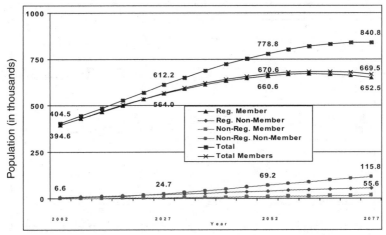

Source: Custom projections based on the December 31, 2002 Indian Register

Some Projection Results

To simplify the presentation of projection findings, the results from the individual subgroup projections have been aggregated to the national level, as well as for the seven main types of membership rules considered in this study. Projection results at the national level are presented for the combined, as well as on- and off-reserve contexts. Results for First Nations using the various types of membership rules are presented for the combined on- and off-reserve populations only.[13]

National Estimates by Location On- and Off-Reserve

Figure 5.1 presents the projected estimates for the combined on- and off-reserve population at the national level by membership eligibility and Indian registration subgroup. The total population (i.e. all survivors and their descendants) is projected to increase throughout most of the 75-year time period reaching a maximum of about 1.371 million (in year 2072). The population eligible for First Nations membership is projected to rise over the initial 50-year period reaching about 987,600 individuals in year 2052. This population is projected to decline to about 914,300 individuals by year 2077.

Individuals who are entitled to Indian registration and eligible for First Nations membership (i.e., registered members) are expected to form a majority of the total population throughout the projection period. This population is expected to grow over the initial 45 year period to about 955,000, but decline to about 858,100 within 75 years. The population eligible for First Nations membership is expected to include a growing number of individuals who do not meet the requirements

Figure 5.3: Projected Population of Survivors and Descendants Off-Reserve by Membership Eligibility and Indian Registration Entitlement, Canada, 2002–2077

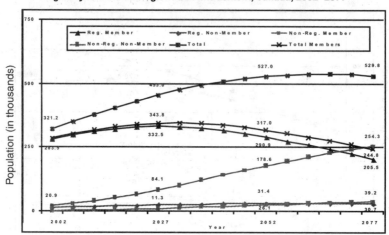

Source: Custom projections based on the December 31, 2002, Indian Register

for Indian registration. This segment of the population, which is estimated to total only about 3,000 individuals in 2002, is projected to increase throughout the period to about 56,200 within 75 years.

The population that does not qualify for First Nations membership is expected to increase throughout the entire time period from the current level of 44,600 to 456,400 individuals within 75 years. Although individuals who are not entitled to Indian registration are projected to form a large majority of those ineligible for membership, the population ineligible for membership is also projected to include a growing number of individuals who qualify for Indian registration (i.e. registered non-members). This latter group is expected to grow from about 20,900 individuals (in 2002) to about 45,100 individuals within 25 years and to about 86,300 individuals within 75 years.

Population changes at the national level are expected to be quite different on- and off-reserve. Population estimates for the context on reserve are presented in **Figure 5.2** (page 109).

Growth in the total population of survivors and descendants on-reserve is projected to occur throughout the entire projection period reaching about 840,800 individuals within 75 years. Rates of growth on-reserve, however, are expected to fall throughout the period and approach zero near the end of the period. The population eligible for First Nations membership is projected to increase for about 60 years peaking at about 688,700 in year 2062. A small decline in this segment of the population is projected to occur over the remainder of the period.

A large majority of the population eligible for membership on reserve is also expected to qualify for Indian registration. This population group (i.e., registered members) is expected to grow for about 60 years reaching about 670,900 in year 2062. This segment of the population is projected to decline gradually thereafter, and number about 652,500 within 75 years.

Growth in the on-reserve population ineligible for membership is expected to occur throughout the projection period. This population, which is currently estimated at about 9,500 individuals, is projected to rise to about 44,700 within 25 years and about 171,300 within 75 years. Although most of those ineligible for membership are also expected to lack entitlement to Indian registration, the Registered Indian component of those lacking eligibility for membership is expected to increase sharply over the period (from about 6,000 in 2002 to about 55,600 within 75 years).

Growth is also expected over the period in the on-reserve population that is eligible for membership but not entitled to Indian registration (i.e. non-registered members). This subgroup is projected to increase from about 500 individuals (in 2002) to about 17,000 individuals over the projection period.

As illustrated in **Figure 5.3**, much more pronounced changes are expected to occur in the composition of the off-reserve population. While the total population of survivors and descendants off-reserve is expected to increase for about 65 years, growth in the population eligible for membership is expected to occur for only 30 years. The member-eligible population is expected to peak at about 345,300 individuals in 2032 and fall to about 244,800 individuals within 75 years (a level roughly 40,000 lower than in 2002).

The off-reserve population entitled to Indian registration and eligible for First Nations membership (i.e., registered members) is projected to increase for only 25 years, peaking at about 332,500 individuals. Over the remainder of the projection period, this population is projected to decline to 205,500, roughly 78,000 lower than in 2002.

The high rates of exogamous parenting which characterize off-reserve populations are expected to result in very rapid growth in the population that lacks eligibility for membership. This population, which is estimated to number about 35,200 individuals in 2002, is projected to rise to about 109,200 within 25 years and to about 285,000 within 75 years. Within about 70 years, those ineligible for First Nations membership are expected to form a majority of the off-reserve population. The vast majority of those lacking eligibility for membership are also projected to lack entitlement to Indian registration.

Population Impacts of Various Types of Membership Rules
As noted by Clatworthy and Smith (1992), the implications of exogamous parenting vary widely among First Nations that employ different types of membership rules. This sub-section of the report provides a brief summary of the projection results associated with First Nations that have adopted different types of membership rules. The results are presented at the national level for the combined population living on- and off-reserve in **Table 5.5** (page 112).

Table 5.5: Projected Distribution of First Nations Population by Type of Membership Rule, Canada, 2002–2077 (Projected)

Population Group	% of Population			
	2002	2027	2052	2077
Indian Act of Equivalent				
Registered Members	96.2	88.0	77.3	67.4
Registered Non-Members	0.0	0.0	0.0	0.0
Non-Registered Members	0.0	0.0	0.0	0.0
Non-Registered Non-Members	3.8	12.0	22.7	32.6
Indian Act or Equivalent but excluding those without acquired rights				
Registered Members	78.7	74.3	67.6	59.9
Registered Non-Members	16.3	11.2	5.5	2.1
Non-Registered Members	0.0	0.0	0.0	0.0
Non-Registered Non-Members	5.0	14.5	26.9	38.0
Unlimited One Parent				
Registered Members	96.4	88.3	77.1	65.9
Registered Non-Members	0.0	0.0	0.0	0.0
Non-Registered Members	3.6	11.7	22.9	34.1
Non-Registered Non-Members	0.0	0.0	0.0	0.0
Unlimited One Parent but excluding those without acquired rights				
Registered Members	81.2	78.9	73.7	67.6
Registered Non-Members	14.3	8.2	3.2	0.5
Non-Registered Members	0.1	4.9	13.3	21.9
Non-Registered Non-Members	4.4	8.1	9.7	10.0
Two Parent				
Registered Members	69.7	49.8	32.3	18.6
Registered Non-Members	27.0	40.6	52.6	63.5
Non-Registered Members	0.0	0.0	0.0	0.0
Non-Registered Non-Members	3.3	9.6	15.1	17.9
50% Blood Quantum				
Registered Members	95.6	87.5	76.2	63.2
Registered Non-Members	1.2	2.4	4.6	8.7
Non-Registered Members	0.0	0.0	0.0	0.0
Non-Registered Non-Members	3.2	10.1	19.2	28.1
25% Blood Quantum				
Registered Members	97.9	92.2	83.6	73.9
Registered Non-Members	0.0	0.0	0.0	0.0
Non-Registered Members	2.1	7.0	12.4	15.3
Non-Registered Non-Members	0.0	0.9	4.0	10.9
All First Nations				
Registered Members	93.4	84.2	72.9	62.6
Registered Non-Members	2.9	4.2	5.4	6.3
Non-Registered Members	0.4	1.4	2.8	4.1
Non-Registered Non-Members	3.3	10.2	19.0	27.0

Source: Custom projections based on the December 31, 2002 Indian Register

Some of the main observations concerning the results of this component of the projections are summarized below:

- The number of survivors and descendants ineligible for registration and membership in First Nations that base membership on the rules governing Indian registration (*Indian Act* or equivalent membership rules) is expected to increase sharply throughout the period. Within 25 years this population is expected to number about 89,300, representing about one in every eight individuals. This population is projected to grow to about 207,600 (about one in every five individuals) within 50 years and to about 316,000 (about one in every three individuals) within 75 years.

- The populations of First Nations that use rules equivalent to the *Indian Act* but exclude those whose rights were not protected under the 1985 *Indian Act*, are projected to experience rapid growth on the share of the population that is ineligible for membership. This population, which formed about 20% of the total population in 2002, is projected to increase to about 40% within 75 years.

- All survivors and descendants of First Nations that use unlimited one parent rules retain eligibility for membership. Over the course of the projection period, however, a growing segment of the population eligible for membership is expected to lack entitlement to Indian registration. Within 75 years, more than one in every three members of these populations is expected to lack Indian registration.

- Individuals who are eligible for membership are projected to form a majority of the populations of First Nations that use unlimited one parent rules but exclude those whose rights were not protected under the 1985 *Indian Act*. Within 75 years, however, about one in every four members is expected to lack entitlement to Indian registration.

- The share of the population eligible for membership in First Nations that use two parent membership rules is projected to decline rapidly throughout the period. Within 25 years, those ineligible for membership are projected to be a majority of the population. Most of those who do not qualify for membership are expected to qualify to Indian registration.

- Those who do not qualify for membership are expected to form a growing share of the populations of First Nations that use 50% blood quantum rules. Within 75 years about one-third of the population is expected to lack membership eligibility. About one in every four of those who lack membership eligibility are, however, expected to qualify for Indian registration.

- All survivors and descendants of First Nations that use 25% blood quantum rules are expected to retain eligibility for membership. Within 75 years, however, about one in every four individuals eligible for membership are expected to lack entitlement to Indian registration.

Implications for Service Provision to First Nations Populations

The projection results highlighted in the previous section suggest that the populations of most First Nations are in the process of changing from a context where those who are eligible for Indian registration and membership form a large majority to a context where those who lack eligibility for membership and Indian registration form a large and growing segment of community residents. These latter groups of residents are expected to form a majority of the population in many First Nations communities within two generations.

The emergence of different classes of citizens within First Nations populations raises a number of important questions and issues concerning individual and collective rights, social equality and cohesion, and jurisdictional, financial, and administrative responsibilities for the provision of a wide range of services to various citizen groups. Although the projected changes are likely to impact on First Nations communities and populations in many ways, the main focus of this study relates primarily to two key issues concerning the provision of services to the future populations of First Nations communities:

- The demand for services associated with various classes of First Nations citizens
- The scale of financial resources that would be required to provide comparable levels of services to the various citizen groups comprising First Nations populations

The study's interest in exploring compositional changes in the demand for various services over time emerges from the viewpoint that current policies and related funding mechanisms have evolved within a context where no distinctions between membership and Indian registration existed among First Nations populations. As the impacts of the interplay of membership rules, the rules governing Indian registration, and exogamous parenting unfold, First Nations and other governments are likely to experience growing pressures to provide a wide range of services to groups of citizens who have not traditionally formed a significant component of service demand on First Nations reserves.

How First Nations and other governments respond to these compositional shifts in service demand can be expected to have profound effects on First Nations communities. For example, if First Nations, either by policy (or as a consequence of existing funding mechanisms) decide to restrict the allocation of housing resources to *members* only, will this result in a "forced" exodus from reserve communities of large numbers of young adults and families who do not qualify for membership? Do current policies concerning service delivery jurisdiction and responsibility, and related financial transfer arrangements, allow for the provision of services to all of the groups of citizens which are expected to form part of future First Nations communities? If First Nations desire to provide equal access

Table 5.6: Projected Incremental Resources to Provide Comparable Levels of Service by Type of Service and Population Group, Canada, 2003-2027

Program/Service	Estimated Incremental Service Cost 2003–2007 (millions, 2002 Constant $)				
	Population Group				
	Registered Members	Registered Non-Members	Non-Registered Members	Non-Registered Non-Members	Total
Housing	7,382.5	291.1	27.5	172.6	7,873.5
Infrastructure[1]	1,572.7	110.0	24.7	160.6	1,868.0
NIHB (Pharmacy)	891.3	61.5	23.8	179.0	1,155.6
NIHB (Dental)	362.0	29.0	9.2	63.0	463.2
Education	1,685.8	265.9	90.1	657.9	2,699.8
Post-Secondary Education	927.6	176.6	62.9	483.7	1,650.8
Children in Care	107.3	74.6	31.4	227.1	440.3
Social Assistance	2,540.6	197.9	38.4	261.4	3,038.3
All Services	**15,469.7**	**1,206.6**	**307.9**	**2,205.2**	**19,189.5**

[1] Excludes education facility capital requirements

Source: Custom projections based on the December 31, 2002, Indian Register, INAC Administrative Data, 2001/2002 NIHB Program Annual Reports

to services for all groups of citizens, will new financial arrangements or intergovernmental transfer agreements be required to allow this to happen?

Providing answers to these important questions lies beyond the scope of the present study. In all likelihood, questions such as these will require difficult decisions to be made by First Nations' governments and negotiations with other governments. This study's contribution to the topic is limited to providing some information about the scale of the future demand for specific types of services which may be needed by the various groups of citizens that are expected to comprise First Nations populations, as well as some estimates of the approximate scale of financial resources associated with these services. Who eventually assumes responsibility for funding and delivering services to these various citizen groups remains to be determined.[14]

Resources, data, and methodological limitations do not permit examination of the full range of services directed to or presently available to First Nations populations. The study, however, does consider a wide range of programs and services, including housing, community infrastructure, pharmacy and dental benefits provided under Health Canada's Non-Insured Health Benefits (NIHB) Program, education programming services, post-education education support, services to children in care, and social assistance. Collectively, these programs and services account for a substantial portion of the total resources provided by the federal government to First Nations communities and populations.[15]

Estimating future levels of service demand and costs is a challenging exercise, as both demand and service costs can be influenced by a number of unforeseen factors and events. Among other things, these confounding factors include budgetary restrictions (which serve to limit the number of services provided or the number of individuals who are able to access services), changes to program eligibility criteria and service benefit levels, and changes in regional and local employment and economic conditions (which can alter the nature and level of services required by the population). For the most part, many of the underlying factors which can shape the future demand for and cost of services are quite difficult (if not impossible) to forecast accurately, especially in the medium- and longer-terms. In such contexts, the service demand and cost implications of population changes may be best examined using hypothetical scenarios.

Estimates prepared for this study are based on a specific hypothetical scenario which assumes that both the rate of service utilization (demand) and the unit cost of providing services (i.e. the cost per service or cost per client) remain stable in the future at levels estimated for the baseline year 2002. The scenario also assumes that the future service needs among individuals of different citizen groups within First Nations populations are the same. This scenario allows one to explore the requirements and related costs of providing comparable or equivalent levels of services to all classes of First Nations citizens, regardless of membership or Indian registration status. Service demand and cost implications are explored over a 25-year period spanning the years 2002–2027.

Although minor elements of the methodology vary by the type of service considered, the general approach employed involves three stages, including:

- Estimation of current rates of service use and the average cost per service user (or service)
- Application of rates of service use to the projected population to estimate the future number of service users (or services required) by citizen class
- Application of the average cost per service user (or service provided) to the number of projected service users (or services required) to estimate the future costs of providing the service

Demand and related financial estimates for housing, infrastructure, education, children in care, and social assistance have been carried for the population residing on First Nations reserves, as First Nations administrative responsibilities for these services are generally restricted to reserve residents. Estimates for post-secondary education support services and for NIHB's pharmacy and dental benefits also include the population residing off-reserve, as these programs do not contain residency restrictions.

Results of analysis are presented in **Table 5.6** (page 115). The estimates suggest that the levels of financial resources that would be required to extend comparable levels of services to all subgroups residing in First Nations communities are likely to become quite significant over the next 25-year period. While registered members are expected to account for most of the incremental demand for future services, resources associated with providing comparable levels of the services to population subgroups that lack membership eligibility or Indian registration are expected to approach $3.7 billion over the 2003–2027 period. Most of these resources would be associated with maintaining comparable levels of service to descendants who lack entitlement to Indian registration. Children are expected to form the largest segment of this population throughout the 25-year projection period.

The level of incremental resources required to support comparable levels of service provision among subgroups which lack eligibility for membership or Indian registration are expected to remain modest in the short term, but increase at an accelerating pace in medium- and longer-terms. Within 25 years, more than one-quarter of the projected increase in resources needed to provide the services highlighted in this report is expected to result from service demands associated with residents who lack Indian registration or First Nations membership.

Review and Discussion

As a consequence of the 1985 *Indian Act* changes to the rules governing Indian registration, and the adoption by many First Nations of membership rules which differ from those which govern Indian registration, the populations of most First Nations in Canada are undergoing significant transformations. The nature of change is generally one away from populations which are comprised largely of individuals who meet the requirements for both Indian registration and First Nation membership to populations which also include growing numbers of citizens who lack Indian registration or eligibility for membership or both. Shifts in the composition of First Nations populations are presently pronounced off-reserve and are expected to become significant in many reserve communities over the course of the next generation. Within this time frame, classes of citizens with differing rights and entitlements are expected to become the norm in most First Nations communities.

These population changes appear to raise a number of complex and multi-faceted issues with political, legal, social, cultural, and economic dimensions and ramifications. This study has highlighted some of the potential implications of the expected population shifts within the context of providing services to First Nations residents in the future. In this regard, the study's results suggest that First Nations and other governments are likely to experience growing pressures to provide a wide range of services to groups of citizens (i.e. descendants who lack Indian registration, membership, or both) who have not traditionally formed a significant component of service demand in First Nations communities. How First Nations and other governments respond to this changing context of service demand can be expected to have profound effects not only on individuals but also on many aspects of life in First Nations communities.

At the present time, jurisdictional and financial responsibilities for program and service provision to the various classes of residents that are expected to comprise First Nations communities in the future are unclear. Current First Nations policies surrounding service allocation (e.g. which, in general, tend to restrict or limit services to those who qualify as members) may result in some groups of citizens who lack access to needed services. Similarly, the basis for establishing funding levels under current intergovernmental transfer agreements may not recognize the service needs of all subgroups or classes of citizens residing in First Nations communities. Resulting inequalities among citizen groups with respect to access to services could lead to conflicts, legal challenges, and the erosion of social cohesion within communities.

Although the challenges confronting First Nations in responding to the changing population context have many dimensions, a central issue relates to the principle of establishing comparable levels of access to services among all community residents. In this regard, options available to First Nations within the confines of the *Indian Act* appear to be limited. Under the *Indian Act*, First Nations do (or can) exercise control over some aspects of the issue, including membership and (to some extent) service and program eligibility and allocation policies. Revisions to (or the adoption of) membership rules and the formulation of service allocation policies which are cognizant of the emerging changes in community populations may be an option for some First Nations. Such initiatives could mitigate some of the inequality among classes of citizens but are also likely to require new financial transfer arrangements with the federal (and perhaps provincial) government(s). It is not clear that suitable financial transfer arrangements could be achieved within the context of the current *Indian Act*. As such, First Nations may also want to explore the option of self-government. In theory, self-government financial transfer agreements (SGFTA's) can be configured to enable service provision to all citizens who reside in the community.[16] Intergovernmental negotiations, however, are also likely to be required in the process of pursuing this latter approach.

Endnotes

1　A recent study by Clatworthy (2002) reveals that as of December 31, 2002, more than 114,000 individuals have been added to the Registered Indian population through these provisions.

2　For First Nations that did not adopt rules under section 10 of the *Indian Act*, membership is determined by the rules governing Indian registration. These rules are contained in section 6 of the 1985 *Indian Act* and allow for individuals to be registered under one of two sub-sections, including: section 6(1), where both of the individual's parents are entitled to Indian registration, and section 6(2), where one of the individual's parents is entitled to Indian registration under Section 6(1) and the other parent is not registered. Individuals who have only one Indian parent registered under section 6(2) do not qualify for Indian registration or First Nations membership.

3　This is also the case for those First Nations that have established self-government arrangements. The membership rules of self-governing First Nations are not considered in this study.

4　There is some existing evidence of the presence of conflict surrounding First Nations member-ship issues. Litigation involving citizen challenges to specific provisions of some First Nations membership rules has been undertaken (e.g. Corbière, Perron, Starlight [Sawridge], and L'Hirondelle [Tsuu T'ina]). Disagreements among citizen groups over membership issues have also been reported in other First Nations contexts (e.g. Buffalo Point and Kahnawake).

5　Some aspects of the relationship between Indian registration and First Nation membership are also discussed by Wherret (1990) and Smith (1991). Case studies exploring the longer-term populations of the membership rules of specific First Nations have been undertaken by Clatworthy (1991, 1998, 1999, 2001, and 2002b) and by United Anishnaabeg Councils (1999).

6　Several features found in some membership rules, although examined, were not incorporated into the typology. These included additional "discretionary" criteria (e.g. cultural/ language tests, tests of character, and considerations of context [e.g., reserve residency, availability of community resources]) that are applied to some applicants, provisions, and conditions for admitting other "non-descendants," and the mechanics of administering the rules. They noted that some of these other features could, depending upon how they are applied, have considerable impact on the population that is accepted into membership. The full impacts of these other features on future populations, however, cannot be determined.

7　First Nations that adopted membership rules prior to June 28, 1987 were required (at a minimum) to admit into initial membership individuals whose rights to membership were protected by the 1985 *Indian Act* (i.e. those with acquired rights). This included all those who were eligible to be on the band list as of April 17, 1985, all individuals who reacquired registration under the 1985 *Indian Act* and who had been removed from the Indian Register prior to April 16, 1985 as a consequence of their (or their mother's) marriage to a non-Indian, and individuals whose both parents were original or reinstated members and who traced their descent entirely through these members. All First Nations that adopted membership rules on or after June 28, 1987 were required to admit into membership all individuals who were entitled to Indian registration at that time, including all those who qualified for registration under the revised rules of the 1985 *Indian Act*.

8　Clatworthy and Smith reported that 85 (or roughly 36%) of the 236 First Nations that had adopted membership rules at the time of their review, elected to exclude this group of descendants from initial membership.

9　The remaining 62 First Nations, whose rules were not approved, do not appear to have submitted revised rules to the department. Most of these non-approved rules were submitted prior to 1993.

10　The survey was administered via telephone over the November 1, 2002 to January 30, 2003 time period to First Nations staff responsible for Indian registration or First Nation membership. Contact was made with 215 (or 93%) of the 232 First Nations that were identified to have current membership rules adopted under section 10 of the 1985 *Indian Act*. Interviews were completed for 212 of those contacted (three First Nations declined to be interviewed for the study).

11　In addition to those First Nations which had formally approved amendments or revisions to their membership rules, 86 First Nations reported that they were actively considering changes to their membership rules. Twenty-six of these First Nations reported changes that were considered to be major and would impact on significant numbers of individuals. In all of these cases, the proposed changes would extend membership eligibility to additional groups of individuals who were denied membership under the original membership rule.

12 In addition to discretionary provisions, other factors are likely to influence the actual population of First Nations members. For example, membership in most First Nations is not automatically granted upon birth and individuals are required to apply to become members. Some individuals who meet all of the conditions necessary to become members, may not apply to become members for many reasons (see Clatworthy "Brokenhead" this volume for more comments on this issue).

13 The projection results presented in this study derive from a specific set of models that assume a gradual decline in fertility, gradual improvements in life expectancy, and stable rates of exogamous parenting over the course of the projection period.

14 The study is not attempting to suggest that services to all of these citizen groups will be necessarily assumed by any level of government. The possibility exists that some individuals or groups may be required to do without services or to pay directly for these services themselves.

15 Although not comprehensive, the range of programs and services addressed in the study is believed to be sufficiently broad to illustrate the nature and scale of changes in service needs (demand) and the related financial implications of these changes.

16 Although self-governing financial transfer agreements may allow for resolution of some service provision issues, it is likely that such arrangements can be structured to provide full equality for all citizen groups. For example, differences among residents with respect to income and sales tax exemption and Non-Insured Health Benefits (which are limited to those who are Registered Indians) are likely to remain.

References

Clatworthy, S. J. 1991. *Modeling the Future Population Eligible for Indian Registration and Band Membership: Selected Communities of the Meadow Lake Tribal Council*, Meadow Lake Tribal Council, Saskatchewan.

Clatworthy, S. J. 1998. *Population and Membership Projections: Mohawks of Kahnawake*, Intergovernmental Relations Team, Mohawk Council of Kahnawake, Mohawk Territory of Kahnawake.

Clatworthy, S. J. 1999. *Population Implications of Proposed Revisions to the Blood Tribe Membership Code*, Blood Tribe Membership Review Committee, Blood Tribe, Alberta.

Clatworthy, S. J. 2001. *Re-Assessing the Population Impacts of Bill C-31*, Strategic Research and Analysis Directorate. Ottawa: INAC.

Clatworthy, S. J. 2002. *Implications of First Nations Demography: Recent Trends and Projected Population Changes*, prepared for the Strategic Research and Analysis Directorate. Ottawa: INAC.

Clatworthy, S. J. 2002b. *Population Implications of Proposed Revisions to the Peigan Nation Membership Code*. Brocket, Alberta: Peigan Nation Membership Review Committee.

Clatworthy, S. J. and A. H. Smith. 1992. *Population Implications of the 1985 Amendments to the Indian Act*, Ottawa: Assembly of First Nations.

Nault, F. and J. Chen 1993. *Household and Family Projections of Registered Indians, 1991–2015*. Ottawa: INAC.

Smith, A. H. 1991. *Bill C-31 Impact Study: Meadow Lake First Nations*, prepared for the Meadow Lake Tribal Council, Meadow Lake, Saskatchewan.

United Anishnaabeg Councils 1999. *Impacts of the Authority to Determine Band Membership*, prepared for Strategic Research and Analysis Directorate. Ottawa: INAC.

Wherret, J. 1990. *Indian Status and Band Membership*. Ottawa: Political and Social Affairs Division, Library of Parliament.

Barbara Dorey

Barbara was born in Truro on January 25, 1952. Her parents are Levi and Mary Bridget (Johnson) Gloade and are Millbrook First Nation Band members. Barbara resided in Millbrook until the age of twenty, when she lost her Indian status through marriage to a non-native. Barbara and her husband resided off the reserve but the marriage ended in divorce.

Barbara remembers receiving a letter from the Department of Indian Affairs stating that she was no longer considered an Indian as defined under the Indian Act, *and she was not entitled to any benefits. She was asked to sign the letter stating that she was in agreement with the change and once the Department of Indian Affairs received the signed letter, she would be sent a cheque for $70. After reading the letter, and in total disbelief and disagreement that the Department of Indian Affairs would send out such a letter, Barbara consulted some members from the band and her employer at the Union of Nova Scotia Indians to get some feedback. This letter was never signed, but after reviewing the band membership list several years later, she found out that her name was marked on the list with red ink stating she was no longer a member.*

As the only daughter of a family of eight brothers, being told that you are no longer a band member was not only shocking but heart breaking, and left her with a feeling as an outcast. It was difficult enough being faced with racism while attending school, but facing this through the community was not an easy thing to accept.

In 1975, Barbara became involved with the Native Council of Nova Scotia and was elected Secretary-Treasurer for five years. The position has given her more of an insight of what many native women faced when they got married to non-natives or lost their rights through enfranchisement and made her want to fight for their rights even more. In 1982, Barbara remarried but still resided off-reserve and had one daughter and adopted a son. In 1985 Barbara was reinstated through Bill C-31; she received assistance from the Millbrook Band and built a house on the reserve in 1987. Receiving some assistance from the Millbrook Band was a great help in starting their home, but being classed as Bill C-31 was still a label and she felt discriminated against.

To this day, Barbara remains on the Millbrook First Nation and has raised two beautiful and strong supportive children. Bill C-31 has caused many problems for women and their children and they were denied their rights for years, and are still being faced with the problem today. She stated that women should be compensated and the injustice should have never been done.

Part Four:
Legal Issues and Future Directions

6

Indian Registration: Unrecognized and Unstated Paternity

Michelle Mann

Introduction

Since the enactment of Bill C-31 in 1985, the provisions of the *Indian Act* relating to Indian[1] registration and Band membership have been the source of litigation and policy challenges.

Bill C-31 was intended to address gender discrimination arising from previous provisions of the *Indian Act*,[2] which provided that an Indian woman who married a non-Indian man lost her Indian registration and band membership, as did their children. By contrast, an Indian man who married a non-Indian woman did not lose these entitlements, nor did his children, while his wife could actually gain Indian status and band membership.

While Bill C-31 attempted to deal with this gender-based discrimination, it has not been entirely successful. Allegations of gender-based discrimination remain, now focused on subsections 6(1) and 6(2) of the *Indian Act*.[3] These allegations include issues relating to Indian status, band membership, and the stigmatization and exclusion of Bill C-31 reinstatees. Another significant gender concern is that the patrilineal legacy of the *Indian Act* provisions survives in current federal policy relating to the registration of children with "unstated" or "unrecognized" paternity.

The current *Indian Act* now contains two main categories of Indian registration. Children born after 1985 are registered as Status Indians under subsection 6(1) if both parents are or were entitled to registration, and under subsection 6(2) if one parent is or was entitled to registration under subsection 6(1). Thus, section 6 translates into a loss of registration for successive generations where both parents are not Registered Indians or are not recognized as such.

Following the 1985 amendments, Indian and Northern Affairs Canada (INAC) registry policy was changed to require the father's signature on the birth form and other forms of proof of paternity, in the absence of which the child's registration would be determined solely on the basis of the mother's entitlement.

As a result, many children are either registered incorrectly, or not registered at all where paternity is not established in accordance with the Registrar's policy at INAC. Non-reporting or non-acknowledgment of a Registered Indian father may result in the loss of benefits and entitlements to either the child or his or her subsequent children through the loss of registration.

Ultimately, Indian registration confers tax benefits for those with reserve-based property, membership in bands whose membership is still determined by INAC, and access to national programs such as post-secondary education and the Non-Insured Health Benefits Program. These benefits conferred by registration and Band membership are often of great importance to women as primary caregivers of children.

Given high rates of unstated and unrecognized paternity in the First Nations community, fundamental questions arise concerning the Registrar's policy and the determination of registration and accompanying Band membership for many children born after 1985.

The Registrar's Policy

Subsequent to the 1985 amendments, INAC registry policy was changed to require proof of paternity, in the absence of which the child's registration would be determined solely on the basis of the mother's entitlement. The INAC policy pertaining to Indian registration is similar across all regions. Currently the Registrar accepts the following birth evidence as it relates to proof of paternity.[4]

5.1.5 Births—All births must be accompanied by:

- (i) a Vital Statistics birth record or extract which identifies the parent(s) by name,* but:
    - (a) if the named father is claimed to be incorrect, the applicant must contact Vital Statistics to obtain an amended birth registration that either changes the name of the father or is silent on paternity; or,
    - (b) if the birth document is silent on paternity but Indian paternity is claimed, then statutory declarations by the parents (see (c) and (d) below and examples for mother and father at Annex C) confirming paternity will be required to substantiate the claimed father;
    - (c) statutory declarations must always be completed and witnessed in front of a person authorized as a commissioner for the taking of oaths (either by the Province or Territory) such as a lawyer, Notary Public or Justice of the Peace, or by an INAC official authorized under s.108 of the *Indian Act* to witness statements of this kind;
    - (d) if the father (for (b) above) is deceased, the Registrar will require statutory declarations from at least two close relatives of the deceased father (e.g., grandparent, aunt, uncle, sibling, etc.) who are aware of the circumstances of the child's birth and who can identify the father from their own personal knowledge. Each statutory declaration is to describe: how the person making the declaration came about this knowledge; identify what relationship they have to the child; and, provide their full name, date of birth, and band name and number.

- (iii) a completed *Child Application for Registration as an Indian* form with the signed Parental Consent Statements by the parent(s) or legal guardian, whether Indian or non-Indian, requesting the child's registration and indicating in which Registry Group (of which parent) they wish the child to be registered.

Thus, while the two-parent rule is contained in the *Indian Act*, the evidentiary and administrative requirements for proof of paternity are established entirely as a matter of INAC policy. As noted by the Standing Committee on Aboriginal Affairs and Northern Development (1988: 46:15): "There is no provision in the amended *Act* that stipulates particular evidentiary requirements at the initial application stage for entitlement to registration or band membership."

Nonetheless, non-reporting or non-acknowledgment of a Registered Indian father may result in the loss of benefits and entitlements to either the child or his or her subsequent children through the loss of registration.

For example, if a First Nations woman entitled to subsection 6(1) registration has a child with unestablished paternity, that child is automatically entitled to subsection 6(2) registration. If the First Nations woman is registered under subsection 6(2) herself, then her child is not entitled to registration as a Status Indian. Similarly, the child of a non-registered woman with an unnamed registered father will not be entitled to registration.

Critical Impacts

The gravity of the unstated paternity problem is evident in statistics gathered indicating unstated fathers for children born to subsection 6(1) registered women. Clatworthy (2003a:2–3) found that an analysis of the Indian register for children born to women registered under subsection 6(1) between April 17, 1985 and December 31, 1999 indicated roughly 37,300 children with unstated fathers. This number represents about 19% of all children born to subsection 6(1) registered women during that same period.

Further, while direct numbers were not available for children with unstated fathers born to subsection 6(2) registered women, Clatworthy (2003a:3) estimates that as many as 13,000 may have unstated fathers and are therefore ineligible for registration. Clatworthy (2003a:4) has also observed that during the 1985–1999 period, about 30% of all children with unstated fathers were born to mothers under 20 years of age.

More specifically, a study (Clatworthy 2001) prepared for the Manitoba Southern Chiefs Organization (SCO) highlights the impacts of the operation of subsections 6(1) and 6(2) as they interact with high rates of unstated paternity.

More than 29 percent of the Registered Indian population of SCO First Nations is registered under section 6(2). Among children (aged 0–17 years), section 6(2) registrants form more than 48 percent of the population.

> The high concentrations of SCO children registered under 6(2) result in part from very high rates of unstated paternity. More than 30 percent of all SCO children born since Bill C-31 was enacted have unstated fathers, a rate nearly twice the national average (iii).

Clatworthy's conclusions (2001:v) for SCO First Nations included a finding that with an ever-increasing number of descendants not entitled to registration, sometime during the fifth generation, no further descendants will be so entitled.

The benefits conferred by registration and membership are of great import to First Nations women, who remain most often the primary caregivers of children. Aboriginal women in Canada experience lower incomes and higher rates of unemployment than Aboriginal men or other women, and in 1996, Registered Indians had by far the highest proportion of single mother families (Hull 2001: x). In 1996, more than 25% of Registered Indian children lived in single mother families, compared to 14% of non-Aboriginal children (Hull 2001:xi). Aboriginal women aged 15–24 years were found to be more than three times as likely to be single mothers than the general population in that age group, with about one in three Aboriginal mothers single (Hull 2001: xi).

There are also additional non-tangible benefits that registration may facilitate such as personal, community, and cultural identification:

> I want my children to experience the feeling of belonging because before that, I don't feel that we did, I did, I didn't belong. And my children would like to have status whether there's anything involved in that, except its sort of a recognition kind of a thing. They would like to have it and I think they should have it. There's sort of an unspoken thing for people who have status, its legal. (Huntley and Blaney 1999:40).

While many First Nations women and their children experience the detrimental effects arising from unstated or unrecognized paternity, teenage mothers and their offspring may suffer disproportionately. The negative impact on First Nations women and their children resulting from the two-parent rule and proof of paternity requirements arguably constitutes discrimination based on gender and family status.

Focus group participants in hearings held by the Special Representative on First Nations Women's Issues found the requirement for First Nations women to identify the paternity of their children to be "offensive, degrading, discriminatory, and a potential violation of the rights of Aboriginal women to privacy" (Erickson 2001:27).

In addition, the two-parent rule, and its resulting impacts of reducing the registered population over two generations of successive out-parenting is perceived as further governmental attempts at genocide, assimilation, and gradual elimination of the Registered Indian population (AFN 1999).

Critical Causes

Having established the detrimental impacts experienced by women and their children with unstated or unacknowledged Indian paternity, it is crucial to consider why this situation is occurring, and what can be done to address it. The causes underlying unstated paternity are too great to cover in the detail they merit in this chapter, but they range from administrative issues to a decision not to name the father by the mother.

Unacknowledged paternity can be said to arise where the mother names the father but not in accordance with the requirements of provincial Vital Statistics or INAC policy, thereby causing paternity to be considered unstated. Frequently, in the literature, the language of "unstated paternity" subsumes both the categories of unacknowledged and unstated paternity. Clatworthy (2003b) estimated that approximately 50% of unstated paternity cases are considered to be unintentional on the part of the mother, while the other 50% are deemed intentional.

"Administrative" Difficulties

On the administrative end, problems have been identified with the registration of birth form, which is completed by the mother in hospital (except in Quebec) and names the father along with other details of the birth. Where the birth occurs outside of a medical facility, the parents have 30 days to file the form. Administrative requirements differ between regions, but in most provinces the registration of birth form must be signed by both parents where they are not married. Where the parents are married, most jurisdictions require only one parent's signature (Clatworthy 2003a:14).

Where the form is not signed by both as required, Vital Statistics in that province contacts the parent(s) by mail informing them of the requirement. Where the signature is still not collected within approximately 60 days, the father's name is stricken from the birth registration, if it was present (Clatworthy 2003a:14). The mother may have provided a name but been unwilling or unable to obtain the father's signature, leading to unacknowledged paternity.

The requirement for the father's signature on the birth registration form is highly problematic for those parents living in remote communities without medical facilities. Where the mother must travel outside of the community to give birth, the father may not attend and therefore not be present to sign the birth registration.

Vital Statistics staff in all of the regions contacted for this study confirm that they receive many birth registrations which contain the father's identity, but which have not been signed by the father or accompanied by a joint request form. Subsequent efforts by Vital Statistics to obtain signed documents frequently meet with no response (Clatworthy 2003a:17).

In those remaining areas of the country, Vital Statistics requires only the mother's signature on the birth registration form, but requires that unmarried parents file a joint request form with both signatures where the father is to be acknowledged. Again, Vital Statistics sends out a reminder and if the joint request form is not received within roughly 30 days, the fathers' information is stricken from the birth registration form.

The difficulties and expense inherent in amending birth registration information are also identified as a cause of unstated paternity. Clatworthy (2003a:14–15) noted that most regions allow for changes to be made free of charge during the first 60 days after registration. Changes may still be made after this time by filing a joint request form, affidavit, or declaration of paternity document, containing the father's particulars and signed by both parents. However, requirements in most regions for witnessing and notarization along with administrative fees render amendment to birth registration complicated and potentially expensive.

Problems with registering the father with Vital Statistics then lead to problems with obtaining Indian registration given that INAC's requirements include birth registration showing the father's name.

As noted earlier, where the birth document is silent on paternity but Indian paternity is claimed, INAC requires statutory declarations by the parents to substantiate the father. However, statutory declarations remain problematic given that commissioners of oaths are not easily located in remote communities and generally charge a fee for their services. In addition, registration of a birth with INAC requires a completed *Child Application for Registration as an Indian* form accompanied by signed parental consent statements by both parents, where paternity is stated.

Clatworthy (2003a:17) also pointed to "lengthy delays" between birth registration and Indian registration as creating additional barriers to paternal identification as the passage of time may create increased difficulties in amending birth registration. Such difficulties include relationship problems between the mother and father, increased evidentiary requirements, and charges or fees.

"Substantive" Difficulties

At the opposite end of the spectrum is the situation whereby the mother decides not to state the father, or the father refuses to acknowledge paternity. Underlying causal factors may include the mother and father having an unstable relationship, concerns about confidentiality in a small community, and the mother's concerns about child custody and access, or her own registration and membership (Clatworthy 2003a:18). In addition, the pregnancy may be the result of abuse, incest, or rape, in which case the mother will likely be unwilling or unable to identify the father:

> Thus, single mothers concerned with protecting their children's birthright face a difficult choice: either they submit to an invasion of their privacy and the ensuing social repercussions which may arise in the context of a patriarchal society or they forfeit their children's right to status. Although, it may not be in a father's interest to acknowledge his child, if he fears being held financially responsible, for example, or happens to be married to someone else, an affidavit signed by him acknowledging paternity must be produced in order to register a child as "Indian." The mother may also not wish to disclose the identity of the father, in particular, in cases of sexualized violence. Not only dehumanizing, but to put a woman into the position of having to ask her rapist for the confirmation of his deed

is more than absurd. Regardless of the circumstances, women are placed at the mercy of the father's consent (Huntley and Blaney 1999:24).

It has also been noted that single First Nations mothers often feel that the father's background should not be a factor where he is not an active member of the family and that to require his acknowledgement is culturally inappropriate.

If one does not name the father of one's child, it is assumed the child's father is non-Indian. This is racist, sexist and is directly against women's cultural rights. Culture is transmitted largely through women ... and therefore a child with an Indian mother is an Indian regardless of biological paternity. (Holmes 1987:25).

Charter Compliance

Section 15

The most relevant section of the Charter is subsection 15(1):

Every individual is equal before and under the law and has the right to the equal protection and equal benefit of the law without discrimination and, in particular, without discrimination based on race, national or ethnic origin, colour, religion, sex, age or mental or physical disability.

As far back as 1988, the Standing Committee on Aboriginal Affairs and Northern Development noted residual sex discrimination in the requirement for unmarried Indian women to name the father of their children to establish their children's entitlement to registration and band membership (Standing Committee 1988:46:35).

The case of *Villeneuve, McGillivary v. Canada* deals directly with the unstated paternity issue: a re-amended statement of claim was filed with the Federal Court in 1998, though the case does not appear to have progressed further. According to the statement of claim, the plaintiffs challenged the entitlement to registration of a child who was born to a Registered Indian mother and father. The mother, however, elected to keep the identity of the plaintiff's father undisclosed. Accordingly, the child was registered under subsection 6(2) of the *Indian Act* as having only one Registered Indian parent. Among other allegations, the plaintiffs claimed that Canada has violated their right to equality under the law by following a departmental policy that discriminates against applicants for Indian registration on the grounds of both sex and family status. One remedy sought was that the policy regarding proof of paternity be declared of no force and effect.

In *Gehl v. Canada (Attorney General)*, the plaintiff Lynn Gehl brought a claim against the government for her denial of registration on the basis that her father had unstated paternity, leaving him registered under subsection 6(2). Partnered with a non-registered person, her father was then unable to pass registration on to his daughter, the plaintiff. In this case, Ms. Gehl argued that she was discriminated against on the basis of her family status, given that a distinction is created between Aboriginal children of wed and unwed parents. A burden is imposed upon children of unwed parents and their offspring in the form of a more onerous requirement of proof than that imposed on other applicants for registration. She further alleged that the negative presumption of paternity is based on stereotyping of Indians of unwed parents that goes to their human dignity. Finally, she alleged a breach of her section 15 equality rights to be registered as an Indian and a breach of her Aboriginal rights under s. 35 to be an Indian and member of her Aboriginal community. Unfortunately, this case was not decided on the merits by the Ontario Court of Appeal, which found that it had been brought in the wrong form to the wrong court.

Similarly, section 3 of the *Canadian Human Rights Act,* which prohibits discrimination on the grounds of sex, marital, and family status among others, would also apply were it not for section 67 which exempts the *Indian Act*. In 2000, the *Canadian Human Rights Act* Review Panel (p. 135) recommended removal of section 67 from the Human Rights Act, but to date it remains.

The Trociuk Case

A section 15 Charter equality case that may have implications for federal policy is *Trociuk v. Attorney General of British Columbia*, a 2003 decision of the Supreme Court of Canada. In this case, an estranged non-Aboriginal father and mother of triplets were battling over the mother's legislated right to fill out and submit the statement of live birth on her own, marking the father as "unacknowledged by the mother." She alone chose and registered the children's surname, pursuant to the British Columbia *Vital Statistics Act*, and the father was precluded from having the registration altered to include his particulars.

In what appears to be a first in Canada, section 15 equality rights under the Charter were successfully employed by the father to defend the interests of men. The court found that the statutory absolute discretion conferred on British Columbia mothers to "unacknowledge" a biological father on birth registration and in naming children discriminated on the basis of sex and could not be defended by the saving provisions of section 1 of the Charter. Such a provision violated the human dignity of biological fathers.

However, as the Supreme Court duly noted, there are circumstances where a biological father will be appropriately unacknowledged.

There may be compelling reasons for permitting a mother to unacknowledge a father at birth, to exclude his particulars from the registration, and to permanently preclude his participation in determining the child's surname. Such is the case of a mother who has become pregnant as a result of rape or incest. (para 25)

The court then cited a justice who heard the case at the British Columbia Court of Appeal level.

Newbury J.A. held, and counsel for the respondent, Reni Ernst, argued, that in cases where a mother has good reasons for unacknowledging a father, providing the latter the opportunity to dispute the unacknowledgment would lead to negative effects. Newbury J.A. reasoned that such an opportunity would be "a serious incursion into the interests of the mother" and would not be in the best interests of the child. (para 26)

Finally, the court concluded:

> An application procedure could be designed to control the particular negative effects on mothers that may flow from post-unacknowledgment applications. Such effects include unwanted public disclosure of the identities of fathers who have been justifiably unacknowledged, and confrontation in court between mothers and men who have caused them harm. Prowse J.A. has proposed a procedure that would eliminate both these effects. The legislature could provide that a judge in chambers would alone determine whether a father has been justifiably excluded, based solely on affidavit evidence. (para 38)

It is noteworthy that the Supreme Court considered that such a procedure could be said to have ameliorative purposes or effects for two disadvantaged groups pursuant to subsection 15(1) of the Charter: women who have valid reasons to unacknowledge a father, and their children (para 27). Such an ameliorative procedure would not be discriminatory in its treatment of biological fathers.

International Compliance

Over the years, INAC has endeavoured to develop viable policy options that are responsive to both pending domestic litigation challenges and Canada's international commitments; commitments that many Aboriginal women say are being broken.

> The Aboriginal child deprived of his or her status, or of band membership, is thus deprived of the right to take part in the life of his community, contrary to the provisions of Article 27 of the *International Covenant on Civil and Political Rights*, to the almost identical provisions Article XII of the *American Declaration of the Rights and Duties of Man*, which binds Canada since it became a member of the Organization of American states, in January of 1990 and of article 30 of the *Convention on the Rights of the Child* (NWAC and QNWA nd: 9).

Two separate but interconnected groups are impacted by the Registrar's unstated paternity policy: children of unwed parents, and their mothers. Those international covenants considered most applicable are canvassed below.

The *Universal Declaration of Human Rights* as the first of the modern human rights treaties forms the basis for the more specific conventions that followed. Article 2 of the Declaration provides for freedom from discrimination on the basis of numerous characteristics, including sex and birth, while Article 7 states that all are equal before the law and are entitled without discrimination to equal protection of the law. Article 25 might provide fodder for an international challenge to the unstated paternity policy, given the implications for the mother and child's standard of living where there is a denial of registration:

> (1) Everyone has the right to a standard of living adequate for the health and well-being of himself and of his family, including food, clothing, housing and medical care and necessary social services, and the right to security in the event of unemployment,

sickness, disability, widowhood, old age or other lack of livelihood in circumstances beyond his control.

(2) Motherhood and childhood are entitled to special care and assistance. All children, whether born in or out of wedlock, shall enjoy the same social protection.

With respect to children who may be denied registration as a result of unstated or unrecognized paternity, the *Convention on the Rights of the Child* may apply. Article 2 of the Convention provides that state parties shall respect and ensure the rights within, without discrimination of any kind, irrespective of the child's or his or her parent's sex, or birth. Article 8 protects a child's right to preserve his or her identity, including nationality, name, and family relations as recognized by law and without unlawful interference. Article 30 provides that children of Indigenous origin "shall not be denied the right, in community with other members of his or her group, to enjoy his or her own culture."

The *International Covenant on Civil and Political Rights* provides protection from discrimination on the grounds of sex and birth in Article 2, while Article 26 provides the standard equality before and equal protection of the law provisions. Article 17 addresses individual privacy rights:

(1) No one shall be subjected to arbitrary or unlawful interference with his privacy, family, home or correspondence, nor to unlawful attacks on his honour and reputation.

(2) Everyone has the right to the protection of the law against such interference or attacks.

As noted by the Quebec Native Women's Association (2000:12):

Consequently, the administrative policy requiring that unmarried women name the father of their child, failing which, the father is presumed to be non-Indian is incompatible with Canada's international obligations. This policy forces the mother to reveal the identity of the Aboriginal father to avoid gravely penalizing her child. It constitutes arbitrary interference with her privacy, contrary to the provisions of Article 17 of the *International Covenant on Civil and Political Rights*.

Article 27 of the *International Covenant on Civil and Political Rights* guarantees that persons belonging to ethnic minorities may enjoy their culture in community with other members of their group. Article 27 was the basis for the success of *Sandra Lovelace v. Canada* at the United Nations Human Rights Committee in 1981, where Sandra Lovelace challenged the now infamous *Indian Act* provisions wherein a woman lost Indian registration upon "marrying out." In 1985 the government responded to this international criticism with Bill C-31, restoring registration to these women.

In fact, in 1999, the Human Rights Committee was still commenting on Lovelace:

The Committee is concerned about ongoing discrimination against Aboriginal women. Following the adoption of the Committee's views in the Lovelace case in July 1981, amendments were introduced to the *Indian Act* in 1985. Although the Indian status of women who had lost status because of marriage was reinstituted, this amendment affects only the woman and her children, not subsequent generations, which may still be denied membership in the community. The Committee recommends that these issues be addressed by the State party (para 19)

Most recently in 2003, the Committee on the Elimination of Discrimination Against Women expressed "serious concern" "about the persistent systematic discrimination faced by Aboriginal women in all aspects of their lives." The committee urged Canada to accelerate its efforts to eliminate discrimination against Aboriginal women, particularly with respect to remaining discriminatory legal provisions and the equal enjoyment of their human rights to education, employment and physical and psychological well-being. It urged Canada to combat patriarchal attitudes, practices, and stereotyping of roles relating to Aboriginal women and requested "comprehensive information on the situation of Aboriginal women" in Canada's next report (paras 361–362).

Critical Options

This paper proposes a variety of options that explore ways to address the needs of First Nations women and their children with unstated paternity, in relation to registration and in a manner consistent with the legal environment.

It is the opinion of the author that the numerous challenges cannot be resolved without addressing INAC policy in a fairly fundamental way.

1. Maintain the Status Quo

The first option is self-explanatory: maintain the status quo, do nothing, but wait and see where litigation and political pressures take INAC. Advocates of this approach posit that it avoids making premature changes that will run counter to the demands flowing from current, unresolved challenges.

The least proactive of all options, it does not address what is likely to be increasing litigation on the issue and the possibility of a high court decision rendering the policy inoperable. It also does not address the political environment, in which many First Nations' men and women increasingly challenge the legitimacy of the federal government's defining "Indianness." Nor does it address the children who suffer for the actions or oversights of their biological parents under a policy that is not in their best interests.

2. Departmental Prioritization

Departmental prioritization of the unstated paternity issue could include more targeted research and exploration of policy options, including the involvement of focus groups and vetting by stakeholders, most particularly within the First Nations community and by First Nations women.

Although some modest research as well as educational and administrative initiatives regarding unstated paternity have been undertaken, the issue requires greater commitment from the Department. While recognizing that unstated paternity issues have regional and First Nation–specific characteristics, INAC could develop and implement a national initiative with stakeholder input.

The Report of the Special Representative recommends that the government conduct a Bill C-31 impact study and that the terms of reference for this study be developed with Aboriginal people at the grassroots (Erickson 2001:33). The Special Representative also calls for more involvement of and funding for Aboriginal women's groups so that they can make submissions to government and participate in consultation processes (Erickson 2001:50). The Aboriginal Women's Action Network (AWAN) has also called for related national conferences, qualitative research projects, and evaluation of INAC's implementation of C-31(Huntley and Blaney 1999:75).

While departmental prioritization is an improvement on the status quo, the unstated paternity issue was flagged as discriminatory by the parliamentary Standing Committee as far back as 1988 (p.46:35), allowing sufficient time in the intervening years to address this failing. Departmental prioritization does not address the volume of youth being inappropriately registered or denied registration altogether every year and the resulting impacts on their quality of life and well-being. Nor does it take into account pending and anticipated litigation on the issue.

3. Educational Initiatives

Any education initiatives pertaining to paternity and Indian registration must be targeted to both men and women. Men must receive an equal educational focus, since they are the fathers whose signatures may be missing or withheld. As noted by a participant at an Aboriginal Women's Roundtable on Gender Equality:

> Our biggest problem is our men who are our leaders. They have never lost status, so they need to be educated about this. However, the challenge is how are we going to educate them? This fight has to have the Chief's support. Our job is to protect the next seven generations and we can start the education process right in our own homes (SWC 2000:6).

Clatworthy (2003a:20–22) noted an absence of printed informational material concerning birth, Indian registration, and unstated paternity for distribution to expectant parents, as well as a need for community-based group workshops, information sessions, and other educational initiatives. It is suggested that initiatives specifically focused on teens and pre-teens might begin to address their disproportionate representation in cases of unstated paternity.

Women participating in the Special Representative focus groups commented on the need to educate Aboriginal women on the implications of marriage and paternity for their children. Here, the suggestion was that Canada make funding available to Aboriginal women's organizations to develop these educational materials, and that the government ensure they are widely distributed across Canada (Erickson 2001:22–23 and 31). These women also felt they did not receive adequate information pertaining to government policy changes and consultation processes and recommended that information be more thoroughly disseminated to the grassroots level (Erickson 2001:48).

INAC could also enhance the role of Indian Registry Administrators (IRAs) who discover and obtain the appropriate supporting documents and signatures for "field events"[6] in their community then report these events to the regional office or enter the events directly in the Indian Register. IRAs are based in First Nations communities and are therefore well positioned to undertake local education initiatives.

While education is generally a valuable initiative, it will not address the current litigation environment, nor will it likely impact upon the ongoing loss of, or incorrect, registration in the near future. Most importantly, while educational initiatives will address some situations in which paternity is unstated, others will remain, such as situations in which the mother will not or cannot identify the father.

4. Remedy "Administrative" Issues

Administration of the provincial *Vital Statistics Act* contributes to unstated and unacknowledged paternity, given that INAC heavily relies on birth registration for proof of parentage. Addressing some of the following more administrative concerns, (noted by Clatworthy and others), would likely result in a reduction in unstated or unacknowledged paternity:

- Provide accompaniment monies to the father through INAC or band councils when the mother is giving birth outside of the community; he can then be present to sign the birth registration form
- Allow joint request forms for birth registration to be signed in the community prior to the mother leaving to give birth
- Provide more administrative support and interpretation services in communities with respect to preparation of documents, and communications with outside agencies; the government could establish independent local and regional "advocacy" offices or could enhance the role of Indian Registry administrators
- INAC could liase with provincial/territorial Vital Statistics agencies to discuss where changes might be made to some of the more administrative problems faced, including signing the birth registration form, and subsequent amendments
- Use alternatives to notarization for amendments to the birth registration or occasionally provide a commissioner of oaths to the community, or an INAC official authorized under s. 108 of the *Indian Act*

Administrative measures may assist in reducing the numbers of First Nations children with unstated or unacknowledged paternity, but will not address what is arguably the most grievous of situations, where the mother has reason for not disclosing paternity or the father refuses acknowledgment. It also does not address the litigation environment and any discrimination existent via the Registrar's policy.

5. Registrar's Policy Change

While the two-parent rule is contained in section 6 of the *Indian Act* the evidentiary requirements for proof of paternity are contained in the Registrar's policy. Policy is changed far more easily than legislation. The 1970 incarnation of the *Indian Act* provided that the child of a registered mother was entitled to registration unless the child's father was proven non-registered. Nothing in the literature reviewed indicates that this approach opened the "floodgates" to registration for children not so entitled.

As far back as 1988, three years after the Bill C-31 amendments, the Standing Committee (1988:46:20) recommended:

> We recommend that as there is no legal requirement in the *Act* for unmarried Indian women to name the father of their children in order to establish their entitlement to registration and band membership, the practice be discontinued immediately. An affidavit or statutory declaration simply swearing or declaring the status of the father without naming him should be sufficient to satisfy the requirements of the application for reinstatement.

The Quebec Native Women's Association (2000:13) agrees. "There is no excuse for refusing to discontinue this administrative practice. As stated by the Standing Committee, an affidavit or statutory declaration declaring the status of the father without naming him or requiring his signature, should be sufficient."

The Report of the Special Representative also recommends that the federal government abandon its presumption that the father of a First Nations child is not First Nations absent the requisite evidence (Erickson 2001:28). A policy wherein the child of a Registered Indian woman who swears that the father is also registered, is entitled to registration on the basis of both parent's heritage would address the concerns cited by the Standing Committee and by First Nations women's groups. It would remedy any discrimination arising from the current policy and address unstated paternity litigation, while staunching the flow of loss of and incorrect registration pursuant to the policy.

If INAC and various First Nations have concerns about opening the "floodgates" to incorrect registration, then a policy similar to that contained in the 1970 Act could be instituted, notifying Bands of registration by standard form, and allowing them one year to rebut Registered Indian paternity.

At the very least, INAC policy should be changed to include a *Trociuk*-style amendment, wherein women whose pregnancies are the result of abuse, incest, and rape and who want to "unacknowledge" the father, may file an affidavit as to Registered Indian paternity. This would be an ameliorative approach for those women disadvantaged on the basis of sex, and for those children who are disadvantaged based on the conditions of their birth. The requirement of an affidavit from women who have been victimized would necessitate the availability of culturally appropriate trained counsellors in order to minimize the potential for re-victimization. Further input into the development of such a process should be obtained from First Nations women's organizations and such counsellors.

6. Amend the Indian Act

INAC could undertake to open up the *Indian Act* and amend the two parent rule contained in section 6, replacing it with one type of registration that could be determined any number of ways including by descent from one Indian parent. This would address the immediate issues concerning Indian women and unstated paternity, as it would no longer be a determining factor for registration of the children of one Indian parent. This would also effectively abolish the second generation cut-off rule.

The Aboriginal Women's Action Network reported that:

> To categorise is to separate, divide and exclude. With Bill C-31's new class of "Indians" registered under 6(2), in the future, even more people will be excluded and stripped of their rights…
>
> Because of the second generation cut-off rule contained in the amendment, Bill C-31 has been called the Abocide Bill. In fact, since more and more people fall under the 6(2) category, some bands may only preserve their numbers if their members choose to marry (or have children with) Status Indians. Generation genocide is another term which has been used to describe the long-term effects of the legislation (Huntley and Blaney 1999: 54).

It would also accord with the feelings of some First Nations' women that registration should be determined by the mother. "Women at this focus group feel that if the mother is a Status Indian, then her child should be registered as a Status Indian. One woman stated 'it isn't the government's business who the child's father is.' Another woman stated that 'it should be the women's right to decide the status of their children.'" (Erickson 2001:29)

The women also commented on the divisive nature of categories of registration such as subsection 6(1) and 6(2) created by Bill C-31, with the recommendation that "the categorization of Status Indians should be eliminated." They recommended that subsections 6(1) and 6(2) be repealed and replaced with a provision that states that all persons of Indian ancestry are entitled to be Indian under the *Act* (Erickson 2001:86).

The Aboriginal Justice Inquiry (1991:c. 5) suggested:

> Any person designated as a full member of a recognized First Nation in Canada be accepted by the federal government as qualifying as a Registered Indian for the purposes of federal legislation, funding formula and programs.
>
> The category of so-called "Non-Status" or "unregistered" Indians should disappear. It is thoroughly inappropriate for the federal government to possess the authority or to legislate in such a way as to divide a people into those it will regard legally as being members of the group and those it will not, on grounds that violate the cultural, linguistic, spiritual, political and racial identity of these people.

The *Indian Act* should be amended to entitle any person to be registered who is descended from an Indian band member.

It is beyond the scope of this chapter to propose a new registration scheme for the *Indian Act*, though it appears likely that in years to come the *Act* will be subject to increasing challenge. Changes to the *Act* could circumvent some if not all registration-related litigation; however, passing legislation in this area not only takes years but is also not guaranteed to succeed. Legislative amendment may be on the horizon, but is not sufficiently timely to offer the best solution for the unstated paternity issue in the here and now.

7. Remove Registration from the Indian Act

Distaste for the entire registration system emerged in focus groups held by the Special Representative, wherein Aboriginal women voiced the alien nature of the *Indian Act* to Aboriginal culture. These participants felt that the registration and membership provisions of the *Act* should either be amended to respect traditional ways (such as matrilineal heritage) or the *Act* should be abolished altogether in favour of traditional laws (Erickson 2001:23). It has been suggested that the *Indian Act* provisions be replaced with First Nations governance and citizenship codes.

Removal of registration from the *Indian Act* could accord with the trend in jurisprudence pertaining to treaty rights, indicating that entitlement will be determined on whether an individual claimant has a "substantial connection" to the Indian band signatories and descent from one of the original signatory Indians.[7] Courts across Canada have indicated that non-registration under the *Indian Act* is not to be equated with treaty non-entitlement, indicating that there are other more important determinants. A similar rationale could be applied in determining entitlement to INAC's programming base for Registered Indians.

The *Indian Act*'s determination of Indian registration is likely to be subjected to increasing legal and political challenge in the years to come. However, even more so than amendments to the *Indian Act*, the removal of registration from the *Act* and the subsequent development of alternative First Nations approaches is likely to be a gradual and painstaking process, rendering it a less tenable option for addressing unstated and unacknowledged paternity.

Conclusion

The Registrar's policy regarding evidentiary requirements for proof of paternity should be amended to allow an unmarried First Nations woman to swear an affidavit or declaration that the other parent of their child is a Registered Indian. At the very least, the Registrar's policy should be changed to include a *Trociuk*-style amendment.

Further policy and legal analysis should be conducted to ascertain whether this policy change should also apply to non-registered parents (Aboriginal and non-)

who claim a Registered Indian parent of their child, and to determine ways to curb possible abuse.

Further input into the development of such a process should be obtained from First Nations women's organizations and culturally appropriate trained counsellors in order to minimize the potential for re-victimization. First Nations women's and other representative groups are key stakeholders and should be consulted throughout the development of any policy and legislative change, educational initiatives, or administrative approaches. Where necessary, they should receive funding to facilitate their involvement.

Systemic racism and sexism erect barriers to the lives of Aboriginal women and their children, creating and perpetuating their inequality in Canadian society. The many challenging issues faced by Aboriginal women and their children, including poverty, violence, and poor health, do not stand alone, but are rather inextricably interconnected and indivisible from the systemic and pervasive nature of Aboriginal women's inequality in Canadian society.

The roots of First Nations women's systemic inequality are both broad and deep. While Bill C-31 was intended to weed the *Indian Act* of existing gender-based discrimination, its replacement with discriminatory federal policy pertaining to the registration of the children of First Nations women with unstated and unrecognized paternity remains an ongoing cause of oppression of both First Nations women and their children.

Endnotes

1 First Nations and "Indian" are both used to indicate peoples with Indian status pursuant to the *Indian Act.*

2 R.S.C. 1970, c. I-6, as am.

3 Commonly referred to as the "cousins" and "siblings" impacts.

4 Indian and Northern Affairs Canada. 2003. *Policies on Indian Registration*. Ottawa: Indian and Northern Affairs Canada.

* (note from source document) Vital Statistics ultimately requires a paternal signature where parents are unmarried, see section on causes.

5 Section 7, which provides that "Everyone has the right to life, liberty and security of the person and the right not to be deprived thereof except in accordance with the principles of fundamental justice," may also be applicable.

6 An event occurring on or after April 17, 1985 and delegated by the Registrar to field officers to enter into the Indian Register.

7 See for example, *Simon v. The Queen*, [1985] 2 S.C.R. 387.

References

Aboriginal Justice Inquiry. 1991. *Report of the Aboriginal Justice Inquiry of Manitoba*. Winnipeg: Government of Manitoba.

Assembly of First Nations. 1999. *Resolution: Future Impact of Indian Act Amendment (Bill C-31) on First Nations Population*. Ottawa: Assembly of First Nations.

Assembly of First Nations. 2001. *Transcription: Discussing Bill C31 at the 22nd annual general assembly*. Halifax: Assembly of First Nations.

Brooks, Cheryl. 1991. *In Celebration of Our Survival: the First Nations of British Columbia*. British Columbia: UBC press.

Canadian Charter of Rights and Freedoms, Part I of the *Constitution Act*, 1982, being Schedule B to the *Canada Act* 1982 (U.K.), 1982, c. 11.

Canadian Feminist Alliance for International Action. 2003. *Canada's Failure to Act: Women's Inequality Deepens. Submission to the United Nations Committee on the Elimination of Discrimination Against Women*. Ottawa: Canadian Feminist Alliance for International Action.

Canadian Human Rights Act Review Panel. 2000. *Report of the* Canadian Human Rights Act *Review Panel*. Ottawa: Minister of Justice.

Canadian Human Rights Act, R.S. 1985, c. H-6.

Clatworthy, Stewart. 1992. *Population Implications of the 1985 Amendments to the* Indian Act, *Final Report*. Ottawa: INAC.

Clatworthy, Stewart. 1994. *Revised Projection Scenarios Concerning the Population Implications of Section 6 of the* Indian Act. Ottawa: INAC.

Clatworthy, Stewart. 1997. *Implications of First Nations Demography: Final Report*. Ottawa: INAC.

Clatworthy, Stewart. 2000. *Paternal Identity and Entitlement to Indian Registration: The Manitoba Context*. Ottawa: INAC.

Clatworthy, Stewart. 2001. *First Nations Membership and Registered Indian Status*. Ottawa: INAC.

Clatworthy, Stewart. 2003a. *Factors Contributing to Unstated Paternity*. Ottawa: Indian and Northern Affairs Canada.

Clatworthy, Stewart. 2003b. *Factors Contributing to Unstated Paternity Lecture*. February 21, [Video].

Concluding Observations of the Committee on the Elimination of Discrimination against Women: Canada. 13-31/01/2003. A/58/38 (Concluding Observations).

Concluding Observations of the Human Rights Committee: Canada. 07/04/99. CCPR/C/79/Add.105 (Concluding Observations/Comments).

Convention on the Elimination of all Forms of Discrimination Against Women. Adopted by the General Assembly, United Nations. December 18, 1979.

Convention on the Rights of the Child. Adopted by the General Assembly, United Nations. November 20, 1989.

Eberts, Mary. n.d. *Aboriginal Women's Rights are Human Rights*. Ottawa: Native Women's Association of Canada.

Erickson, Mavis. 2001. *Where are the Women: Report of the Special Representative on the Protection of First Nations Women's Rights*. Ottawa: INAC.

Furi, Megan and Wherrett, Jill. 2003. *Indian Status and Band Membership Issues*. Ottawa: Library of Parliament.

Gehl v. Canada (Attorney General), [2002] O.J. No. 3393.

Gehl, Lynn. 2000. "'The Queen and I': Discrimination Against Women in the Indian Act Continues." *Canadian Women's Studies*. 20(2): 64–69.

Green, Joyce. 2001. "Canaries in the Mines of Citizenship: Indian Women in Canada." Canadian *Journal of Political Science*. 34: 715–738.

Holmes, Joan. 1987. *Bill C-31 Equality or Disparity? The Effects of the New Indian Act on Native Women*. Ottawa: Canadian Advisory Council on the Status of Women.

Hull, Jeremy. 2001. *Aboriginal Single Mothers in Canada 1996: A Statistical Profile*. Ottawa: INAC.

Huntley, A. and Blaney, Fay. 1999. *Bill C-31: Its Impact, Implications and Recommendations for Change in British Columbia - Final Report*. Vancouver: Aboriginal Women's Action Network.

Indian Act, R.S.C. 1985, c. I-5, as am.

Indian and Northern Affairs Canada, and Statistics Canada. n.d. *Registered Indian Population Projections for Canada and Regions 2000–2021*. Ottawa: INAC.

Indian and Northern Affairs Canada. 1990. *Impacts of the 1985 Amendments to the* Indian Act *(Bill C-31)*. Ottawa: INAC.

Indian and Northern Affairs Canada. 2001. *Aboriginal Women: A Profile from the 1996 Census*. Ottawa: INAC.

Indian and Northern Affairs Canada. 2003. *Policies on Indian Registration*. Ottawa: Indian and Northern Affairs Canada.

International Covenant on Civil and Political Rights. Adopted by the General Assembly, United Nations. December 16, 1966.

Jordan, Elizabeth. 1995. "Residual Sex Discrimination in the Indian Act: Constitutional Remedies." *Journal of Law and Social Policy*. 11: 213–40.

Krosenbrink-Gelissen, Lilianne Ernestine. 1991. *Sexual Equality as an Aboriginal Right*. Fort Lauderdale: Verlag Breitenbach Publishers.

McIvor, Sharon. 1994. "The *Indian Act* as Patriarchal Control of Women." *Aboriginal Women's Law Journal*. 41(1): 41–52.

Morse, Bradford. 2002. "Symposium: 20 Years Under the Charter: Twenty Years of Charter Protection: The Status of Aboriginal Peoples under the Canadian Charter of Rights and Freedoms." *Windsor Y.B. Access Just*. 21: 385–424.

Native Women's Association of Canada, and Quebec Native Women's Association. n.d. *Quebec Native Women and Bill C-7*. Ottawa: Native Women's Association of Canada.

Native Women's Association of Canada. 1988. *Report of the Native Women's Association of Canada on Preliminary Impacts and Concerns Flowing from the Implementation of Bill C-31*. Ottawa: Native Women's Association of Canada.

Native Women's Association of Canada. 1998. *Bill C-31: Unity for Our Grandchildren Conference Proceedings*. Ottawa: Native Women's Association of Canada.

Paul, Pam. 1990. Bill C-31: The Trojan Horse: an Analysis of the Social Economic and Political Reaction of First Nations People as a Result of Bill C-31. Master's thesis. University of New Brunswick, Moncton.

Public History. 2003. *A Select and Annotated Bibliography Regarding Bill C-31 and Aboriginal Women's Concerns Relating to Gender Politics, Band Membership and Aboriginal Identity (Draft)*. Ottawa: INAC.

Quebec Native Women's Association. 2000. *A Presentation to the Special Representative of Indian and Northern Affairs Canada Re: Proposed Changes to the Indian Act and to the Administration of the* Indian Act. Montreal: Quebec Native Women's Association.

Royal Commission on Aboriginal Peoples. 1996. "Women's Perspectives." *Report of the Royal Commission on Aboriginal Peoples*, 4(2): 7–106.

Sandra Lovelace v. Canada, Communication No. R.6/24, U.N. Doc. Supp. No. 40 (A/36/40) at 166 (1981).

Sodhi, Gurpreet Kaur. 1996. *Ignored are the Wives and Children: Voices from Band Councils and Native Organizations during the Special Joint Committee of 1946–1948 and the Standing Committee on Bill C-31*. Ottawa: National Library of Canada.

Standing Committee on Aboriginal Affairs and Northern Development. 1988. *C-31 Fifth Report*. Ottawa: House of Commons.

Status of Women Canada. 2000. *Aboriginal Women's Roundtable on Gender Equality Roundtable Report*. Ottawa: Status Of Women Canada.

Trociuk v. British Columbia (Attorney General), [2003] 1 S.C.R. 835.

Universal Declaration of Human Rights. Adopted by the General Assembly, United Nations. December 10, 1948.

Villeneuve, McGillivary v. Canada, Re-Amended Statement of Claim, August 20, 1998.

7

Indian Status, Band Membership, First Nation Citizenship, Kinship, Gender, and Race: Reconsidering the Role of Federal Law[1]

Wendy Cornet

Introduction

Under the current *Indian Act*, responsibility for defining certain First Nation identities in law is shared between First Nation governments and the federal parliament. This paper examines human rights and governance issues arising from current approaches to defining First Nation identities.[2]

For much of Canada's history, the legal definitions of "Indian" and "band member" have been shaped by governments outside First Nation control. This paper will show that the boundaries of these legal constructs have been defined predominately through criteria reflecting high levels of arbitrariness, both historically and under the current state of the law. Law in this area has evolved from a relatively flexible and gender-neutral kinship-based system (1850–1868) to a patrilineal, patrilocal, and patriarchal kinship-based system involving various forms of gender-based discrimination (1876–1985) to the current blood quantum system with some residual gender-based discrimination (1985). The blood quantum approach is also evident in many band membership and First Nation citizenship laws. In all cases, definitions that rely solely on a simple in-out classification system of individuals based on descent criteria alone, or discrimination on grounds of sex, raise serious human rights issues.

Legal definitions of Indian status, band membership, and First Nation citizenship can impact personal identity at the individual level. Consequently, policy decisions reflected in laws respecting Indian status, band membership, and First Nation citizenship can affect the enjoyment of individual human rights. Collectively, federal and First Nation laws have created numerous different legal classes of people of First Nation descent. This complexity can result in arbitrariness with negative effects on human dignity, personal autonomy, and self-esteem.

Another important consideration is the negative impact of a complex and arcane system of defining First Nation identities (a system flowing from the *Indian Act*) on the capacity of governments at all levels to effectively plan the delivery of vital programs and services such as health and education.

In some ways, the legal concept of "Indian" under the *Indian Act* reflects prevailing societal myths about race and about "Aboriginality" or "Indianness" as categories of race. There has been confusion regarding the distinction between "racial" and "cultural" identities. Many people view the legal concept of Indian status as a foreign notion imposed on First Nations people. Many (but not all) people of First Nation descent reject the term "Indian" as a marker of identity and prefer the term "First Nation."

Difficulties can arise when individuals discover that the law does not accommodate their self-perception of cultural identity, whether that law is federal or First Nation in source.

The Role of Federal Law in Defining First Nation Identities

Law is a product of society and some aspects of Canadian law reflect societal assumptions about race. The notion of "Indian" in the sense of a "North American Indian race" is a social and legal abstraction. The influence of socially constructed notions of race is evident in the history of Indian Affairs policy and the *Indian Act* itself.[3] The application of the term "Indian" to a multiplicity of diverse cultures, nations, and language groups is a striking example of how colonialism and other social forces have created and defined racial categories. The notion of "Indian" lumps a diverse array of distinct peoples Indigenous to North America into one legal and racial category—without regard to their own distinct cultural and political identities. In this way the legal concept of Indian status under the *Indian Act* has contributed to the "racialization"[4] of First Nation peoples—meaning that the law has contributed to the imposition of a generic racial category on diverse peoples Indigenous to Canada.[5]

An important policy question is whether the goal of ensuring the equality and cultural rights of First Nation peoples is well served by the continued use in statutes of the racial term "Indian" (and the federal role of defining this term) or whether these goals would be better met by First Nation concepts of First Nation citizenship and the use of criteria such as culture and family relationships (kinship) as well as descent.

Historically, the legal category of "Indian" has served as the basis for specialized legal treatment, sometimes with a positive impact on the rights of First Nation people, and sometimes with a negative impact. In the past, this specialized legal treatment often involved discrimination—legal distinctions with negative consequences for the peoples concerned, such as denial of the right to vote (a denial of an individual civil and political right) or denial of nation recognition (a denial of a collective right to a specific cultural and national identity). At one time, "Indian" status meant "not a person," and denoted a legal incapacity in regard to many civil and political rights and freedoms. The legal consequences attached to Indian status have evolved over time. More recently, Canadian law has recognized the need for specialized legal treatment of Indians/First Nations as peoples—not races—to protect the fundamental cultural, social, economic, civil, and political rights of First Nations as nations and peoples. (An example of this change is the entrenchment of Aboriginal and treaty rights of the Aboriginal peoples of Canada in section 35 of the *Constitution Act*, 1982.) This policy goal is consistent with international human rights norms respecting the equality of all peoples and their right to self-determination.

The *Indian Act* continues to provide a legal framework to define individuals in and out of identities such as "band member" and "Indian." Federal law currently does this by creating an objective standard of "Indianness." This standard is applied in an either/or type classification system based on the circumstances of a person's birth. This approach carries a great potential for arbitrariness and discrimination. Any set of rules defining a legal identity based primarily on descent will involve a degree of arbitrariness—whether it is Indian status, band membership, or citizenship. The greater the degree of arbitrariness, the greater is the potential for harm to individual identities and rights.

The federal rules now governing Indian status and band membership rely heavily on descent-based criteria, with rigid cut-off rules to address situations of Indian–non-Indian parentage. There is little provision under the current *Indian Act* for alternate eligibility criteria. In the case of Indian status, for persons born after April 16, 1985, descent is the only criteria, apart from adoption and some limited exceptions provided by section 4(1). The simplicity of descent-based criteria presumably makes administration of entitlement less complex than systems requiring assessment of factors such as cultural knowledge or degree of connection to a community. However, this simplicity is traded off for the complexity of delivering diverse government services and programs through varying criteria of Indian status, First Nation membership/citizenship, or reserve residency for eligibility or funding purposes. Federal and First Nation law-making and policy-making face the same challenge in this regard.

Arbitrariness in definitions of Indian status and membership/citizenship has long been a concern of many First Nations women activists and organizations—whether the discrimination is based on sex, descent, marital, or family status. Of course, it is true that Aboriginal rights by definition are the rights attached to persons connected to the Indigenous peoples in control of their territories prior to European colonization and this necessarily involves descent criteria to determine entitlement. However, the rigid descent rules that now typify Indian status entitlement and most band membership rules are a relatively recent development. This rigidity has the unfortunate consequence of perpetuating colonial notions of race and also fails to respond to the needs of "bi-racial" or "multi-racial" children.

Federal laws, policies, and funding criteria may influence First Nation–controlled decisions about band membership criteria. The colonial legacy of racial categorization may also influence First Nation decision-making in some cases. Carole Ambrose-Goldberg has commented on the influence U.S. federal law can have on tribal identities and definitions in the United States: "Law is one potentially powerful outside influence on political identity. Explicitly, law may establish categories of people eligible for benefits or subject to burdens according to particular understandings of ethnicity or nationality. These definitions may in turn provide incentives or disincentives for groups to organize politically along particular lines" (Ambrose-Goldberg 1994, 1123–1124). Ambrose-Goldberg notes that in the U.S., federal legislation began supplanting treaties in the early nineteenth century and finally took over after 1871. The result was national legislation that focused on group rights for Indians as a whole (that is, for Indians as a racial group) rather than the rights of individual tribes (that is, distinct peoples with rights to maintain their distinct cultures, modes of political organization, law, etc.) (Ambrose-Goldberg 1994, 1141). Ambrose-Goldberg makes the following conclusion about the impact of this race-focused legal approach on the Indian nations themselves: "By classifying all the many native peoples as 'Indians,' the first European invaders generated an idea that has in turn created a reality in its own image, through non-Indian power and native response ... the racially inspired policies of non-Indians began to reproduce in Indians the original European race-based conceptions" (Ambrose-Goldberg 1994, 1140).

For a long period, aspects of the Indian status and band membership provisions supported federal policy goals of forcibly assimilating First Nation people as individuals. First Nation women were a key target of assimilative policies launched through previous *Indian Act* provisions governing Indian status and band membership entitlement. Section 12(1)(b) of the pre-1985 *Indian Act* is perhaps the most infamous example. This provision removed Indian status from any woman marrying a person without Indian status and from her children. While section 12(1)(b) was often rationalized as necessary to protect the reserve base from exploitation by non-Aboriginal husbands of Indian women, there is no evidence of alternative measures ever being considered to address this concern until the legislative process that led to the 1985 amendments.

For some time, First Nation people have struggled to reassert control over their personal identities as individuals and their collective identities as nations or peoples. First Nation women activists and organizations have fought for fair and non-discriminatory systems of determining Indian status and band membership, whether controlled by the federal government or First Nation governments. Despite the removal of much of the sex-based discrimination from the *Indian Act*, the concepts of "Indian" and "band member" remain problematic and residual sex discrimination is still evident.

The federal government and many First Nations have expressed interest in moving towards a system that recognizes First Nation citizenship as a legal concept in place of the *Indian Act* notion of band membership. Future policy reforms by the federal government or First Nation governments to reduce arbitrariness should first determine the relevance of notions of "descent" and "race" in the development of any new definitions of First Nations identity and the relevance of alternative criteria such as cultural knowledge and connection to community. Policy work in this area must also consider how any proposed reforms may impact men and women differently (e.g., due to the continuing impact of past discriminatory laws).

Race Creation, Gender-based Discrimination, and Legal Indian Status

A review of Canadian case law reveals a lack of clarity on whether the legal category of "Indian" under the *Indian Act* refers to a racial group, or diverse cultural and political entities. This can be seen by comparing the 1983 decision of the Supreme Court of Canada in *Martin v. Chapman*[6] (which discusses the legal concept of "Indian" in the racial terminology of "Indian blood") to the 1999 decision *Corbière v. Canada*[7] (where the Court references both race and culture as part of the legal conception of "Indian").[8] This is a critical area of legal analysis that requires clarification (through legislation, judicial decision, or both) if Aboriginal rights within the Canadian legal system are to be understood and analyzed as rights of peoples or nations, and not as "race-based rights." This would not affect the capacity of human rights law to sanction harmful discriminatory action arising from the ongoing social phenomenon of racial categorization and discrimination aimed at the members of the diverse Indigenous nations as "Indians."

The concept of "race" as it has been popularly used in European and European-based societies has changed substantially over the centuries. As Constance Backhouse explains, it was originally used to mark differences of class within European society and also to delineate different cultures and societies who often did not look markedly different from one another.[9] In this sense it simply referred to persons connected by common descent or origin. Backhouse explains: "The word 'race' originally denoted 'family,' and was applied only to noble or important dynasties—the race of the Bourbons and the race of David for example. The term underwent 'a semantic journey of extraordinary proportions' when it expanded during the nineteenth century to categorize large groups of people who were not related directly through kinship, but who shared specified traits. Early classifications based almost exclusively on skin colour had enumerated four separate races: Europaceus albus, Asiaticus luridus, Americanus rufus, and Afer niger" (Backhouse 1999, 42). Later work relied on a combination of physical features such as hair texture, skin colour, eye colour, and shape of nose, and resulted in classification systems of at least seventeen "main races" (Backhouse 1999, 42 citing Otto Klineberg).

With the advent of European colonization of large parts of the globe, the concept of race evolved as a means of rationalizing different and unequal treatment of people based on their physical appearance and cultural distinctiveness relative to people of European descent. With the growth in European scientific activity in the nineteenth century, and the ongoing thrust of colonialism, considerable effort was expended to prove some biological or genetic foundation to the then prevailing systems of racial classification based on physical appearance. These efforts utterly failed. As many authorities have concluded, race is a social construct with no scientific foundation (Lopez 1994, 1).

The dehumanizing process of classifying other people into arbitrary racial categories and discriminating against them based on such imposed categories is distinguishable from the process of people self-identifying as nations or distinct peoples based on shared attributes which may include kinship ties, language, cultural values, histories, and laws. In the latter situation, the people or nation concerned have agency in asserting fundamental rights that are protected by domestic and international law. Such fundamental rights include the right of peoples to self-determination, the related Aboriginal and treaty rights of First Nations under the Canadian Constitution, and rights under international human rights covenants relating to language and culture.

When the *Indian Act* was first enacted in the late nineteenth century, Euro-Canadian social and legal norms often assigned persons whose ancestry was outside Europe (including First Nation people and people of Asian and African descent among others) to various racial categories deemed not "white." "White" as a racial category became a standard of privilege and the standard for full social, economic, and political rights, against which other "races" were identified, defined, and ranked by decision-makers such as judges or Members of Parliament or Legislatures who considered themselves "white." Assignment to a racial category other than "white" often triggered some form of legal disadvantage such as barriers to voting rights, immigration, or certain kinds of employment. The history of the evolving nature of legal definitions of racial categories and how these were manipulated to secure and perpetuate privilege by people asserting a racial identity as "white" throughout the nineteenth century and half of the twentieth century has been documented by several authorities.[10] It is also evident that the racialization of First Nation peoples through the *Indian Act* began to eclipse the Crown's recognition of Indigenous nations and the treaties the Crown had entered into with them.

The legal definition of "Indian" has evolved from its inception in colonial law in 1850 to the 1985 *Indian Act* amendments from a flexible, broad definition relying on a degree of self-identification and community acceptance to an increasingly narrow definition dependent almost solely on descent-based criteria. Over this period, three distinct approaches can be identified: 1) a flexible gender-neutral and non-unilineal kinship-based system; 2) a patrilineal and patriarchal kinship-based system with various manifestations of sex discrimination; and 3) a strict descent-based system (non-unilineal) with blood quantum requirements and some residual elements of gender-based discrimination.

While the current Indian status entitlement system does not rely on outward physical characteristics to classify people, its almost exclusive reliance on strict descent-based criteria arguably constitutes a form of race classification. High levels of arbitrariness characterize systems of race classification. With its focus on individual descent histories and its exclusion of relationship criteria (e.g. relationship of individuals to families or to communities) the current *Indian Act* creates an objective but rigid and arbitrary standard of "Indianness"—one that is to be determined by federal law alone and applied on a national basis to a diverse group of nations or peoples. This approach unfortunately implies the existence of some trait or characteristics that make "Indians" inherently different from those deemed "not Indian." The current system offers a binary choice between the categories—"Indian" and "not Indian" based solely on the circumstances of a person's parentage. Within the category of "Indian," two sub-categories have been created which in turn imply the existence of "degrees of Indianness"—Indians registered under section 6(1) of the *Act* and Indians registered under section 6(2). Indians registered under section 6(1) can pass on Indian status to their children, regardless of who they marry. As noted above, Indians registered under section 6(2) can only pass on Indian status if the other parent is registered under either section 6(1) or section 6(2).

The current *Indian Act* reinforces the notion of "Indian" as a racial category in the following ways:

- By specifically referring to "Inuit" as a "race" excluded from the definition of "Indian," section 4(1)
- By relying strictly on descent-based criteria to determine eligibility for persons born after 1985
- By creating subcategories of "Indianness"—"6(1) Indians" and "6(2) Indians" in common parlance today—with different capacities to transmit Indian status
- By establishing a system that leads over time to an escalating separation of Indian status from connectedness to the group identity of band or First Nation
- By separating the determination of "Indian" identity from connection to First Nation land rights

From 1876–1985 Indian status under the federal *Indian Act* was primarily determined by a patrilineal kinship system. The result was that gender-based discrimination was the key tool for meeting the federal policy goal of controlling and narrowing the class of people of First Nation descent who would be entitled to Indian status under the *Indian Act*. Under this system, federal law determined both entitlement to Indian status and band membership, and there was an almost total match between those entitled to Indian status and band membership. Entire nuclear families (husband, wife, children) could move in or out of Indian status and band membership, based on the status of the father or husband. Descent from a male person with Indian status or marriage to a male with Indian status were the primary means of individual entitlement. Conversely, marriage by an Indian woman to a non-Indian male resulted in loss of Indian status to herself and her children.

The 1985 amendments to the *Indian Act* re-introduced non-unilineal (or "cognatic") descent principles whereby descent is now traced through both maternal and paternal ancestors. Because this approach would dramatically increase the number of persons entitled to Indian registration, the federal policy goal of controlling the number meeting the definition of "Indian" is now met by degree of descent rules. These begin to operate in the first generation of Indian and non-Indian parentage and lead to disentitlement if there are two successive generations of Indian and non-Indian parentage. The only deviations from descent criteria are provisions respecting adoption (in the *Act*'s definition of "child") and the provision that deems band members without Indian status to be "Indians" for several key provisions of the *Act* (section 4.1).

There is still residual sex discrimination in the determination of Indian status. The children of women, who "married-out" prior to 1985 and were reinstated under the 1985 amendments, are treated differently than the children of men who married out prior to 1985. The children of women who married out prior to 1985 are registered under section 6(2) while the children of men who "married-out" are registered under section 6(1). This means that successive generations of inter-marriage results in termination of Indian status one generation earlier for women than for men who married out prior to 1985. In addition to problems arising from provisions of the *Act* itself, there are issues arising from DIAND's policy respecting "unacknowledged paternity" and "unstated paternity." Although the *Act* does not address evidence of paternity, federal policy does. Where a mother cannot establish to the satisfaction of the Department, the Indian status of the father of her child (or who chooses not to) federal policy provides that only on the mother's Indian status will be relied on to determine which subsection to register the child. This policy effectively amounts to deeming the father as not having status as an "Indian" under the *Indian Act*. A raft of gender equality issues are raised by this policy, which have been explored by others.[11]

Rules Governing Entitlement to Band Membership

Under the *Indian Act* diverse First Nations, identified as "bands," are subject to a more or less uniform system of local governance and reserve land regulation.[12] The recognition of distinct "band" entities and brief references to custom bands and treaties is the closest the *Indian Act* comes to recognizing diverse Indigenous cultural or political entities.

Prior to 1985, all band members were deemed to belong to the category of "Indian." The *Indian Act* now allows the development of separate legal rules to govern Indian status and band membership. Indian status remains determined solely by the federal rules set out in sections 6 and 7 of the *Indian Act*. Band membership continues to coincide with Indian status for bands not taking control of their membership rules, as provided by section 10 of the *Act*. Bands who do assume control over their membership codes may develop rules different from those determining Indian status (within certain parameters). For these bands, band membership can mean something different than Indian status.

The vast majority of bands appear to rely heavily on descent-based criteria as a pre-condition to entitlement either because their membership rules are governed by the *Indian Act*, or where control of membership has been assumed, the rules rely on descent-based rules.

Some bands restrict eligibility criteria to specific descent rules. Others provide for some opportunity for the admission of persons not meeting the standard descent criteria by establishing other criteria such as:

- Demonstrated knowledge of the nation's language
- Demonstrated knowledge of the nation's customs and traditions
- Length of residence among the nation
- Social and cultural ties to the nation
- Support from a majority of electors voting by secret ballot on the application
- Existence of close family ties within the nation
- Is self-supporting or alternatively, can make a valuable contribution to the band, or is a caring parent who can participate in the betterment of the reserve
- A native or non-native adopted child of a person eligible to be a band member[13]

First Nations have taken a range of approaches in defining the initial charter group of persons automatically eligible for band membership. Different cut-off dates have been established for determining the charter group from which descent would be traced to determine the eligibility of future generations. Different terms to name the initial charter group of band members have been used, e.g. "original members" (Adams Lake Indian Band) or "traditional citizens" (Fort Nelson Indian Band). Different approaches have been taken to the relevance of Indian status to eligibility for band membership. The Skeetchestn Indian Band requires both the applicant and at least one of the applicant's parents to have Indian status, in addition to other requirements (Gilbert 1996, 180).

The separation of Indian status from band membership and the differing trends across First Nations in the numbers entitled to each legal status, results in a complex array of legal rules to determine access to many important legal rights and benefits. This is a complex legal field that both nations and individuals must cope with. Indian status determines eligibility for several significant social programs such as the Non-Insured Health Benefits. Band membership determines eligibility for many political and civil rights on-reserve such as voting in band council elections and the right to hold an individual land allotment. It is also important to note that the loss of capacity to transmit Indian status or band membership to children due to "out-marriage" affects women more than men, given rates of Indian/non-Indian parenting are considerably higher for females than males, both on- and off-reserve (Gilbert 1996, 180).

The combined effect of rigid, yet differing descent-based rules for Indian status and band membership, creates a complex legal and policy environment for federal, provincial, and First Nation governments. This complicates the planning and delivery of government services and programs on- and off-reserve. The separation of Indian status from band membership is creating an increasingly incoherent system that fails to reflect the family relationships of First Nation people on- and off-reserve. Yet another set of legal rights are defined in terms of treaty beneficiary rights for First Nations who have entered treaties with the Crown. In addition, some federal programs are based on funding criteria determined by the number of people resident on-reserve. Moving to a legal system based on recognizing nations and First Nation citizenship could provide an opportunity to rationalize at least some of these overlapping legal statuses and funding criteria.

Equality Rights, Notions of "Difference," and Legally Created Identities

As a matter of personal identity, each person of First Nation descent is entitled to choose an identity as Aboriginal, First Nation, or any other. Some people are comfortable with one or more of the generic terms commonly used today such as First Nation, Aboriginal, or Indigenous. There are also individuals who refer to themselves as "Indian." Still others, with equal legitimacy, do not identify with any of these generic terms and relate only to their specific national identity (such as Mi'Kmaq or Nisga'a).

The personal right of individuals to identify themselves is distinct from considering the legal and social consequences of identities created and defined in law, especially by governments outside the control of the group being defined. Each individual has the right to shape their own identity to the extent they are able, or wish to, beyond the influence of their parents, families, cultures, and nations. However, the capacity of individuals to assert this freedom can be affected by the broad powers of government to create and define legal categories of people (subject to constitutional restraints such as the Charter guarantees of equality or Aboriginal and treaty rights).

Citizenship, band membership, and Indian status are all legally defined categories that necessarily involve defining some people in, and some people out of each category as well as the rights and benefits attached to each. The first step to begin addressing concerns about the arbitrariness of current rules relating to Indian status and band membership is to understand how "difference" is typically identified and created by Western (meaning, European-derived) systems of law. The analysis in this chapter relies on the legal theory of American equality rights theorist, Martha Minow on Western understandings of "difference."[14] Minow provides several examples demonstrating how categories of difference are created and defined by law, and how these are often culturally bound. Western notions of human difference in turn have influenced the development of equality rights theory—the legal theory that identifies when different treatment amounts to discrimination contrary to human rights norms.

Minow observes that the creation of different abstract categories of people is a common function of the law in European-derived legal systems. She notes that the operation of American law in any field typically involves distinguishing things, situations, and people from other things, situations, and people and does so through the establishment of abstract legal definitions or concepts. However, she points out that difference is a comparative term and that the very idea of difference implies a reference point to make any given comparison (Minow 1990, 22). That is, a finding of difference and the assigning of a person to one group rather than another implies difference from some standard of comparison. Minow states that a legal system that purports to value individual equality constantly poses the "dilemma of difference": sometimes ensuring real or substantive equality requires treating people the same regardless of personal traits and sometimes equality requires acknowledging and accommodating differences between people.

Western legal theory, for example, tends to construct dichotomous (opposing) categories such as gender and sex (male/female). By comparison, in at least one major Aboriginal language, there are no words to connote "male" and "female" (Henderson 1996, 1). Further, the idea of "Indians" and "bands" are products of European colonial law and did not exist prior to European arrival in the Western Hemisphere. The legal creation of "Indians" has created a need to identify "non-Indians" and a process of distinguishing between the two legal categories of people. The problem of identifying difference is inherent in issues relating to entitlement to Indian status as well as band membership and First Nation citizenship. It is inherent in determining when such distinctions amount to discrimination.

Equality rights theory in Canada responds to the dilemma of difference by identifying legal distinctions that harm human dignity and personal autonomy. For example, a decision to exclude a person from a benefit under the law because of a personal characteristic—such as sex or race—in a way that implies the person is of less value because of that personal characteristic, can be a form of discrimination.

Laws and government decisions which impair human dignity carry the potential to negatively affect self-esteem and the process of identity formation in young people. Policy makers should consider the impact on young First Nation people of having to cope with, and find their place in, a confusing array of legal statuses somehow related to their family histories (e.g. Status Indian, Non-Status Indian, C-31 Indian, 6(1) Indian, 6(2) Indian, band member, non-band member, Treaty Indian). Some of these legal categories may overlap when applied to a particular individual and some may not. A further consideration is that multiracial children not only face the complexities of identity formation in a race-conscious society, but also a legal system that establishes multiple categories of First Nation people. The key focus of policy reform should be on moving away from legal categories that racialize people into categories and subcategories. Instead, policy could promote the development of First Nation–controlled legal systems that define citizenship in ways reflecting First Nation cultural identities while respecting the fundamental dignity and equality of First Nation men, women, and children. This may require development of kinship rules that meet the contemporary needs of the family situations of First Nation people. Movement in this direction would be consistent with the conclusions of the Royal Commission on Aboriginal Peoples, which stated that the distinctiveness of Aboriginal people is cultural and political, not "racial": "Aboriginal peoples are not racial groups; rather they are organic political and cultural entities. Although contemporary Aboriginal groups stem historically from the original peoples of North America, they often have mixed genetic heritages and include individuals of varied ancestry. As organic political entities, they have the capacity to evolve over time and change in their internal composition."[15]

Determining when a distinction in law or policy amounts to discrimination is not always easy. While all discrimination necessarily involves some form of identifying difference between two categories of people, not all legal distinctions amount to discrimination under Canadian law (whether the Charter is being applied or federal or provincial human rights legislation).

The purpose of Canadian anti-discrimination law is to identify and provide remedies for arbitrary legal distinctions that impose real disadvantage—disadvantage based on negative stereotypes attached to a personal characteristic, such as sex or race, or multiple personal characteristics at the same time. When the result of applying such stereotypes and disadvantage is impairment of a person's dignity as a human being, discrimination is usually found to exist as a matter of law. For example, a provision of the *Indian Act* that prohibited off-reserve band members from voting in band council elections has been held a violation of section 15 Charter equality rights in *Corbière v. Canada*.[16] The exclusion of band members living off-reserve from participation in a key part of the political life of *Indian Act* bands was found to be an impairment of the human dignity of the members affected, because the exclusion: 1) suggested that off-reserve band members were less worthy as band members and 2) perpetuated a longstanding stereotype that off-reserve band members are necessarily more culturally assimilated than members resident on-reserve.

Martha Minow's theory of how the law creates and shapes notions of "difference" can be used to better understand Indian status and band membership issues in Canadian law. Drawing on theories from a range of disciplines including sociology, law, and psychology, Minow describes "a social relations approach" to addressing perceptions of difference within an equality rights framework (Minow 1990, 12). Minow suggests that a social relations approach to law focuses on identifying the relationships and interdependency of people, as an essential part of the context for making decisions on rights related questions. A social relations approach takes into consideration the dynamic and evolving nature of human relationships, and adopts the view that legal distinctions do not necessarily, and often do not, reflect differences inherent in the people assigned to different legal categories. In a Canadian context, this suggests that rigid in/out definitions will likely not take account of the diversity of family relationships nor how the mobility of First Nation people to seek employment or education off-reserve often influences their choice of partners.

The arbitrariness of strict descent-based criteria perhaps could be alleviated by moving away from strict either/or classification approaches determined only by descent and instead develop codes that reflect the inherent nature of human relationships as dynamic, evolving, and interconnected. It may also help to keep in mind that legal distinctions between "Indian" and "non-Indian" under the *Indian Act* do not necessarily reflect real differences inherent in the persons concerned.

Notions of Citizenship

Citizenship is a legal status that brings with it a specific political identity and specific rights and obligations. The definition of citizenship and its rights and responsibilities are controlled by the government of the nation in question. Citizenship is a legal concept determined by specific events (such as being born in a certain territory or being born to parents with a particular citizenship or meeting the requirements of a naturalization process) and not by qualities inherent in a person.

Prior to 1947, there was no such thing as Canadian citizenship, as all Canadians were simply considered British subjects (Young 1997). The British common law system historically determined an individual's entitlement to citizenship by the place of birth (jus soli), regardless of the citizenship of the parents. European countries whose legal systems derive from Roman law historically relied on the citizenship of the parents (jus sanguinis) to determine the citizenship of a child. Other countries such as Japan have similar rules.

Canadian law provides three means of acquiring Canadian citizenship: 1) being born on Canadian soil; 2) being born to at least one parent with Canadian citizenship; and 3) if not automatically entitled by birth (either by place of birth or by blood) through "naturalization."

The notion of band membership does bear some resemblance to the concept of citizenship. Traditionally, entitlement to band membership and Indian status has been determined by the specifics of the parents' entitlement to band membership and Indian status. Since the 1985 amendments to the *Indian Act*, bands have been able to take control of their membership rules and use criteria other than descent either in addition to, or as an alternative to, descent criteria. Unlike Canadian citizenship, birth in a First Nation's territory such as a reserve typically does not confer band membership. Given the small numbers of people of First Nation descent relative to people with no First Nations descent on a national basis, such rules could undermine the transmission and survival of First Nations cultural values.

First Nation citizenship codes can determine access to civil, political, and social rights within First Nation communities. First Nation citizenship, like band membership, raises difficult policy issues involving personal identities. When personal identities do not match the legal rules determining citizenship rights, lack of access to important cultural rights tied to civil, political, and social rights within First Nation communities are felt as particular hardships by persons falling outside definitions of band membership or First Nation citizenship. Citizenship and band membership codes necessarily involve establishing rules for the inclusion or exclusion of individuals. Like citizenship laws of other nations, citizenship codes likely will be the focus of ongoing controversy and feelings of hurt and injustice by those seeking inclusion but failing to meet citizenship requirements. However, First Nation lawmakers could seek to reduce arbitrariness through codes that focus on relationships and connection to community as well as descent, and by continuing dialogue within their communities on citizenship issues.

There has been a strong interest in moving away from the *Indian Act* concept of "bands" and "band membership" to a more respectful terminology of "Nation" and "First Nation citizenship." First Nation representatives have said that the system of bands imposed by the *Indian Act* does not reflect the traditional nations in which Indigenous people organized themselves prior to colonization. The Royal Commission on Aboriginal Peoples noted that before colonization there were approximately 80 to 90 distinct peoples or nations in the territory now known as Canada. The 600 plus bands recognized under the *Indian Act* do not necessarily reflect the traditional political organization of First Nations in Canada, as nations. While Aboriginal nations are understood to often encompass more than one *Indian Act* band, there is a noticeable trend particularly in federal legislation, to equate the legal term "band" with "First Nation." The term First Nation citizenship today is often used to refer to the same unit as band membership.

The Royal Commission on Aboriginal Peoples concluded that First Nations have the right to determine their membership as an element of their inherent right of self-government. Significantly, the Commission also concluded this right is limited by two requirements: 1) to ensure no discrimination between men and women, and 2) there should be no reliance on minimum blood quantum as a "general pre-requisite" for citizenship: "Under section 35 of the *Constitution Act, 1982*, an Aboriginal nation has the right to determine which individuals belong to the nation as members and citizens. However, this right is subject to two basic limitations. First, it cannot be exercised in a manner that discriminates between men and women. Second, it cannot specify a minimum blood quantum as a general prerequisite for citizenship. Modern Aboriginal nations, like other nations in the world today, represent a mixture of genetic heritages. Their identity lies in their collective life, their history, ancestry, culture, values, traditions, and ties to the land, rather than in their race as such."[17]

Kimberley Tallbear has argued against the use of rigid blood quantum criteria in contemporary First Nation laws on membership or citizenship and against assumptions that equate race with culture or blood quantum with transmission of culture. She states that prior to colonization, there were First Nations that used nonracial criteria to determine citizenship such as "marrying into the community, long-term residence within the tribal community, and the assumption of cultural norms such as language, religion, and other practices" (see Tallbear 20012000).

The types of band membership rules described in Clatworthy's studies of band-designed membership codes are different in some important ways from the legal definition of Canadian citizenship. Entitlement to Canadian citizenship is determined by birth in Canadian territory. In addition, it can be acquired by persons born outside Canada if born to a Canadian or meeting the requirements of naturalization. By contrast, band membership and Indian status are largely determined by descent from persons with Indian status or band membership, regardless of where a person is born. Band membership can be extended to persons not entitled to it by birth if the band membership rules so provide. The fact of colonization and its resulting loss of land and control over traditional territory place First Nations in a very different situation than Canada with respect to "immigration" norms and citizenship. Presumably acquisition of citizenship by birth in First Nations territory is not attractive to many, because of the threat of being overwhelmed eventually by non-Aboriginal people. Canada, on the other hand, promotes immigration and acquisition of Canadian citizenship as a social and economic benefit to the country as a whole.

It should also be kept in mind that descent has been a relevant factor for passing on Canadian citizenship, and cut-off rules have been used regarding children of Canadian citizens born abroad. Gender-based discrimination in the operation of such rules has been found unconstitutional. A sexually discriminatory rule that permitted a married Canadian father to pass on his citizenship but not a Canadian mother was found an unconstitutional violation of section 15 in *Benner v. Canada*.[18]

First Nation citizenship as a concept could invoke notions of political membership, cultural affiliation and family relationships rather than colonial notions of race based on rigid descent rules alone. Legislation to introduce a new system of nation recognition to replace the current system of band recognition would be consistent with the right of First Nations to self-government and self-determination and could include provision for human rights protection. Concerns about the need to respect equality rights within the nation (whether gender equality concerns, treatment of on- and off-reserve members, or other differences) could be addressed by the application of the *Canadian Human Rights Act*, the Charter or First Nation–designed human rights instruments consistent with international human rights standards.

Conclusion

The number and complexity of legal statuses for First Nation people have grown over the years. New forms of arbitrary discrimination in definitions of Indian status and band membership have replaced old ones. The various legal statuses for Aboriginal people under Canadian law—such as "Indian," "band member," and "treaty beneficiary"—overlap but do not always coincide.

Arbitrariness could be reduced by focusing more on the relationships between people as a context for developing laws to determine First Nation identity categories such as membership or citizenship. This would mean focusing on the contemporary context and manifestation of First Nation kinship and determining how this is relevant to citizenship. Such a focus may involve taking account of factors such as degree of participation in the life of the community, residence in community, community acceptance, contributions to the First Nation, or support of family in the community or other community members. Other objective factors might include an assessment of cultural knowledge or knowledge of the nation's language. Any or several such factors could be used as alternative criteria for people not meeting descent-based criteria. While some First Nations already have incorporated such criteria into their band membership codes, rigid descent criteria still appear to be the predominant and only determinant for many membership codes to date as the work of Stewart Clatworthy demonstrates.

Aboriginal people must cope with layers of legal identities beyond their control but vital to their lives. Understanding these rules and falling within the recognition they offer can mean the difference between being able to reside on-reserve or not, being able to buy a house on-reserve or not, having access to post-secondary education, employment training, and other programs. The current level of complexity and arbitrariness in the legal rules governing Indian status and band membership also creates impractical burdens for administrators and leaders of First Nations, and confusion and conflict for First Nation individuals attempting to find their way through a mass of technical rules coming from federal and First Nation sources.

At a broader level, the concepts of Indian status and band membership themselves are problematic. The legal notion of "Indian" perpetuates the notion of a universal "Indian" race and undermines recognition of the distinct nation status of the diverse First Nations of Canada. Similarly, the notions of "band" and "band membership" do not promote recognition of First Nations as nations.

Some alternative policy choices to revise the Indian status and band membership provisions under the current *Indian Act* could include:

1) Focus on eliminating residual sex discrimination in the existing system including addressing policy issues respecting: a) " unstated paternity"; b) discriminatory treatment of the children of Indian women who "married out" before 1985 with respect to Indian status and band membership; and c) discriminatory treatment of children of female "illegitimate" children with respect to band membership

2) Recognize two legal sources for Indian status entitlement by amending section 4.1 of the *Indian Act* so that: a) all persons with band membership as determined by bands would be deemed "Indians" for all provisions of the *Indian Act* and other federal purposes such as funding formulas; and b) persons without band membership would continue to be eligible for Indian

status according to federal law

3) Eliminate the concept of Indian status and use band membership/First Nation citizenship as the primary legal status for federal and constitutional matters relating to First Nations

4) Replace Indian status and band membership systems with First Nation citizenship codes as determined by First Nation laws

Historically, First Nation women have been subject to various forms of discrimination in regard to Indian status and band membership entitlement. Any initiative to examine law and policy relating to Indian status and band membership will require a gender-based analysis to address the various layers of discrimination to which women and children reinstated under the 1985 amendments to the *Indian Act* have been made subject—including discrimination based on sex, race, marital status and family status. To address concerns about the need to protect against new forms of sex discrimination in future laws, the *Canadian Human Rights Act* could be amended to ensure a fuller application to First Nation laws, pending the development of First Nation human rights codes consistent with international human rights norms. An interpretive clause to take account of the need to balance individual rights with collective Aboriginal, treaty and self-government rights would likely be required (as recommended by the *Canadian Human Rights Act* Review Panel). The addition of new responsibilities would require additional resources to ensure that access to the Commission's complaint process by First Nation people is more than theoretical. Locally accessible mechanisms—such as mediation, tribunals, and courts—to deal with conflicts over membership or citizenship decisions are also needed.

A policy shift respecting the concept of Indian status under the *Indian Act* (without affecting the different legal meaning of "Indian" under the *Constitution Act*, 1867 and *Constitution Act*, 1982) would require a fundamental rethinking of the role and purpose of federal legislation in this area. This may involve new legislation or a treaty process providing a procedure for recognizing First Nations without again contributing to the racialization of the diverse nations concerned. The same legislation could require that citizenship codes respect fundamental human rights.

There could be advantages to ultimately eliminating the federally created legal statuses of "Indian" and band membership and moving to recognize First Nation citizenship more broadly than it is now. Returning to the use of one primary legal status to identify beneficiaries of rights in relation to First Nation lands and self-government would reduce the multiple combinations and permutations of Indian status and band membership within the same families.

Overall, it is a fair conclusion to say that First Nation people as a whole are not well served by a legal category like Indian status, which has done much to contribute to the myth of a single biologically based North American Indian race. In addition, the growing demographic dissonance in Canada between those entitled to

Indian status and those entitled to band membership will be an increasing challenge for governments (federal, provincial, and First Nation) charged with delivering programs and services to First Nation people whether on- or off-reserves.

Endnotes

1 This paper is a revision and updating of an unpublished paper by the author entitled "First Nation Identities and Individual Equality Rights: A Discussion of Citizenship, Band Membership, and Indian Status," January 2003.

2 Issues relating to the inherent right of self-government are not discussed in any depth due to limitations of space.

3 For discussions on the social construction of "race", see Omi and Winant (1986), Jackson (1987, 3), Lock (1999, 83), Lopez (1994, 1), Powell (1997, 99), and Tallbear (2001 and 2000).

4 The term "racialization of identity" is used by Cheryl Harris in her article, "Whiteness as Property," p. 1709.

5 See also Turpel-Lafond (1997, 64–66) and Cornet (2003, 121–147) .

6 [1983] 1 S.C.R. 365 (S.C.C.).

7 [1999] 2 S.C.R. 203 (S.C.C.).

8 For detailed discussion of this issue see, Cornet (2003).

9 See also Backhouse (1999, 5) and Lock (1999); Margaret Lock also provides a review of the historical meanings of race and notes its early usage to determine matters of kinship and thus its concern with descent and genealogy, not outward physical appearance.

10 See for example, Backhouse (1999) or McCalla and Satzewich (2002, 25).

11 The demographic trends in regard to unstated paternity and some of the program and policy implications of these trends are examined by Clatworthy (2003) and Mann (2005).

12 However, there are opportunities to opt out of the *Indian Act* reserve land system and establish a First Nations–designed land management regime under the *First Nations Land Management Act*, S.C. 1999, C.24.

13 These observations are based on the codes reviewed in Gilbert (1996). Any of these membership codes since may have been modified.

14 Martha Minow is an American legal expert on the nature of equality and on issues of identity and equality rights. See in particular, Minow (1990).

15 Report of the Royal Commission on Aboriginal Peoples, Volume 5, Chapter 3.

16 *Corbière v. Canada*, [1999] S.C.J. No. 24, 2 S.C.R. 203, (1999) 173 D.L.R. (4th) 1, 239 N.R. 1, [1999] 3 C.N.L.R. 19 (S.C.C.).

17 Report of the Royal Commission on Aboriginal Peoples, Volume 5, Chapter 3.

18 [1997] 1 S.C.R. 358.

References

Ambrose-Goldberg, Carole. 1994. "Of Native Americans and Tribal Members: The Impact of Law on Indian Group Life." *Law & Society Review,* 28: 1123–1148.

Backhouse, Constance. 1999. *Colour-Coded: A Legal History of Racism in Canada, 1900–1950.* Toronto: UTP.

Clatworthy, Stewart. 2003. *Factors Contributing to Unstated Paternity.* Ottawa: INAC. *I*Cornet, Wendy. 2003. "Aboriginality: Legal Foundations, Past Trends, Future Prospects." in Joseph Magnet, ed., *Aboriginal Rights Litigation.* Markham: LexisNexis Canada Inc. 121–147.

Gilbert, Larry. 1996. *Entitlement to Indian Status and Membership Codes In Canada.* Toronto: Carswell.

Jackson, Peter. 1987. "The idea of 'race' and the geography of racism" in *Race and Racism: Essays in social geography.* London: Allen and Unwin, 2–22.

Harris, Cheryl. 1993. "Whiteness as Property." *Harv. L. R.* (106): 1709–1791.

Henderson, James [sakéj] Youngblood. 1996. "First Nations' Legal Inheritances in Canada: The Mikmaq Model" *Manitoba Law Journal* (23): 1.

Lock, Margaret. 1999 "Genetic Diversity and The Politics of Difference" *Chi. Kent L. Rev.* (75): 83–111.

Lopez, Ian. 1994. "The Social Construction of Race: Some Observations on Illusion, Fabrication, and Choice." *Harvard Civil Rights – Civil Liberties Law Review* (29): 1–62.

Mann, Michelle M. 2005. *Indian Registration: Unrecognized and Unstated Paternity*, Ottawa: Status of Women Canada.

McCalla, Andrea and Vic Satzewich. 2002. "Settler Capitalism and the Construction of Immigrants and 'Indians' as Racialized Others" in Wendy Chan & Kiran Mirchandani eds., *Crimes of Colour: Racialization and the Criminal Justice System In Canada*. Peterborough: Broadview Press.

Minow, Martha. 1990. *Making All The Difference: Inclusion, Exclusion and American Law*. Ithaca and London: Cornell University Press.

Omi, Michael and Howard Winant. 1986. *Racial Formation in the United States*. New York and London: Routledge.

Powell, John A. 1997. "The 'Racing' of American Society: Race Functioning as a Verb Before Signifying as a Noun" *Law and Inequality*. (15): 99.

Tallbear, Kimberly. 2000. "Genetics, Culture and Identity In Indian Country," Paper presented at Seventh International Congress of Ethnobiology, Athens Georgia, 23–27 October 2000 (available for download on the Website of the International Indigenous Institute for Resource Management <**www.iiirm.org/publications/pubs.htm**>).

Tallbear, Kimberley. 2001. "Racialising Tribal Identity and The Implications For Political and Cultural Development," presented at the Indigenous Peoples and Racism Conference, Sydney Australia, 20–22 February 2001 (available for download on the Website of the International Indigenous Institute for Resource Management <**www.iiirm.org/publications/pubs.htm**>).

Turpel-Lafond, Mary Ellen. 1997. "Patriarchy and Paternalism: The Legacy of the Canadian State for First Nations Women" in Andrew and Rodgers (eds.) *Women and the Canadian State*. Montreal and Kingston: McGill-Queen's University Press.

Young, Margaret. 1997. *Canadian Citizenship Act* And Current Issues (BP-445E). Ottawa: Library of Parliament Research Branch, Law and Government Division.

Notes on Contributors

Erik Anderson

Erik Anderson has served as a senior research manager and policy analyst for both the Privy Council Office and INAC. Much of his career has been spent examining and writing about the issues of Bill C-31, Aboriginal and treaty rights, and identity and gender equality. Most recently Erik has helped lead the policy development on the matrimonial real property issue on reserves for INAC. Erik has written about the impacts of the diamond industry in the Northwest Territories, health and well-being of Aboriginal communities, and the historical Inuit–Government of Canada relationship. Erik received an MA in History from the University of Northern British Columbia in 1996 in the area of Aboriginal contact history of religion.

Dan Beavon

Dan Beavon is the director of the Research and Analysis Directorate at INAC. He has worked in policy research for 20 years and has dozens of publications to his credit. He manages an Aboriginal research program on a variety of issues, increasing the amount and quality of strategic information available to the policy process. Much of his work involves complex horizontal and sensitive issues requiring partnerships with other federal departments, academics, and First Nations organizations.

Martin J. Cannon

Martin J. Cannon, PhD, is an Assistant Professor of Sociology and Equity Studies in Education at the Ontario Institute for Studies in Education (OISE) at the University of Toronto. He is a citizen of the Six Nations of Grand River Territory, and has been writing since 1995 about his experience as a Status Indian and the descendant of a woman who lost and later re-acquired Indian status. He is author of "The Regulation of First Nations Sexuality" (1998); "Bill C-31: Notes toward a Qualitative Analysis of Legislated Injustice" (2005); and "First Nations Citizenship, *An Act to Amend the Indian Act* and the Accommodation of Sex-Discriminatory Policy" (2006).

Stewart Clatworthy

Stewart Clatworthy operates Four Directions Project Consultants, a Winnipeg-based management consulting firm specializing in socioeconomic research, information systems development, and program evaluation. Since 1980, Stewart has completed numerous studies on Aboriginal demography and migration, population, membership and student enrollment projections, and socioeconomic, housing, and employment conditions. Through this research, he has gained a national reputation as a leading scholar of Canadian Aboriginal socioeconomic and demographic circumstances.

Wendy Cornet

Wendy Cornet (née Moss) resides in Ottawa and heads a local consulting firm, Cornet Consulting & Mediation Inc. She has 36 experiences as a policy analyst and researcher specializing in government relations, human rights, and legal issues affecting Aboriginal peoples, and she has a special interest in conflict resolution. She received her LLB in 1983 (UBC) and has worked for several national and regional Aboriginal peoples organizations and for government on issues relating to the *Indian Act*, northern and Inuit issues, land rights, self-government, human rights as well as constitutional and international indigenous issues. She is the author of several journal articles, book chapters, and major reports on Aboriginal issues and has conducted and facilitated numerous workshops on Aboriginal issues.

Jo-Anne Fiske

Jo-Anne Fiske engages questions of Aboriginal policy research through inter-weaving a number of perspectives: legal and medical anthropology, feminism, and critical theory. She has written on issues of the role of women in self-government, legal and governance traditions, health policy, and contradictory impacts of federal policy on the status of Aboriginal women in Canada. Currently she is at the University of Lethbridge where she is Dean of Graduate Studies and a member of the Women's Studies Program. Her recent work has appeared in *Policy Sciences*, *Atlantis*, and in several anthologies. She is co-author with Betty Patrick (Chief of the Lake Babine Nation) of *Cis Dideen Kat: When the Plumes Rise, The Way of the Lake Babine Nation*.

Evelyn George

Evelyn George is a member of the Lake Babine Nation of BC and majored in First Nations Studies and is doing her thesis in the MA program at University of Northern BC. She has been involved in several publications with Status of Women Canada, along with several studies in governance, program evaluation, and needs assessment on behalf of the First Nations of the interior BC. Before going to university, Evelyn was a political leader of the Old Fort Nation and worked with youth at Babine Elementary Secondary School. During her research for Status of Women Canada on a project called Seeking Alternatives to Bill C-31: An Investigation of Matrilineal Models of First Nations Citizenship and Community Membership Policies, she experienced the impact of Bill C-31 on the remote communities of northern BC.

Gerard Hartley

Gerard Hartley is one of the founding owners of Public History, an Ottawa-based historical research firm that was established in 1995. Since 2001, Gerard has been the senior manager and lead analyst on a major company project for Indian and Northern Affairs Canada that addressed the historical development of the federal government's Indian policy in the period leading up the 1985 *Indian Act* amendments. Gerard Hartley has a BA in history from the University of Prince Edward Island and an MA in history from Queen's University.

Michelle M. Mann

Michelle M. Mann is a Toronto-based lawyer, writer, television host/commentator, and consultant. She holds a BA in history from the University of Guelph, an LLB from the University of Ottawa, and was called to the Bar of Ontario in 1996. Michelle has practiced law in both the public and private sector, and is former legal counsel to the federal Department of Justice and the Indian Claims Commission. Michelle has authored several published governmental reports and book chapters on Aboriginal and human rights issues. She is a freelance legal affairs writer and columnist, as well as a legal and political affairs television host and commentator.

Jerry White

Jerry White was Chair of the Department of Sociology at the University of Western Ontario until June of 2006. He is currently Professor and Senior Adviser to the Vice President (Provost), and the Director of the Aboriginal Policy Research Consortium (International). Jerry is the co-chair of the 2006 Aboriginal Policy Research Conference (with Dan Beavon and Peter Dinsdale) and a member of the Board of Governors for UWO. He has written and co-written 11 books and numerous articles on health care, and Aboriginal policy, the most recent being *Aboriginal Conditions* (UBC Press) and *Permission to Develop* (TEP). He is co-editor of the *Aboriginal Policy Research* series.